Fame-Dropping

Fame-Dropping

Five Decades of Encounters with the Eminent

James C. Humes

Hamilton Books

Lanham • Boulder • New York • Toronto • London

Copyright © 2019 by The Rowman & Littlefield Publishing Group, Inc.
An imprint of The Rowman & Littlefield Publishing Group, Inc.
4501 Forbes Boulevard, Suite 200, Lanham, Maryland 20706
Hamilton Books Acquisitions Department (301) 459-3366

6 Tinworth Street, London SE11 5AL, United Kingdom

Library of Congress Control Number: 2018965145
ISBN: 978-0-7618-7079-1 (pbk. : alk. cloth)
ISBN: 978-0-7618-7080-7 (electronic)

∞™ The paper used in this publication meets the minimum requirements of American National Standard for Information Sciences Permanence of Paper for Printed Library Materials, ANSI/NISO Z39.48-1992.

Printed in the United States of America

Contents

Introduction

On December 20, 2010, Conservative MP Jonathan Aitken met me for drinks at the Sloane Club in Chelsea. As we sipped our cocktails, he told me that he had some important advice to offer. Jonathan had been head boy at Eton—in other words, Captain of School, a position of high visibility and prestige—and he entertained similar ambitions for my grandson James. He knew the director of admissions for Eton, and assured me that he would tell him that James Quillen would do Eton proud. But in return, he told me that I had to promise to do something for him. When Jonathan was ten (as he related), he found a valise in his grandmother's attic. He opened it. It contained papers addressed to his yet-unborn great-grandson a century after he was writing. Jonathan's grandfather had been governor of the Sudan and both in and out of government service. Over the years, he had become acquainted with the statesmen of the day, and wrote down his observations of them.

An accomplished statesman in his own right, formerly an adviser to Queen Elizabeth, Jonathan had a way of giving friendly advice the weight of an official directive. He told me that as someone who had been on the fringes of history, I should jot down my observations for my grandson and name-sake, James, and his siblings, to read and study one day.

In accordance with his suggestion, this chronicle is a collection of my observations and comments about some of the great men and women of my day whom I met and talked to. I am imposing some restrictions: It is limited, with a few exceptions, to noteworthy figures of the twentieth century. I owe the title to Jonathan Aitken's sending me the book *Dropped Names* by Frank Langella, who played Nixon in the *Frost/Nixon* movie. *Dropped Names* contains Langella's personal impressions of the star personalities he had met.

Chapter One

The White House

Dwight David Eisenhower: Supreme Allied Commander in World War II and America's Thirty-Fourth President

My first interest in a political campaign arose in 1951, when General Eisenhower was battling Bob Taft for the Republican nomination. Although my family was distant kin of Taft through his mother, Helen Herron, I was swept up by the glamour of the "I Like Ike" phenomenon. Yet my first meeting with Eisenhower was an unhappy one. In the summer of 1956, as a Young Republican in Washington, DC, I served as an usher at a thousand-dollar-a-plate fundraising dinner held at the Washington Coliseum (known at the time as the Uline Arena). Some of Ike's aides told me that the president needed to find a men's room. Eager to help, but not wanting to seem like I didn't know what I was doing, I took a guess, pointed to the right, and rushed ahead of the presidential party. To my dismay, I found it was the ladies' room. I yelled, "Everyone out!" and saluted beside the open door, hiding the telltale sign. The president, sighting an unfamiliar environment, glared at me with his icy blue eyes, and strode on.

Contrary to the genial smiling image he portrayed on TV, Eisenhower was a flinty five-star general. My wife Dianne, who worked for him as a secretary outside the Oval Office in 1957–58, said the staff was more scared of Ike than of Governor Sherman Adams, his brusque front man, especially on days when Ike resumed the role of general by wearing a brown suit. One time a new secretary wore pants, and on seeing her, Ike uttered his curse: Hell's bells! He was as purely male as his wife Mamie was feminine. She loved wearing pink and playing canasta with the girls. Ike liked golf and bridge with the boys, although his friends didn't enjoy partnering with him in bridge because he'd bark at their mistakes. Yet "Eisenhower" (German for "hewer of iron") could easily morph into Ike at a public event: a Norman

Rockwell painting of a seventy-year-old Huck Finn. His grandson, David, told me that his grandfather always came up grinning, having learned that trick while fighting when he was a boy. They can never lick you if you're smiling, as Grandpa Ike told David.

My only long conversation with Eisenhower took place during October 1962 in Gettysburg, when I was a candidate for the Pennsylvania Assembly. Keystone State gubernatorial candidate Bill Scranton (who knew him slightly, for he had served under U.S. Secretary of State John Foster Dulles) arranged the meeting; he had told Ike that I was the best of young leaders. Fixing his eagle eyes on me, the general asked if I was going door to door in the campaign. I nodded "yes." He told me to list my likely voters on a card, and then urge them on to the polls.

While Ike's critics may have painted him as a "do-nothing president," his eight years of peace and prosperity (as well as six balanced budgets) comprise a record for any president to emulate. Not to mention two keys to that booming economy: The St. Lawrence Seaway Act (which Ike signed into law in May 1954) opened the heart of our country to the Atlantic, and the National System of Interstate and Defense Highways (authorized in June 1956) shortened the links to all American cities. Liberals have compared the extent of these two achievements to the great scope of Kennedy's Peace Corps and Johnson's Great Society, and found them lacking. But conservative substance and results often prove greater than symbolic progress by the left.

The Democrats also faulted Ike for not being intellectual like Adlai Stevenson. But he was knowledgeable. When President Johnson's domestic policy aide Joe Califano was about to go up to Eisenhower's home in Gettysburg to brief him on policy, LBJ gave him this advice: Listen to Ike and make a note to yourself every time he frowns, or looks at the sky. LBJ knew that Ike was a wise old man, irrespective of the crap the Democrats repeated about him in campaigns.

While at Gettysburg in 1967, I witnessed one example of the former president's wide reading. A retired general, commenting on Vietnam, claimed to quote Herodotus on the Peloponnesian War: "You can't be an armchair general twenty miles from the front."

Eisenhower thanked him for these words of wisdom, which had clearly piqued his interest. When the general had left, Ike told me that, first of all, it was Aemilius Paullus, not Herodotus, who had written this; second, it referred to the Punic Wars, not the Peloponnesian War; and third, this general had misquoted the author. When I asked why he didn't correct the general, Ike said that he didn't want to embarrass him. He had learned in the military that sometimes it's best to hide your ego as well as your intelligence.

The British military historian John Kerrigan said Eisenhower was the man he most admired in history. If not an intellectual by academic standards, he was a wise leader, insightful and prudent.

Richard Nixon: America's Thirty-Seventh President

Of all the leaders for whom I drafted speeches, the brightest was Richard Nixon. He was also the best read in history and biography. Nixon was like the motivating teacher or professor you once had, not the one who gave you easy A's, but the one who insisted, "This is not your best—you can do better." As I once said about speechwriting, "Reagan edited for style, Nixon for substance."

Nixon was an introvert in an extrovert's profession. He disdained small talk, and despised fools. He was awkward on social occasions. The only small talk he could engage in comfortably was on sports. Being somewhat reticent himself, he was distrustful of my 'showboating' side. His favorite in our family was my wife, Dianne; Nixon's former office manager Loie Gaunt told my daughter Rachel on a visit to Yorba Linda in 2009 that Dianne reminded him of his own wife, Pat.

He was attracted to intelligent and independent-minded people who had ideas, even if they disagreed with him. He had no use for rigid lefties, or doctrinaire right-wingers who spouted clichés. Although he could be stilted and stiff at receptions and parties, he could be warm in cerebral settings. He was more expansive on those occasions than Gerald Ford, George H. W. Bush, or Ronald Reagan.

Nixon could be brusque and even curt in his dealings if he was focused on something else. Yet he was also quite considerate. Hundreds of letters attest to his handwritten notes to orphans and Vietnam War soldiers, as well as notes to the daughters of both JFK and LBJ, and his calling on Ted Kennedy Jr. (the senator's son) after the young man lost his leg to cancer. The press knew nothing of these gestures.

In 1959, Nixon asked me where I thought we would be with China in twenty years. His diplomatic overtures to China a dozen years later, culminating with a personal visit in 1972, would open the door to normalized relations with the communist behemoth. As British Prime Minister Harold Macmillan stated, this was probably the greatest diplomatic feat of the last century.

While the liberal media painted him as a hard man of the right, Nixon was actually the most progressive president since Franklin D. Roosevelt. Setting time frames and goals for Affirmative Action programs, creating the Environmental Protection Agency, giving the District of Columbia the vote, providing female collegiate athletes with opportunities to excel, ending the draft, and beginning the withdrawal from Vietnam: These were among his initiatives and accomplishments. To this day, our biased media has cast all Republican presidents as stupid—except Nixon. They knew he was smart, just wicked.

Nixon revealed his knowledge of history when discussing his proposed negative income tax with Senator Daniel Patrick Moynihan, a sociologist and diplomat who was one of his closest advisors. This wealth-redistribution program would have outflanked anything dreamed up by the liberals. Citing the words of Disraeli, Nixon told him that the Republicans would outdish the Whigs.

On my sixtieth birthday, Tricia Nixon Cox gave me a note card that she had found in her father's desk drawer after his death. Written on the card were ten political maxims Nixon had derived from his knowledge of great leaders, such as Pericles, Franklin, Churchill, MacArthur, and others—the essential rules for leadership and negotiation. These "Ten Commandments of Statecraft" had guided Nixon through conflicts in Asia, Russia, and the Middle East.

> A President needs a global view, a sense of proportion, and a keen sense of the possible. He needs to know how power operates, and he must have the will to use it.
>
> If I could carve ten rules into the walls of the Oval Office for my successors to follow in the dangerous years just ahead, they would be these:
>
> 1. Always be prepared to negotiate, but never negotiate without being prepared.
> 2. Never be belligerent, but always be firm.
> 3. Always remember that covenants should be openly agreed to but privately negotiated.
> 4. Never seek publicity that would destroy the ability to get results.
> 5. Never give up unilaterally what could be used as a bargaining chip. Make your adversaries give something for everything they get.
> 6. Never let your adversary underestimate what you would do in response to a challenge. Never tell him what you would not do.
> 7. Always leave your adversary a face-saving line of retreat.
> 8. Always carefully distinguish between friends who provide some human rights and enemies who deny all human rights.
> 9. Always do at least as much for our friends as our adversaries do for our enemies.
> 10. Never lose faith. In a just cause faith can move mountains. Faith without strength is futile, but strength without faith is sterile.
>
> Having laid down these rules, I would also suggest that the President keep in his desk drawer, in mind but out of sight, an eleventh commandment: When saying "always" and "never," foreclose the unique exception; always leave room for maneuver. A President always has to be prepared for what he thought he would never do.
>
> —Richard M. Nixon[1]

Julie Nixon Eisenhower: Daughter of Pat and Richard Nixon

Julie Nixon Eisenhower manifests all the grit of her father and the grace of her mother. She combines the resolve of Richard Nixon with the radiant warmth and compassion of Pat Nixon.

Julie is a fighter. She pleaded with her father not to resign. A Nixon never quits, she told him. The flag of family and its ultimate vindication kept flying. That conviction remains as steadfast and strong in the present day as it did in the past during the national ordeal of Watergate.[2] As long as she lives, so will Richard Nixon's vision of a world where conflicts are stabilized into an uneasy, if unsettling, truce between the aspirations of the free and the malice of America's adversaries—those who work to sap our nation's strength and vigor amid the surging tides of change.

Julie voices the opinions her father would have held against those at home and abroad who attack our Constitution, particularly our right to free speech and expression. Like her father, she abhors the academic who—instead of championing free speech—challenges this value in a posture of "political correctness." Both Julie at Smith College and her husband David Eisenhower at Amherst experienced their Ivy League campuses dissolving into diatribe and dissent. The hatred of America and its morals has not waned but worsened since Nixon's time. Riots and protests confront many a speaker who is not a certified leftist.

Julie has manifested the values of her father and family in her role as a mother and nurturer. I was invited to the home of Julie and David Eisenhower outside of Philadelphia when their children were young. On this visit, Julie's daughter Jennie gave a rousing rendition of "Button Up Your Overcoat." Jennie would carry her theatrical talents to the stage and to the screen, appearing on Broadway and in several Hollywood movies.

Julie is true to her ideals, and does not let friend or foe get in the way of her opinions. She turned down pleas from Pennsylvania Republicans to run for the position of U.S. senator from the Keystone State. As Julie explained, she is a loyal Republican, but a mother first and foremost. Family has always been her greatest priority.

And her integrity is not tempered by political affiliation. In the 1990s, when President Bill Clinton was under constant attack from Republicans, based on accusations of graft and corruption during his time as governor of Arkansas, Julie refused to join in. Her poise and aplomb earned her grudging praise by many a Democrat. As a presidential daughter, she is a model for emulation. She combines a vivacity of spirit with a valor of steel. She embodies the qualities of both her parents, and her life is a testament to each of them.

Gerald Ford: America's Thirty-Eighth President

Gerald Ford was an ordinary man who did the right job at the right time. Dictatorship may depend on one man, but the greatness of democracy is that of ordinary men and women doing their jobs extraordinarily well. Ford was an example of that. I first wrote speeches for him in the summer of 1976. He seldom corrected my drafts, but sometimes he had the annoying habit of ad-libbing to make it seem like he wrote the address himself. One such text praised Pat Moynihan's tenure at the UN. I wrote that "Ambassador Moynihan stripped the pretense of democracy from the dictators in Africa." In delivering the speech, Ford ad-libbed that Pat had called a spade a spade! Other remarks displayed prescience and a simple eloquence. When Ford returned from Philadelphia following the Bicentennial Celebration, and heard the news that not one protest or demonstration had marred the occasion, he turned to his wife Betty and said that America was healed.

I got to know Ford while working with ghostwriter Trevor Armbrister, for whom I suggested the title *A Time to Heal* from Ecclesiastes for the former president's autobiography. Ford was an innately kind man. When cruel things were said about him, he shrugged them off. The only two people he expressed dislike for were Nixon's defense secretary, Jim Schlesinger, and White House Counsel John Dean. He had little respect for Reagan's competence. He did admire Nixon, particularly in foreign policy, but unlike Nixon, he read little. When I would give him a quotation from Churchill, Truman, or Lincoln in hopes of expanding his conception of the presidency, he'd brush it off. To the media, all GOP presidents are backward, and they tried to portray him as stupid. But Ford ranked higher in his Yale Law School graduating class than either Cyrus Vance or Sargent Shriver, his classmates. He would amaze me by recalling a military appropriations bill signed ten years earlier, with numbers correct almost to the decimal point. He told me he pardoned Nixon, not for his sake, but for the country's, knowing that the pardon would defeat him in 1976. Years later, Ted Kennedy praised this much-criticized pardon as an act of statesmanship and courage.

The most influential address I ever drafted was not in the White House, and not for a serving president. When I was in Vail, Colorado in 1977 helping Ford with his memoirs, he asked me to write a speech for the thirty-second anniversary of Winston Churchill's Iron Curtain Speech, to be delivered at the site of the original event in Fulton, Missouri. In Europe, the communists were threatening to win elections in France, Italy, and Spain, while from the other side of the Iron Curtain, the Soviets were promoting "communism with a human face." Unlike every president since Harry Truman, who had stood beside Churchill at tiny Westminster College while the British statesman outlined the dire threat posed by communism, President Carter refused to take a stand on the European elections.

At that time in Washington, to save electricity, Carter had the lights in the Capitol dome turned off. In Ford's speech, which I drafted, the former president alluded to turning off the Capitol dome's lights in Washington to save energy, and raised the specter of parliaments in Rome, Paris, and Lisbon dousing the lights of free debate in the absence of democracy. These remarks echoed the words of British Foreign Secretary Sir Edward Grey on the eve of World War II: The lamps are going out all over Europe. Clearly, the communists thought that a minority could gain power in Western Europe, as they once had in the East. For the speech I had drafted, "Canopy of Tyranny," Ford spoke at Westminster College on October 29, 1977, to a standing-room-only crowd of more than four thousand people. His words resonated with supporters of democracy and human rights around the globe, including those at the Holy See; the speech was later featured prominently in the Vatican's daily newspaper, *L'Osservatore Romano.*

Zbigniew Brzezinski, President Carter's foreign policy advisor, later told me that if France, Italy, and Spain were painted red on a map of Europe, his boss could forget about re-election. And this "Second Iron Curtain Address" may have had an effect: Soon after, Carter changed his position and declared that the election of communist parties in Europe would be a disaster. Fortunately, the communists did not win a plurality in any European country.

The most surreal experience I ever had as a writer also involved a speech for Gerald Ford, which was delivered at New Haven, Connecticut, in October 1978. GOP Congressman Ronald Sarasin was running for governor to unseat Ella Grasso, and Ford had been invited to speak on behalf of his former House colleague. But what made the occasion weird for me is that I drafted all the speeches delivered that evening: the one by Sarasin, the introduction of Ford by the Connecticut GOP state party chairman, and the featured speech by former President Ford. Eloquence at short notice—such is the life of a White House ghostwriter!

Ronald Reagan: America's Fortieth President

Ronald Reagan was the most amiable president I ever met, but also the most aloof. When I first encountered him in 1973, I was promoting my book *Instant Eloquence,* and my law-school friend Chuck Manatt hosted a reception for me at the Beverly Hilton. Reagan speechwriter Pete Hannaford took me in for a quick handshake with the governor. It was perfunctory, with no injection of personality. I told the governor to note my "soul shakers" in the book—anecdotes from history for closing talks inspirationally. One of those "soul shakers" became his favorite—words taken from John Winthrop's sermon, "A Model of Christian Charity," in which the future governor of Puritan Massachusetts expressed his intent to build a city upon a hill.

In 1975, I helped Reagan with his remarks before the World Affairs Council in Philadelphia. He had left the California governor's office in January of that year, and the speech was designed to showcase his knowledge of foreign policy—with an eye towards his presidential ambitions. Having worked on this speech, I was an unwitting participant in one of the greatest bloopers in the history of public speaking. I had adapted Reagan's address from the work of a foreign-policy think-tank apparatchik—reshaping the stiffly bureaucratic language into something that, if not quite poetic, was certainly conversational and simple. One theme to be emphasized was the Third World, in terms of enlarging America's policy vision towards less-developed nations. But wherever I had drafted the phrase Third World, Reagan mistakenly ad-libbed Third World War!

Reagan never addressed me by name. He would call me that Churchill fellow, and then proceed to tell me a Churchill anecdote. If he seemed simplistic to the left, he was. He was guided by simple beliefs: love of God, love of country, and the American way of life—free markets and a free world. Reagan changed America and all of humanity. In making communism a dirty word and capitalism a good one, he provided a benchmark for every president who succeeded him.

A story he told me about his youth may be instructive. Reagan was attending church in Dixon, Illinois with his mother and brother on an August day so sweltering that you could have fried eggs on the courthouse steps, Reagan recalled. As the preacher climbed the stairs to the pulpit, he saw Reagan pull at his necktie and collar. The pastor looked out at his congregation, and then, pointing downwards with his finger towards the infernal regions, he said: "It's hotter down THERE!" His Sunday sermon concluded, the reverend walked out of church. If brevity was the point of this anecdote, it also illustrated Reagan's basic groundings in God and family.

George H. W. Bush: America's Forty-First President

The first President Bush was the quintessential aristocrat. Despite his adoption of Texas as his political base, he remained the Andover and Yale man, with a family-bred sense of *noblesse oblige*. He was the English public school Tory transformed for American political life. But to Margaret Thatcher he was a "wet," the type of moderate Establishment conservative she despised. She manifested her suspicions of President Bush when she saw him in August 1990, against a backdrop of the events that led to Desert Storm the following January. Turning to America's leader, she told him not to go wobbly on her! Thatcher, who once remarked that consensus is a euphemism for cowardice, knew that Bush was conditioned to accept the views of his State Department: the same ones who advised Reagan to oppose Britain's defense of the Falklands in 1982.

I first got to know Bush in 1972, at a dinner with my distant cousin John Humes, Nixon's ambassador to Austria, at the Chevy Chase Club. The gracious and congenial Bush recruited me to write speeches, and once took me to dinner with him at the Alfalfa Club. He was not a natural extrovert like his son George Jr., or his secretary of state and chief of staff, Jim Baker. But he worked at knowing names and storing away personal data about all his friends and employees. While I did write some speeches for him, and once accompanied him to Indianapolis, I was pushed aside in favor of Spiro Agnew's former pen Vic Gold—who in all fairness was a superior writer.

On one occasion, George Bush met me at The Brook in Manhattan, where I introduced him to my daughters Mary and Rachel. We soon fled this private club in favor of Burger King, because too many people at The Brook called Bush "Poppy"—his nickname from prep school and Yale. It has been forgotten that Bush was not only a Phi Beta Kappa at Yale, but an All-American first baseman whose hero was the courageous Lou Gehrig, a star player for the New York Yankees before he succumbed to the tragic illness that bears his name. In his quest for the presidency, Bush is said to have penned more notes than Chase Manhattan. When he dropped by my office in Philadelphia and found I wasn't there, he took the time to leave me a handwritten note. This old-school habit was extended to beloved family pets as well: As Vice President, Bush had Millie, his springer spaniel, forward a letter marked with her paw print to our springer spaniel, Edward. When I last saw George and Barbara Bush in Philadelphia, Barbara told me that her husband did not cry when he lost to Clinton, but when Millie died at age twelve of pneumonia, he wept.

George W. ("Dubya") Bush: America's Forty-Third President

I knew Dubya as "George" when his father was vice president. This was in 1988, when I was working on the senior Bush's presidential campaign. If you had told me then that Dubya would one day be president for eight years—double his father's tenure—I wouldn't have believed you.

That does not mean I don't recognize his assets. He is one of the most likeable people, a type for whom the Spanish use the word *simpatico,* whose weak translation is "nice." *Simpatico* suggests empathy, and a willingness to engage with the people. Compared to his father, to whom he was fiercely loyal, he is more extroverted, more gifted in the small talk of camaraderie. Like Jim Baker (a comparison he wouldn't enjoy), he listens more than he talks. He has nicknames for everybody. Mine was "Winston." He called me in Colorado to say that he was sending me a picture of himself with the bust of Churchill, and that he enjoyed looking at my hero every day in the Oval Office.

During the years when his father was vice president, Dubya urged me to regale him, in my Churchill imitation, with anecdotes about the British Prime Minister. Besides Churchill, our other topic of conversation and mutual interest was baseball. He liked my trivia question, "What all-time hitting statistic will never be surpassed?" The answer is Tigers outfielder Sam Crawford's 309 triples, because ever since the dead-ball era in the 1920s, the game has not encouraged scoring triples.

Dubya asked me how I would improve his father's speeches. I told him, "Your father doesn't like delivering speeches. He thinks it's all B.S." I added that the senior Bush should "reveal more of himself, even though he has inhibitions about bragging. One story he should use is about floating in the Pacific, not knowing whether he'd be rescued, after being downed by a Japanese Zero." His father's narrow escape from death has since become one of the best-known anecdotes about our forty-first president.

When Dubya asked me what I admired most about Churchill, I replied, "Doing what's right, regardless of the polls." He nodded. Indeed, if I could make one comparison with his father, Dubya was less guided by the thinking of the Establishment consensus. He was also more of a natural politician.

The success of the second Bush presidency and its invasion of Iraq will be determined by historians. If Iraq does become a viable representative republic—the first in the Middle East—it will be a success. When Obama prematurely withdrew, democracy turned to dictatorship. As of 2018, President Donald Trump's near-defeat of the Islamic State in Iraq bodes well for the future of Iraq and its people.

Harry Truman: America's Thirty-Third President

By 1960, former President Truman had evolved from the sober postwar statesman into the legendary "Give 'em hell, Harry" persona. His upset victory over Governor Thomas Dewey first triggered the change. The David Susskind interviews in 1961 completed this portrait of the new Harry, whom the adoring media loved. Gone was the one-time haberdasher and party loyalist under Kansas City's Prendergast machine, who later toiled as the workhorse (not the show horse) on the Senate committee investigating war contracts.

He had no use for President Eisenhower, who turned—in his opinion—on the Democrats who made him, and then—as the GOP standard bearer—attacked the Democrats' mess in Washington. He despised Vice President Nixon, the probable GOP candidate that year, for his political hatchet attacks—which in Truman's mind impugned his patriotism.

In May of 1953, Dianne and I had a guest visiting us from England: Edward Moulton-Barrett, great-nephew of poet Elizabeth Barrett Browning, and a leader in Britain's small Liberal Party. I took him—courtesy of Vice President Nixon—to lunch in the Senate Dining Room. At the next table,

Senator Stu Symington was chatting with his fellow Missourian, ex-President Truman. Truman was supporting Symington in his presidential primary race against the Democratic favorite, John Kennedy.

Having a foreign visitor with me emboldened my hand. I went over to the table, and said: "Mr. President, this is Edward Moulton-Barrett, a Liberal Party leader in London, and a great admirer of your leadership for the free world." I added, "Though I'm a Republican, I too am appreciative of NATO and the Marshall Plan. Someday I hope to go into politics. Can you give me some advice?"

Truman looked into my eyes, and told me to read American history and tell the truth. History, he said, was the subject to study: not political science. Politics, he told me, is not a science but an art.

In 2012, I had dinner with his nephew John Truman, a lawyer in St. Louis. He divulged two fascinating insights. The first was that Bess Wallace Truman always let her husband know he had married above himself. Her mother, Margaret Wallace, even sported a Dewey button in the 1948 campaign. The second was that Truman told him late in his life he knew he would be president when he accepted the vice presidential nomination in 1944—which is why he didn't want it. In fact, as John told me, everyone in the Senate knew that FDR wouldn't serve out his term.

John F. Kennedy: America's Thirty-Fifth President

To my wife and I, who were working for Vice President Nixon, Senator John Kennedy—only one door away in the Old Senate Office Building—was the archrival. In May of 1960, she and I attended an Alec Guinness double feature at the Georgetown Theater on Wisconsin Avenue. We had just finished watching *The Lavender Hill Mob* when the second feature, *The Man in the White Suit*, appeared on screen. To my right, I heard that familiar Boston twang telling the woman seated beside him that Alec Guinness was his favorite actor. It was Senator John Kennedy. When my wife and I were leaving the theater, I was accidentally tripped by his foot, and he said he was sorry. I replied brusquely, "That's quite all right, Senator Kennedy."

I thought about that incident with a pang of guilt when I heard of the assassination, sitting in the Masonic Lodge in Williamsport. The next day, I was asked to deliver his eulogy in the Pennsylvania State House. The ninety-year-old House Parliamentarian thought it was the most eloquent speech he had heard in his lifetime. But, to be fair, no one else in all that time had been asked to deliver a eulogy after an assassination.

> His grace and eloquence brought politics and public service to the campus—the cigar smoke of the political causes was replaced by the sunshine of college ideals. As Simonides wrote, "Go, stranger, and in Sparta tell / That he in faithful public service fell."[3]

Kennedy was an eloquent, charming man who was murdered before he had completed any substantial record. As a president, he did little. His apologists give him credit for dodging a nuclear war with Khrushchev. The fact is that his Bay of Pigs blunder let Castro have the Soviet arms that caused the crisis. Kennedy had to let Turkey dismantle our missiles pointed at the Soviets in order for Cuba to withdraw theirs. Moreover, there was no civil rights progress under Kennedy. The Great Society was Johnson's achievement, but Kennedy was the first presidential martyr to be as widely mourned as Lincoln.

Spiro Agnew: Nixon's Vice President

Of all the politicians I wrote for, Agnew was the best at delivering comic one-liners. He combined a Buster-Keaton-like poker face with a superb sense of timing. Today he is ridiculed as a right-wing buffoon and a crook. Both are unfair caricatures. He was elected governor of Maryland in 1966 against a rival who had the backing of Alabama Governor George Wallace. Agnew had the support of moderates, including his fellow governor, Nelson Rockefeller of New York. During the urban riots of 1968, Agnew, as governor, cracked down. Agnew originally supported Rockefeller, but when Rockefeller subsequently dropped out (without informing him), the disgruntled Agnew switched to Nixon. Nixon knew that he would need "northern ethnicity" at the convention, in the form of the Italian John Volpe, governor of Massachusetts, or the Greek Agnew (Anagnostopoulos at the time of emigration) to counteract the appeal of Wallace with northern city Democrats. Conservative leaders Strom Thurmond and Barry Goldwater preferred Agnew. It is now nearly forgotten that New York Mayor John Lindsay, a liberal Republican, nominated Agnew in 1968.

As for being a "crook": Agnew was simply a product of the Democrat-dominated Maryland system. A governor's salary was only twelve thousand dollars. It was the practice for a percentage of state contracts to go to the governor's office, to be used for political expenses (Christmas cards, office parties, etc.). As vice president in 1969, Agnew insisted on the percentage owed him in 1968, a mistake for which he was indicted and convicted.

My brother Sam had been county administrator under Agnew, who was executive of Baltimore County when he ran for governor. While Sam virtually ran the office during Agnew's campaign, as he told me, he never interfered with his boss's decisions. Nixon took the high road in his war against the media, and delegated Agnew to attack the administration's enemies. Nixon writer Pat Buchanan wrote Agnew's initial speeches, but William Safire was responsible for the famous rant against effete intellectual snobs and nattering nabobs of negativism. After that, Agnew became the bête noire of the media.

I flew with Agnew to Williamsport, Pennsylvania, for one of his many personal appearances in 1969. On being introduced to me, he shook his head, and said that I couldn't possibly be the brother of Sam Humes (which, of course, I was). I worked on his proposed remarks with a former writer for Rockefeller. In his talk, Agnew cited the Frenchman Albert Camus, who believed that one's service to society makes a job a vocation. Unexpectedly, Agnew pronounced Camus "KA-muss." When a reporter shook his head in puzzlement, I told him that "Kamus" was an early Athenian philosopher.

Nelson Rockefeller: Governor of New York and Ford's Vice President

My first glimpse of the billionaire governor of New York was in the spring of 1960. Local business leaders had selected Herman Schneebeli, a Buick dealer in Williamsport, to replace Congressman Alvin Bush in this safe Republican district after the latter's death. Schneebeli, a diminutive businessman, was in danger of losing when Democrats chose handsome Williamsport lawyer Dean Fisher (who had once clerked for my father) to oppose him.

Schneebeli had one card to play: He had roomed with Nelson Rockefeller at Dartmouth. In my capacity as a part-time Nixon staffer, I drove up from DC to observe. Rockefeller landed in a small plane at the airport in Wellsboro on the Pennsylvania northern tier. He was met by Schneebeli, and Rockefeller embraced him with a warm hello. The two climbed into a car and drove south in a motorcade to Williamsport, stopping at various places on the way. I saw Rockefeller at our final destination, and congratulated him on winning the governorship—saying that I had worked for New York Senator Ken Keating. He was grateful, but in moderation: The only man who could afford to say thanks-a-million said thanks-a-thousand. Rockefeller was a shortish, stocky fellow, but not fat. His eyes were narrow slits, but his powers of observation were keen, and his energy was boundless. The billionaire governor was a born campaigner.

Despite those personal gifts, and billions in the bank, he lost the nomination to Nixon twice: in 1960 and again in 1968. But in spite of their contrasts in background and style, the two were not different politically. Rockefeller, like Nixon, was a moderate Eisenhower Republican, and a strong Cold War anti-communist. Both were ambitious men aspiring to the presidency, but the Rockefellers' wealth was no match for the network of Republican loyalists Nixon had amassed over many years. If Rockefeller had one fault, it was the arrogance of wealth and privilege: something he had in common with the Kennedys.

Yet Rockefeller did have a gift for leadership. I asked Nixon in 1975 if there was one person who could take over the executive office from day one without any adjustment or training period. He answered, John Connally—

who had served as both governor of Texas and secretary of the treasury. Then he paused, before saying that one would need to include Nelson as well. In 1977, I asked Ford the same question. He gave the same answer, but put Rockefeller first and Connally second.

At the 1964 convention, when it was clear that Goldwater would be the nominee, I met with Jack Welles, Rockefeller's campaign manager. Rockefeller had given indications that he would not support Goldwater in the election. I told Welles this was a mistake; Rockefeller only had to give a pro-forma endorsement, as Governor Scranton would do. If he didn't, I explained, he would have difficulty being nominated at the Republican Convention in four years. I thought at that time that Nixon, with his loss for governor in 1962, was out in 1968, and the moderates might need Rockefeller after all.

Nixon did endorse Goldwater, and campaigned for him through that doomed endeavor. Rockefeller sat on his hands in what everyone knew would be Goldwater's loss. Four years later, the Republican convention went for Nixon over Rockefeller.

As in his divorce from his first wife during the 1964 campaign, Rockefeller revealed his egotism and a belief that money can paint over all problems. His own tenure at the White House would be spent as second-in-command for the down-to-earth and much-loved Gerald Ford.

Dick Cheney: Dubya's Vice President

I first met Dick Cheney on the Monday before the election in 1976. He was then Ford's chief of staff and I was a Ford speechwriter. I was with attorney J. D. Williams, and we met Cheney for lunch at the Hay-Adams Hotel in Washington.

Cheney was reconciled to Ford's defeat. He had looked at the latest polls, and the most recent debate had been unfortunate. The spillover from Ford's gaffe on Poland in the debate had aborted an upward trend for the president. It may have been easy to mistake the feisty Poles for a free people, but the reality of Soviet rule in the East was graven in iron as a major determinant of American defense readiness and foreign policy.

Cheney revealed that Ford did not believe he had stated that Poland was not under Soviet control, and he had forced Ford to look at the tape. He was never an obsequious aide; he was blunt and never sugarcoated the facts. When Williams offered him a place in his law firm, Cheney shook his head, but Williams later made a place for Cheney's daughters, Mary and Liz, as interns in his firm, Williams and Jensen.

Cheney's is not a likeable personality. His brusque demeanor often puts off even would-be friends who approach him. When he was Reagan's secretary of defense in 1990, he spoke at the Union League of Philadelphia—a pro-Republican private club—where he was honored with their most prestigious medal. I went to his room to give him a signed copy of my Churchill biography, *Churchill: Speaker of the Century*. He opened the door, took the book, and closed the door in my face. He never even penned a thank-you note, although he later told friends of mine how much he enjoyed it.

In 1995, friends who were pushing him for president organized a dinner fêting would-be campaign donors from the American Enterprise Institute. He was briefed on potential financial backers who would be there. But Cheney had no time for small talk or backslapping, and the presidential event collapsed.

In 2000, Congressman John LeBoutillier and I predicted that George W. Bush might pick someone like Dick Cheney or Senator Dick Lugar for vice president. Our reasoning was that the son Bush felt that the GOP tended to pick running mates who became liabilities, not assets; for example, Spiro Agnew and Dan Quayle, simply based upon where the potential VP lived. If that was the case, credentials and not geography should be made the determining factor. Certainly, Indiana and Wyoming were solidly Republican. But Lugar—a respected leader in foreign affairs—and Cheney—who had served as secretary of defense, presidential chief of staff, and congressman—possessed the gravitas that young Bush lacked. Cheney, as head of the screening committee for potential vice presidential running mates, was nowhere considered in the pundits' speculation.

But LeBoutillier thought Cheney might fare well in comparison to other suggested candidates, and win Bush's trust in the course of their long discussions. The choice of Cheney was received with approval by the Washington press establishment. Years later, Cheney would become another bête noire for the liberal press. But he proved his mettle by becoming the first "deputy president" under George W. Bush—a co-thinker and co-planner of presidential decisions.

During his days as secretary of defense, Cheney came to share the Pentagon's distrust of the State Department. The tenure of Colin Powell and later Condoleeza Rice at State only confirmed those views. In Cheney's eyes, the State Department's positions were products of consensus, which was almost a synonym for cowardice—or, at the very least, blame-shifting to avoid responsibility.

The decision to invade Iraq was George Bush's, but it was also Cheney's. The two men firmly believed that Saddam Hussein was a megalomaniac dictator in command of weapons of mass destruction, which he had already used his against his own people. The war in Iraq split the Republican Party, and brought on the hatred of the world press.

But this can be said about Cheney: He was the most consequential vice president in history. If Iraq develops into a viable representative republic— the only such majority-Muslim government in the Middle East—he and Bush will be regarded favorably by historians, even if their achievement was purchased at heavy cost.

Milton Eisenhower: Diplomat and Educator

Eisenhower's brother Milton deserves mention alongside presidents I have known and admired, as one of Ike's most trusted and influential advisors. When the former supreme allied commander and Columbia University president was running for America's highest office, some of the intellectual left circulated the canard that when Columbia trustees were searching for a president after the death of Nicholas Murray Butler, and the name Eisenhower came up, they were thinking of the academic Eisenhower, not the military one.

I mentioned the apocryphal tale to Milton. He laughed, and assured me that among the Eisenhower brothers, Ike was the smartest.

This exchange took place in Baltimore, early in 1967. I was meeting with Milton in the president's residence at Johns Hopkins University, in my capacity as Director of the Citizens for Nixon. At the general's request, his brother Milton was made chairman, and his son, Colonel John Eisenhower, became president of the Citizens campaign.

Milton's answer to me may have been due to his innate modesty, or because he idolized his older brother. Of the six boys reared in Abilene, Kansas, the third-born, Dwight, and Milton, the youngest, would end up the closest. The sibling rivalry that often surfaced between the older brothers never existed between Milton and Ike. Milton was his kid brother, and Ike was very proud indeed of Milton's academic career.

That affection ripened in the 1920s, when both young men found themselves in Washington: Ike as a mid-level officer in the War Department, and Milton as an academic PhD in the Department of Agriculture. Both were frustrated by the snail's pace of bureaucracy, and developed a bias against professional politicians.

While their government jobs barred them from taking part in politics, both were Republicans, by background and locale. Of course, not all career military types concealed their politics. General Douglas MacArthur, the army chief of staff for whom Ike served as an aide in 1932, was a Republican. In 1936, MacArthur had Major Eisenhower come to the Philippines to be his deputy. He bet Ike that President Roosevelt would lose to Governor Alf Landon of Kansas. Ike replied that Landon would not even carry his home state of Kansas—and he was right. Milton relished telling that story to me.

The ties between the two brothers were renewed again when Ike left the White House in 1961. Milton had left the presidency of Penn State for Johns Hopkins, which was no more than car distance from Baltimore, as it was from Gettysburg.

Milton was not one to vent his political opinions. But it is worthy to note that he hired Malcolm Moos to be a professor at Johns Hopkins. Moos, an admirer of Theodore Roosevelt, had written a history of the Republican Party. It was Milton who suggested that Moos do some speechwriting for his brother. Moos was the principal drafter of Eisenhower's Farewell Address, including Ike's warnings against the military–industrial complex.

Left-wing critics of Nixon hinted that President Eisenhower had little affection for Vice President Nixon. Yet Milton would offer only praise for Nixon, who was soon to become one of his extended family. Julie Nixon would marry David, Ike's only grandson, just before Christmas in 1968.

As a military man, Ike was not fond of professional politicians, but as Milton pointed out to me, they are the ones who announce for the presidency and get nominated. Ike detested Barry Goldwater, and bore a special animus for Nelson Rockefeller, for attacking Ike about the so-called missile gap between America and the Soviet Union. Milton held Nixon in high regard, and considered him to be the most qualified, the most experienced, and the most knowledgeable about foreign policy. What Milton didn't reveal was Ike's doubts about his electability. It was John Eisenhower who told me this, shortly before his father's death.

Milton said Mamie was a fervent fan of Nixon. She was thankful to Nixon for restricting Ike's speaking commitments for Vice President Nixon in 1960 to only three, as she believed it had extended her husband's life.

I had both dinner and breakfast with Milton. He had been, I think, a lonely widower since the death of his wife Ruth a few years before. He came off as avuncular, with a soft-spoken wisdom that eschewed negative personal comments about any of the political figures of the day, including Nelson Rockefeller or John Kennedy. He had kind words to say about Truman and Johnson, both of whom he knew. His fair and dispassionate judgment is what made him a popular appointment to many presidential commissions.

The next morning, Milton related some stories about his childhood in Abilene. Ike was not the storied fist-fighter in neighborhood brawls, but was a superb athlete. He played baseball for the Kansas State League, earning money to defray some travel expenses to and from West Point. His skill bore comparison to that of at least one Hall of Famer. Ike was impossible to strike out—like Willie "Hit 'Em Where They Ain't" Keeler, he would spray-hit to all fields—and he was a hard one to throw out at first because of his speed. How many people know that Ike once tackled Jim Thorpe? Smiling with his eyes, Milton was clearly a fan of his older brother.

Ed Meese: Reagan's White House Counsel and Attorney General

The name "Ed Meese" is almost synonymous with intrigue at the Reagan White House—a reputation he scarcely deserves. Behind his genial smile and affable personality lay a sadness. His son's early death had traumatized both parents, but perhaps it enhanced and empowered his patience in listening to others, and giving them the warmth of his approval and encouragement.

One complaint against Reagan's White House counsel was that he was disorganized (I can identify with that). The other was that he was "too nice a guy." Jim Baker, the moderate Republican and original Bushie, teamed up with Deputy Chief of Staff Michael Deaver to squeeze Meese out of the White House. In my opinion, Deaver was a social climber who had won Nancy's favor, and was not a real conservative.

Meese, who had been Reagan's counsel when he was governor of California, was Reagan's political conscience. In my dinners with him, I never heard him criticize anyone, including Deaver, Baker, or Secretary of State George Shultz. He would smile at any suggestion of mine about them, and say that his forte was not office politics.

He let himself be outmaneuvered by the president's wife, Nancy, who disdained the rumpled Meese, and responded to Deaver the courtier and Baker the Ivy Leaguer, even though Meese had been a Reagan advisor. Baker, as chief of staff, was a gatekeeper who only opened the door to Shultz's foreign-policy priorities after the Baker–Deaver team had Secretary of State Alexander Haig removed.

Meese may have been too sweet a guy for political infighting. But he was Reagan's guardian of conservative principles.

George Cleveland: Grandson of Grover Cleveland

Grover Cleveland is my favorite Democratic president. It was a delight to meet his grandson, who—with his walrus moustache and rotund figure—is a dead-ringer for the only Democrat between Lincoln and Taft. Grover Cleveland was also the only president in American history to have non-consecutive terms. Benjamin Harrison defeated him in 1888, but Cleveland beat the incumbent in 1892.

Perhaps my warm spot for President Cleveland stems from the fact that we lived in an old Victorian mansion in the Germantown section of Philadelphia, which was used by the ailing Cleveland when he was recovering from cancer surgery for a malignancy of the jaw. One of the surgeons who attended him was W. W. Keen of Washington, whose namesake and grandson was also a friend of ours.

A singular exception to most politicians, Cleveland never pandered to interest groups or sacrificed political principle. As one who had never served in the Civil War, he manifested courage in vetoing a pension bill for Union veterans, due to its large number of fraudulent claims. As sheriff of Buffalo, Cleveland hung two convicted murderers with his own hands. He could have delegated the distasteful task to an assistant. But, as George Cleveland told me, his grandfather said he had been elected to do the job and he did it.

When, as governor of New York, Cleveland ran against the Republican James Blaine, the Republicans circulated the rumor that Cleveland had fathered an illegitimate child. One campaign song went: "Ma, ma, where's my Pa? Gone to the White House, ha, ha, ha." When I met his grandson George in 2002, he divulged the true story. A child had been born out of wedlock, to a mother who had been seen with both Cleveland and his law partner. But since Cleveland was not married, he assumed the parentage, even though it has generally been accepted by later historians that he was not the true father. In the campaign, Cleveland said that since Blaine had led a spotless private life, even though his public record was soiled with corruption, it might be best to send him back to the type of life for which he was best qualified. On the other hand, Cleveland hoped that the voters would honor his record in public service as governor by voting him in for another term.

Cleveland was not a gregarious, backslapping politician like Blaine, but even if he was not always liked, he was respected, even by his enemies. When the Democrats nominated the pro-silver-and-easy-credit orator William Jennings Bryan to run against William McKinley, Cleveland, a pro-gold Democrat, was conflicted. He announced that he was still a Democrat, but very still. Among my most cherished possessions is one of the letters Grover Cleveland wrote as president.

Cleveland's speech announcing his veto of a high protective tariff is one of the greatest presidential addresses of all time. Republicans believed that such tariffs embodied a sacrosanct principle, guaranteeing economic progress—and providing the government with a source of revenue prior to the creation of an income tax. Cleveland told them that it was a condition that confronted them, not a theory: American families shouldered the burden when they paid inflated prices for goods protected by high tariffs. Cleveland's controversial move was courageous.

George Cleveland did not know his grandfather, who had died at Princeton, New Jersey, in 1908. (A student at Princeton, David Lawrence, later the founder of *U.S. News & World Report*, broke the news to the world.) But George did remember his grandmother, Frances Folsom Cleveland, who lived until 1947. She kept her beauty to the end, as he told me. She was the only First Lady to be married at the White House.

George also said that the Baby Ruth candy bar was not named after Babe Ruth, the "Yankee Slugger," but in honor of his great-aunt Ruth, who—when born in New York City—became a national sensation.

His father had told him that his grandmother, Frances, was a gracious hostess, sure and confident in herself. Our youngest First Lady—only twenty-one at the time of her marriage—she bore her much-older husband five children.

One story I heard demonstrates Frances Cleveland's sense of humor. At a White House luncheon, a young State Department type stared at his pear salad, which had a bug nestled inside the pear. Should he flick it away and draw attention to it? He decided to eat his salad, bug and all. George Cleveland's grandmother laughed telling the story, saying she had recommended the young man to her husband for a diplomatic post, due to his grace and aplomb under pressure.

Margaret Truman: Daughter of Harry Truman

Harry Truman's daughter possessed the manners of her mother, but the mettle of her dad. Well-mannered and soft-spoken, she had nothing of the "Give 'em hell, Harry" persona her father projected to the public. But like her mother, she also held firm views. One thing Margaret did impart to me was that Bess Truman never forgave her husband for running in 1948, and remained in Independence, Missouri, for most of the next four years.

I met Margaret at an Upper East Side dinner party in the fall of 1973. She and her husband, Clifton Daniel, the managing editor of *The New York Times,* were the only Democrats in attendance. At that time, the Nixon presidency was under attack, with new Watergate revelations breaking out each day.

As a former Nixon speechwriter, I was subjected to harsh questioning by New York Republicans at the table, all of whom had supported Dewey against Margaret's father, but were saying how they wished they had supported Truman. Much to her husband's disgust, Margaret refused to attack Nixon. She recalled the heavy toll the Republican attacks had taken on her own family when President Truman was accused of corruption and malfeasance.

Margaret told me that when she was in the White House, she pledged that she would never criticize an incumbent president publicly, because she knew what it was like to be in the White House under the brunt of such an attack. Her husband countered that he was well aware of what she thought of Nixon, having heard her opinion of him many times. Margaret reacted angrily. That had been pillow talk, she told him: comments made privately, and never to be repeated. He smirked and waved his hand in dismissal. Margaret confirmed that yes, she was a Democrat, and everyone knew that Nixon was not one of her favorite people. But this had nothing to do with her empathy for the commander-in-chief and his family.

Years later, Julie Nixon Eisenhower asked me for advice at the time when Clinton was under attack for his business dealings as governor of Arkansas, and his affair with Monica Lewinsky. She wanted to know how she should respond. I replied, "Quote Margaret Truman."

Pamela Churchill Harriman: Democratic Mega-Donor and Clinton's Ambassador to France

In the summer of 1969, when I was a White House speechwriter for Nixon, I was invited to lunch by an acquaintance, Dan Davidson. He had worked with former New York Governor Averell Harriman in fashioning a peace offer to North Vietnam in the closing days of President Nixon's campaign the previous year. Davidson, a slender, bespectacled, dark-haired young man, had attended Groton—like Harriman and FDR. Roosevelt gave the New York railroad heir his first government job, as an officer of the National Recovery Administration.

Davidson gave me an address—somewhere in Georgetown, I gathered. I arrived at the door and knocked. To my surprise, it was the home of Pamela Harriman—Winston Churchill's daughter-in-law—who provided a festive lunch with lemon sole and a white wine. Davidson, it turned out, often dined with the Harrimans. Pamela Churchill Harriman, if not a beauty, was strikingly charismatic in appearance. Her fair, dimly freckled face was topped by auburn hair, and she had a way of riveting her attention on you—rapt with every word you said.

Pamela was attracted to power and money. The governor, if not an influential voice in Nixon's Washington, still had the millions that wielded a power all its own. Although I was a lowly aide in the White House, being a speechwriter for Nixon made me the only one with an aura of power in the room. So, she focused all her attention on me. Her husband, a deaf octogenarian, was seated at the opposite end of the table from us. While he was treated with conjugal respect, she did not involve the silver-haired patrician in our conversation.

Pamela belied her more than five decades. She had the radiant wholesomeness of an English debutante—a role in which she had shone, as the Honourable Pamela Digby. In 1971, when her son Winston Churchill II was visiting, Pamela had him host a dinner for her at Governor Harriman's house, in honor of their recent marriage. My wife and I attended.

When I visited the downstairs powder room, I noticed that the towels bore the name "Pamela Churchill Harriman." Later, I said to my wife, "That is not correct. It should be 'Pamela Digby Harriman.' One does not carry a previous husband's name." My wife replied, "Her marriage may have been annulled, but if you had married a Churchill, you would have hyphenated your name to Churchill-Humes, and kept it even when you divorced her."

Pamela would accrue power in the Democratic Party by initiating the fundraising practice of "bundling." She would invite prospective donors to a dinner party she hosted, at which she would tap them for big contributions and then 'bundle' these funds under her name in packages of as much as one hundred thousand dollars. In this way, she became President Clinton's ambassador to France in 1993. Fluent in French, she had the presence and poise to make a superb envoy. She died while swimming in the embassy pool in 1997, of a massive cerebral hemorrhage.

Thomas Dewey: Governor of New York and Republican Presidential Nominee

I met the former Governor Dewey only once, in Chicago at the GOP Convention in 1960. He had just delivered a rip-roaring attack on Democratic candidate John Kennedy, touching on his youth and inexperience. Dewey mocked Kennedy for comparing himself to Thomas Jefferson, Alexander Hamilton, and Alexander the Great. The only reason Kennedy didn't include Hannibal, Dewey said, was because Hannibal was known for leading elephants across the Alps. Delivered in Dewey's operatically trained bass, this mock-heroic attack won resounding cheers and laughter.

To break the ice, I told him that both my mother and my mother-in-law had taken to their beds in near nervous breakdowns on his defeat in 1948. When I told him I worked for Nixon, Dewey revealed that he was the one who told Ike to take Nixon as VP in 1952 because of his youth, his anti-communist record, and his California origins.

His grandson, Thomas III, a classmate of my daughter's at St. Paul's School in Concord, New Hampshire, told me a revealing story: Just before he died, his grandfather said he wanted Nixon to call him. He said that he could advise him on how to get out of the encroaching Watergate scandal. This advice, if given, came too late to save Nixon from the relentless media-fueled drive to unseat him.

In 1971, Dewey sent a signed copy of one of his *TIME* magazine covers to me at the White House. I had it framed, and I keep it on a wall in my home.

Herbert Brownell: Eisenhower's Attorney General

I met one of America's best-known attorneys general late in his life. We would meet for dinner at the Waldorf Astoria—a hotel in midtown Manhattan—at the regular meetings of the Pilgrims Society, where we both served on the board. I told him I had dated his daughter Joan when she attended

Dickinson. She wasn't interested in politics. Herbert replied that I had dated the wrong one, because Ann, his older daughter, was the political one. On another occasion, I had lunch with Ann, who would inherit her father's executive seat on the Pilgrims.

At ninety, Brownell was still an imposing figure—totally bald, but fit. He told me that his first experience in politics was beating Tammany Hall for a New York state legislative seat representing Greenwich Village. Tom Dewey, his former Columbia law school classmate, was his manager. All the bohemian intellectuals of Greenwich Village backed him. He would be the GOP national chairman during the 1944 Dewey campaign against the dying FDR. In the campaign, as he told me, they mentioned code words like "weary," "tired," and "fatigued" to remind voters of a declining president. Brownell didn't manage the ill-fated 1948 campaign, but he did advise Dewey to hit Truman harder.

As attorney general, Brownell would take responsibility for one of Ike's worst appointments—that of William J. Brennan for Supreme Court justice. While attending a meeting of state attorneys general in Washington, he heard most of Brennan's address, entitled "No Super Legislatures." Later that day, he saw Eisenhower at a Cabinet meeting and recommended Brennan, a Democrat, to be appointed justice. (It was 1956, an election year, and a Catholic Democrat had seemed an opportune choice.) Subsequently, Brownell discovered to his chagrin that Brennan had been echoing New Jersey Chief Justice Arthur Vanderbilt's speech on judicial restraint, which posited that the Supreme Court should not become a third legislature.

My daughter Mary set up lunch for us at The Brook just before Brownell died. Seated next to him was young Tom Dewey, son of the former presidential candidate. Brownell told me that the first time he met General Eisenhower was in France. Brownell had arrived in Paris the night before, and Eisenhower asked him how he entertained himself. Brownell admitted that he had gone to the Folies Bergere. Eisenhower's frown told him that he thought it frivolous for a distinguished member of the New York Bar to be looking at nude women cavorting. Likewise, his daughter Ann did not like this anecdote about her father.

Brownell's most significant decision as attorney general was persuading Eisenhower to send federal troops to Little Rock to safeguard the integration of schools, against the wishes of states' rights governor Orval Faubus.

Alice Roosevelt Longworth: Teddy Roosevelt's Daughter

My best friend (and former congressman) John LeBoutillier took me to Alice Longworth's Massachusetts Avenue townhouse in October 1978. She served us iced tea. John's grandmother, Flora Whitney Miller, had roomed with Alice during World War I when Flora was engaged to Quentin Roosevelt, who was flying in France. (He would die there in a crash.) Alice told John that she had always considered his grandmother to be one of the family.

The beautiful pearl necklace Alice wore had been presented to her by the President of Cuba in 1908. She had me sit next to a cushion that was emblazoned with these words: "If you can't say something good about someone, sit right here by me." At age ninety-three, she was still full of barbs, but she admired Richard Nixon. She called Watergate a farce, and declared that Franklin Roosevelt had wire-tapped his wife Eleanor.

Of her father, she said that he may have ignored her because she was the cause of her mother's death. Alice Hathaway Lee Roosevelt suffered from a kidney ailment that had been masked by her pregnancy, and died on Valentine's Day 1884—two days after the birth of Alice, her only child. She told me that her father could not stand Winston Churchill because they were too much alike—but also out of envy, the way a debutante five years past her season views the new deb of the season. George Washington was her favorite president, while she thought Truman's rival Dewey resembled the little man one sees on a wedding cake. She assessed Eisenhower as a great general but a so-so president. She was for Taft against Ike in '52, although she had contempt for Taft's famous father, who, as she told us, meant well, but feebly. Her opinion of Teddy Roosevelt? Like his daughter, he loved to be the center of attention; he wanted to be the bride at every wedding and the corpse at every funeral.

Diana Hopkins: Daughter of Harry Hopkins, Aide to Franklin Roosevelt

Diana Hopkins spent her formative years in the White House. President Roosevelt had his number-one advisor Harry Hopkins reside close to him, and his family came along to Pennsylvania Avenue. My wife got to know Diana in Blue Ridge, Pennsylvania, a mountain resort town north of Washington. When I served as a speechwriter for Nixon, we all spent time there.

President Nixon had initiated a policy in which all who had once lived in the White House would be invited back to see their former premises. So, the only time my wife and I were ever on the third floor in the private residence was in escorting Diana and her children to see where she had once lived. One room Diana asked to see was the Monroe room, where Churchill stayed in December 1941 just after Pearl Harbor.

On December 24 of that same month, Diana related, one of the White House ushers—a dignified black gentleman—knocked on her bedroom door and told her solemnly that the prime minister wanted to see her. She was frightened to death, but put on her bathrobe and followed him to Churchill's door. The prime minister was wearing a silk robe with green dragons on it. He put down his cigar, stood up and opened his arms, and told her that he was just a lonely old grandfather on Christmas Eve who wanted to hug a little girl goodnight.

On Christmas day, Diana opened a present from Eleanor Roosevelt, her godmother. She had been hoping for a lace-trimmed silk handkerchief or a bottle of toilet water, but instead, it was an Anglican prayer book. She was awed by her tall godmother, with her loud, commanding voice. Eleanor told Diana that she knew the prayer book would be put to good use.

In 1938, Roosevelt had made Hopkins his secretary of commerce. The fifty-one-year-old former social worker was given the Cabinet post with a broad portfolio, allowing him to perform a variety of tasks for Roosevelt. But during the war years, Diana probably saw more of her godmother than she did of her own father. Acting as the eyes and ears of the paralyzed president, Hopkins was constantly in transit—particularly to and from London, where he was FDR's personal intermediary with Churchill. As Hopkins told his friends, it was not easy dealing with the two most colossal egos in the world.

At one point in the war, Churchill called Hopkins to 10 Downing Street for a special ceremony. With a suitably written proclamation, the prime minister dubbed him Lord Root of the Matter. When some vexing problem arose between the two countries, Hopkins would get the president on the line, and it would be resolved in short order. From the summer of 1939 to December 1941, Hopkins was an interventionist, fully aware of Britain's dire predicament. Roosevelt was sympathetic to Britain, but waited for American public opinion to rally behind U.S. entry into the war. Roosevelt, who had won a third term in 1940 pledging that America would not go to war, was not willing to tell America what Britain's defeat would mean for the United States.

Diana told me that Londoners who survived the Blitz in 1940 (before America entered the war) were moved by her father's words from the Book of Ruth: "Whither thou goest, I shall go. Whither thou lodgest, I will lodge. Thy people are my people . . . and thy God my God" (Ruth 1:16). Churchill wept when he heard Hopkins speak. More than any of Churchill's oratory, it assured the British that America would eventually go to war.

Hopkins was eight years older than FDR, and his family thought he would probably die before the president. Wan and sallow-faced, Hopkins was a frail figure wasted by a bout of cancer that prompted the removal of half his stomach. His diet seemed to consist of cigarettes and coffee. Roosevelt, on the other hand, displayed a bonhomie and vigor that belied his failing health. He did not outlive Hopkins, who died in 1946.

While in London, Hopkins had more on his mind than his health or the urgent crises of the war: His son Stephen had enlisted in the U.S. Marines without telling his father. Stephen Hopkins died in February 1944 at Guadalcanal, in a Japanese assault. He was the only White House resident ever to be killed in action.

Stephen had attended the Hill School, a private academy outside Philadelphia. Being a Hill School alumnus myself, I arranged for a brass plaque to be put in the campus chapel. (My grandfather's plaque is there, without any real merit—it was done by his widow's gift.)

At Stephen's commemorative service, I quoted from A. E. Housman's lines on the Ludlow Fair, a poem familiar to Stephen:

"The lads that will die in their glory and never be old."[4]

Stephen's sister Diana was there to honor her brother at the chapel ceremony.

Albert Hayes-Davis: Great-Grandson of Jefferson Davis

In 2015, I was invited to Marshfield, Missouri for the annual spring conclave of descendants of American presidents. Under a loose interpretation of the rules, a descendant of Jefferson Davis might qualify. He was, after all, an *American* president, if not a U.S. president. That is where I met Albert Hayes-Davis.

Jeff Davis's great-grandson was as tall and handsome as his eminent forebear. His grandmother, Davis's daughter, had been asked by her mother to hyphenate her son's name, to keep the name of Davis alive.

Bert Hayes-Davis repeated some family lore to me: Jefferson Davis used to remark on the irony that as secretary of war, a Cabinet post in the Franklin Pierce administration, he had reorganized, refitted, and re-equipped the Union Army that would defeat him only a few years later. Davis, who left the post in 1857, would say that his time spent serving the New Englander Pierce was the happiest time in the course of his public service.

I told him about the experience of my ten-year-old daughter with someone who had once sat on Jefferson Davis's lap in Mississippi in 1874. This was a Mrs. Rathbone of Old Westbury, Long Island, a centenarian and a native of New Orleans who could still re-arrange the plate service in her little dollhouse. Ex-president Davis often visited the family farm in Mississippi, where he spent his last years. The Rathbones were friends of the Davis family. On a wall of the Rathbone house in Old Westbury, my daughter Mary noted a tableau in which the portraits of Jefferson Davis, Robert E. Lee, and Stonewall Jackson were arranged with that of Abraham Lincoln! Mary asked her hostess, "Why do you have a picture of Lincoln next to a picture of Jefferson Davis, Mrs. Rathbone?"

Mrs. Rathbone replied that this was a wise comment for someone Mary's age, and told her the following story. When she was four, sitting in Mr. Davis's lap, and heard the name Lincoln come up in the adult conversation, she asked the former Confederate president if Lincoln had been a bad man. Davis replied that Lincoln had been a good man, but that the two of them had differences, as adults do—disagreements they couldn't overcome.

When he heard this anecdote, Bert Hayes-Davis smiled, and told Mary that he could remember his grandmother saying the very same thing about the two of them.

Harold Stassen: Governor of Minnesota and Presidential Hopeful

At age thirty-two, Harold Stassen was "the boy wonder" governor of Minnesota, the keynoter of the 1940 convention that nominated Wendell Wilkie for president. He seemed certain to one day become the nominee himself, if not president. The closest he came to this was in 1948, when Dewey destroyed him in a debate in which Stassen called for the outlawing of the Communist Party. He ran for governor of Pennsylvania in 1958, hoping to position himself to run for president in 1960. The Republican organization barely beat him. Then, in 1959, he ran for mayor of Philadelphia, and lost. Still, every four years at the GOP Convention, he would maintain a booth. It was a stop on his quixotic quest for world peace.

I would see him often at the Union League in Philadelphia, sitting by himself. He was a lawyer at Stassen and Kephart (where my friend Joe Bongiovanni was a partner). His big client was the American Baptist Convention, whose headquarters was in suburban Philadelphia.

Stassen knew I had worked for Nixon, and one afternoon he told me that he had met him in 1945, in the Pacific, and that Nixon had expressed an interest in working for Stassen in 1948. Stassen characterized Nixon as a bright man, warped by ambition, and reminded me that Nixon had undercut his own Governor Warren on the train from California to Chicago in 1952, in working with Dewey to get the VP spot with Ike. Interestingly, Stassen reminded me of Warren—both were big handed and large headed, showing their Nordic background.

In 1956, Stassen headed a "Christian Herter for VP" movement to stop Nixon. It was aborted when Ike endorsed Nixon for another term as vice president.

I told Stassen that when I was in the White House in 1969, I recommended that Nixon put him on the group planning the twentieth anniversary of the United Nations. Along with Stassen, Arthur Vandenberg had been appointed to the original founding commission by FDR. Nixon was not receptive to the suggestion.

Stassen's tragedy is that he outlived his reputation.

Ted Sorensen: John F. Kennedy's Speechwriter

I didn't meet the writer of John Kennedy's Inaugural Address until 1990, but I had long admired his craftsmanship. While in the Pennsylvania legislature, I had studied the speeches Senator Kennedy delivered in his 1960 campaign.

Sorensen was by then a lawyer for a big firm that was almost catty-corner from The Brook, where I hosted him for lunch. Shy and bespectacled, he seemed ill matched to the hurly-burly of politics. He was also a paradox of sorts. Having come from a Protestant Republican family in Nebraska—the American heartland—he came east to join the Massachusetts Democrat's Senate staff. A pacifist in World War II, he would pen the most hawkish inaugural address in history: "We shall pay any price, bear any burden, meet any hardship, support any friend, oppose any foe to assure the survival and the success of liberty."[5]

One might argue that the internal rhyme and alliterative phrase were more poetical than practical. When I raised that point with Sorensen, he replied that inaugural addresses are poetry, not political science.

He also revealed to me that when he showed his draft to the president-elect in Palm Beach during his Christmas vacation, Kennedy only changed one word, removing "enemy" and substituting "adversary."

Although we were both trained as lawyers, we shared a fascination with words and sounds, and we both manifested that love in crafting sonnets for family birthdays and anniversaries.

By the Reagan eighties, Sorensen had moved away from the Cold Warrior sentiments of President Kennedy to the hard left. Perhaps his third wife, Gillian Martin—a senior advisor for the United Nations Foundation—was a catalyst in that evolvement.

I told Sorensen that one of the electoral gambits I had lifted from his campaign speeches was his use of a poignant historical anecdote to inspire the closing peroration. In my book, *Instant Eloquence* (1973), I called these "soul shakers." (In 2007, I expanded upon this theme with a book of the same title for the Methodist Press, of a hundred such heart-lifting stories.)

Kennedy frequently delivered two Sorensen "soul shakers" at airport stopovers during the 1960 campaign. Standing at the back of the crowd, Sorensen would signal one or the other to the candidate by waving crude pictures of a candle or a sunrise.

The candle alluded to Colonel James Davenport, Speaker of the House in the Connecticut legislature during June 1780, when an eclipse of the sun rendered noon as black as midnight. In that time, more religious than our own, the Connecticut Delegation panicked and motioned for adjournment.

On the campaign trail in Houston, Texas, in September of 1960, Kennedy described what happened next: "Colonel Davenport came to his feet, and he silenced the din with these words: 'The Day of Judgment is either approaching or it is not. If it is not, there is no cause for adjournment. If it is, I choose to be found doing my duty. I wish therefore that candles be brought.'"[6]

The sunrise was a reference to Benjamin Franklin's closing words to the Constitutional Convention in 1787. The eighty-year-old Philadelphian pointed to the chair on which General Washington presided at times. The back of the chair bore the design of a sun sitting low on the horizon. At Sorensen's signal, Kennedy would describe how Franklin then turned to the assembly and assured them that it was a rising and not a setting sun.

Kennedy's Inaugural Address featured one of the most quoted lines in American history: "Ask not what your country can do for you—ask what you can do for your country."[7]

Some may say the Kennedy speech was more poetry than policy, but JFK, through Sorensen, reached heights of eloquence and elegance that would-be speechwriters will always emulate.

H. R. "Bob" Haldeman: White House Chief of Staff

When I was kicked upstairs from the White House to the State Department in 1970, I was given a farewell party. Bob Haldeman came with a present: a bottle of German wine; in other words, non-intoxicating white German grape juice. Both Haldeman and fellow Nixon loyalist John Erlichman were teetotaling Christian Scientists.

Haldeman was an effective and efficient executor of Nixon's wishes and commands. He was quick minded and bright, which one would expect for someone who had headed the largest advertising firm in Los Angeles, J. Walter Thompson. Yet one might also have expected a person from that profession to have more creative imagination. In the 1960 campaign, he led the team of advance men. Two years later, he managed Nixon's losing race for governor, an appointment that had been opposed not only by Nixon's chief of staff Bob Finch, but also by Nixon's wife, Pat.

Haldeman dismissed the people around Finch (such as Nixon adviser Herbert Klein) as soft and moderate. (I was labeled as the Finch type—one reason I didn't last.) John Mitchell concurred with that assessment of us.

Nixon was impersonal and direct with Haldeman; they were not socially intimate. He admired Haldeman's no-nonsense dispatch of assignments. In some ways, Nixon treated Haldeman like he was a modern-day computer. He could ask Haldeman for information or background on people or issues, and Haldeman, in a short time, would give him a briefing. But he didn't like to tell Nixon unpleasant or bad news. This would not serve Nixon well in the later Watergate crisis.

Nixon, like LBJ and JFK before him, would often vent around his underlings. Bob Finch would let it pass, knowing he was blowing off steam.

Haldeman, Teutonic and literal, with no sense of humor, might take a directive given in anger as an order.

Haldeman's range of acquaintance was extensive, and extremely diverse. In 1971, Viscount "Tony" Furness invited me to a dinner for the ninety-year-old Marquis of Salisbury in London. Tony was the son of Thelma, Viscountess Furness, born Thelma Morgan—the twin sister of Gloria Morgan, mother of Gloria Vanderbilt. At one time, Thelma was the inamorata of the Prince of Wales, later Edward VIII, before his marriage to Wallis Simpson. Tony asked me to give his regards to Haldeman, who had been his roommate at Harvard (i.e., the Harvard Episcopal School, a boarding school in Los Angeles).

I last saw Bob Haldeman at the opening of the Nixon Library, as one of a crowd of Nixon scholars and supporters. I was with Jonathan Aitken, Nixon's biographer. Haldeman reminded Jon how Churchill had describe Jon's uncle, Lord Beaverbrook, as a foul-weather friend—in other words, the opposite of a fair-weather friend. And that, Haldeman declared, was the best way to describe the loyal friends of Richard Nixon who had come together that day to honor his legacy.

Tommy "The Cork" Corcoran: Advisor to Franklin Roosevelt

"Tommy," as he insisted I call him, was a member of FDR's "Brain Trust." He drafted most of the New Deal legislation, including Social Security and the Unemployment Compensation Program, which he said he had lifted from David Lloyd-George and Winston Churchill's Liberal social program of 1911–1912.

Corcoran looked like a leprechaun from the Emerald Isle. His Irish Catholic, urban New York background led him to him first support Democrat Al Smith, but astonishingly, he voted for Herbert Hoover in 1932. (He never told FDR.) Corcoran had been called to help draft Hoover's Reconstruction Finance Program, and became miffed when Governor Roosevelt refused to meet with Hoover, remaining adamant in that refusal after his election and until his inauguration in March. Because of this, Corcoran voted Republican for the first time.

By 1972, the widowed Corcoran was romancing Anna Chenault, the widow of General Claire Lee Chenault, who led the Flying Tigers in World War II. A native of China, this Washington hostess was working for Nixon as a partisan of Chinese Nationalists in Taiwan. Lobbyist Corcoran was also for Nixon. He raised money for Nixon in 1972 and at his request, I did some favors for his estranged daughter. Tommy once invited me to share a law office with him.

Corcoran told me this story: After FDR had won the presidency in 1932, Corcoran was visiting retired Justice Oliver Wendell Holmes, for whom he had once clerked. The phone rang, and Holmes told him that the president wanted to pay a call on him. Corcoran hid in a closet when FDR arrived.

FDR asked: What are you doing, Mr. Justice, on this beautiful spring day?

Reading Greek, replied Holmes.

FDR seemed surprised, and asked him: Why would anyone read Greek on this warm, sunny day?

To improve my mind, Holmes answered.

Then the new president had a question for the ninety-year-old jurist, who had fought in the Civil War and sat on John Quincy Adams's lap: Your life, Mr. Justice, spans more than half of the life of this republic. What advice can you give this new president?

Holmes replied: We are in a national crisis, Mr. President. You must marshal your battalions and fight.

Afterwards, Corcoran asked Holmes what he thought of the president, and Holmes told him that FDR was just like his cousin Theodore: first-class temperament and second-class mind.

Herbert "Pete" Hoover III: Grandson of President Hoover

In August 1996, I was invited to speak at the 122nd Birthday Celebration of President Herbert Hoover at West Branch, Iowa, the thirty-first president's birthplace. Oddly, the group organizing the event asked me to deliver my most popular talk—the one on Churchill. Although the lives of the president and Churchill almost exactly coincided—Hoover was born in 1874 and died in 1964—they had little else in common. Moreover, they cordially disliked each other. They had tangled in Belgium where Hoover was organizing his European relief effort. In my talk, I only mentioned their similar life span, and concentrated on what they had in common: a hatred of war's devastation, and a belief that Germany was treated too harshly at Versailles.

In Iowa, I stayed with Pete Hoover, the grandson—called Pete in the sense of "Repeat"—Herbert Hoover III. Pete had grown up in New York City, and spent many Sunday afternoons and other occasions with his grandfather in his suite at the Waldorf Astoria. The president's closest friend was his former chief of staff, Douglas MacArthur, who was also living in the hotel. Sometimes they'd listen to the Army–Navy football game together. The general would supervise Pete's lead-soldier games with his brother. Neither MacArthur nor Hoover were close to President Eisenhower; Hoover had supported Taft in 1952.

I spoke in West Branch on a Saturday. On Sunday, there was a religious service, which was alternately led by clergy of the Protestant, Catholic, Quaker, or other faiths. That year, there was a rabbi. In his sermon, he never mentioned Hoover, although Hoover's family was present.

Afterwards, I accosted him, and asked him: "Why didn't you mention Hoover?" He replied that he disagreed with Hoover's politics.

I asked him: "Did you oppose his relief of starving Belgians? Did you oppose his founding of CARE, the relief organization? Did you oppose his taking no salary as President?" He shrugged, and walked away.

While FDR was known for his love of martinis, Hoover invented the unique variant known as the Gibson. In 1916, before America had entered the war, Hoover had gone to Belgium to supervise the relief of its war-devastated citizens. The Germans, however, refused to give Hoover a pass to travel within Belgium, a neutral nation. But Hugh Gibson, our ambassador in Brussels, arranged to have Hoover meet the Germans in their embassy for lunch. After many drinks, and a lavish meal, no agreement was reached. Gibson suggested that they meet again for dinner. To Hoover, he confided that the embassy staff would serve martinis as a pre-dinner aperitif before the meeting, but that the Americans' martinis, topped with onions, not olives, would be filled with ice water.

After the dinner, preceded by the Americans' faux martinis and the Germans' full-proof ones, Hoover was given his pass.

When Hoover was president, he would serve guests—notwithstanding Prohibition—what he called his "Gibsons." That was the origin of the name Gibson, for an onion-topped gin martini.

The best memory for me of that weekend was the initiation rite the night I arrived: Full-proof Gibsons, named after Hugh Gibson, ambassador to Belgium, were served to us in our screened cabin.

Jack Kemp: Republican Vice-Presidential Candidate

Jack Kemp really *was* "The Happy Warrior." Yes, FDR had famously used this moniker to describe Al Smith in 1924, but Smith was splenetic and sour in person. Bob Dole picked Kemp to be his running mate in 1996, partly because they were opposites. Dole was dour and moody. Jack radiated hope and happiness like Reagan—a natural candidate type whereas Dole was not. Dole picked Kemp to make the Reaganite-movement conservatives happy. It was an awkward marriage. Pairing a balance-the-budget fiscal conservative with the foremost political advocate of supply-side economics did not make for a good fit.

A former all-American quarterback who starred for the Buffalo Bills, Kemp parlayed his football fame to stride across the racial barrier. He was heard not just in the country clubs, but the inner cities. Even the Jewish community liked him a lot more than Bush or Dole. Kemp and not Bush was the movement conservatives' choice in 1988. When Kemp bailed out, banker Lewis Lehrman—1982's barely losing candidate for New York governor— dismantled his Kemp for President organization. Jack's enthusiasm knew no bounds, particularly when he said that if he could speak like me, he would have been president. He introduced me to audiences and friends a couple of times. The last occasion was in 2007 at the home of William Simon Jr., in the California Palisades, two years before cancer ended Kemp's life.

Kemp's only degree was in physical education, but he tried to compensate by quoting Adam Smith, Friedrich von Hayek, and Milton Friedman in his talks. If he just kept it to football, he would have had his audiences in thrall. Because of my British associations, he once asked me to draft an "after-dinner" speech to the Reform Club—one of London's original gentleman's clubs, in Pall Mall. I told him that a speech delivered after dinner should be light, and consist of self-deprecating humor, sketches of well-known politicians, and American football, followed by a sentimental paean to Anglo-American unity. I wrote it that way. Instead, he delivered a forgettable treatise on economics.

Curtis Roosevelt: Grandson of Franklin Roosevelt

In March 2008, I spoke at an FDR symposium in Hyde Park, New York. The president's grandson Curtis introduced me. Curtis was actually the son of Anna Roosevelt Dall, the eldest child of Eleanor and Franklin. Because his mother divorced his father early on, and then later divorced his stepfather, the grandson had taken back the Roosevelt name. Nicknamed "Buzzie," he was born Curtis Roosevelt Dall.

As an octogenarian, he lived near Springwood, the family estate in Hyde Park, where he had spent his formative years. At the time, this was a farm where the Roosevelts raised their own produce and milked their own cows. Curtis learned to ride on a U.S. Army horse. He commented on my book, *The Wit & Wisdom of FDR*, adding some anecdotes of his own. He well remembered, as he said, the twinkle in his grandfather's eye and his delight as a storyteller. FDR loved reading the Charles Dickens classic *A Christmas Carol* aloud every Christmas Eve. In 1941, a member of the multimillionaire du Pont family got married, and FDR was a guest at this wedding. Curtis recalled Roosevelt's glee at the sight of so many rich getting soaked, which was how the populist president described this event. He also told me that FDR also had a gift for mimicry, and was a wicked imitator of his foes, such as patriarch Joseph P. Kennedy and mine-union leader John L. Lewis.

The feud between the Sagamore Hill and Hyde Park branches of the Roosevelt family is legendary, and Curtis told me that his mischievous and acerbic cousin, Alice Roosevelt Longworth, was to blame. He said that contrary to how she was described by the press, his widowed grandmother Eleanor was not dowdy. Curtis lived with her in Paris, where she bought designer dresses in conservative styles and dark colors. He also confided that his own mother, Anna, had a crush on Adlai Stevenson and never liked JFK:

Too much profile, not enough courage, as she put it. Anna hated Nixon, and was mortified when her son John (the only Republican in the family) seconded Nixon's nomination at the 1960 Republican National Convention.

Robert Finch: Nixon's Chief of Staff and Secretary of Health, Education, and Welfare

Bob Finch was Vice President Nixon's chief of staff. Nixon had recruited the Los Angeles lawyer in 1957 as he geared up for the 1960 presidential campaign. The tall, Hollywood-handsome Finch radiated a genial likeability—in short, the assets Nixon lacked. He was a great stand-in to meet key potential Nixon fundraisers or influential state leaders in elegant surroundings when the vice president was unavailable.

Finch had shrewd political judgment. He advised against Nixon's fifty-state campaign as being a waste of time, and later, against a serious error: debating Senator John Kennedy on television. Later, he would urge the defeated Nixon not to run for governor of California in 1962, which led to a second disheartening loss.

When Nixon again sought the presidency, in 1968, he considered Finch as his VP choice. In 1966, Finch had been elected lieutenant governor of California. He finished more than twenty thousand votes ahead of Ronald Reagan, who was elected governor in the same race (but never forgave him). Nixon's rationale for naming Finch was that neither a Rockefeller moderate like Oregon Senator Mark Hatfield nor a conservative southerner like Florida Governor Claude Kirk was right for the GOP ticket. He was talked out of it with the argument that Finch lacked experience in foreign policy. Instead, President Nixon appointed him secretary of that sprawling bureaucratic operation, the Department of Health, Education, and Welfare.

But it was not a good fit for his talents. He had no liking for bureaucratic infighting and competing budget demands. When Finch resigned in 1972, his successor was Caspar Weinberger, later President Reagan's secretary of defense—a master at controlling bureaucratic demands.

In retrospect, Finch never should have left California. He would have become governor in 1970, when Reagan resigned. With his matinee-idol looks, Finch would have swept California, Texas, and Florida to win a presidential election. He was born to be a national candidate, not the manager of a cumbersome bureaucracy.

Robert K. Gray: Eisenhower's Secretary of the Cabinet

Bob Gray was the ultimate courtier. Handsome, with prematurely silver hair, he fell just short of fawning towards those in power. He came to the White

House from Nebraska as a protégé of Fred Seaton, who was later Ike's secretary of the interior.

Accommodating and attentive to detail, Gray had the soul of a bureaucrat. My wife worked for him in his job as the head of patronage in the White House. He was a considerate boss. He lived quietly in Georgetown with his partner. (This was in a time before gays came out.) For his Christmas party, two different sets of invitations had been sent out, with two different addresses. Gray met Cabinet members at the front door, while his partner greeted staff such as Dianne and myself "below stairs," at the cellar entrance. Gray, however, had borrowed our silver service and candelabra for the upstairs, where he would greet the secretary of state and other dignitaries.

At one point I told Dianne I wanted to check on our silver, and went upstairs to mingle with the A-list, including Secretary of State Christian Herter and UN Ambassador Henry Cabot Lodge Jr. Under the watchful eyes of Bob Gray, nothing had gone missing—not even a coffee spoon.

Checkers: The Black and White Cocker Spaniel of the Nixon Family

In August of 1956, I was visiting Jay Clark, whose mother had been a friend of my mother's. Jay lived in the Spring Valley section of Washington, DC, near to where Vice President Richard Nixon and his family lived. On my way to Clark's house, I decided to stop by a butcher shop to pick up several steaks and a large bone. The steaks were for my host and hostess, Jay and his wife Betsy, and the bone was for the famous canine member of the Nixon family, the black and white cocker spaniel named Checkers.

I set off for the Nixon house, and rang the doorbell. A housekeeper answered the door and said that the Nixons were away. I told her that I had come with a gift for the four-legged member of the family.

The housekeeper chuckled, and asked if I meant Checkers. She motioned for me to make my way around to the back door, where the friendly Checkers was eagerly waiting. He was even more friendly when he smelled the contents of the parcel wrapped in butcher's paper: the juicy bone, which, the housekeeper told me, he much preferred to dog food. Salivating with anticipation, he wagged his tail back and forth. I made him sit and offer me his paw before I let him have the bone.

Checkers had been catapulted into the national consciousness during the 1952 presidential campaign, following Nixon's nomination for the vice presidency as Eisenhower's running mate. A "secret fund" established by wealthy Republican donors for Nixon had come to light, jeopardizing Nixon's spot on the Republican ticket. Nixon made the unforgettable decision to go on national television and give a full accounting of his finances to show that he couldn't possibly be using the money to fund a lavish lifestyle. Now known to history as "The Checkers Speech," Nixon's appeal to the public was broadcast on September 23, 1952, and is considered one of the most significant political speeches in the history of American politics.

Nixon said that he used the funds only for campaign expenses, thereby saving money for the American taxpayer, and that any gifts he received were always instantly returned, with one exception: Checkers, a gift to Nixon's little girls from a man in Texas. Before delivering this speech, he wasn't sure whether he would yield to the pressure to resign from the ticket. He decided to ask viewers to write in to the Republican National Committee and state their views as to whether he should remain the VP candidate. The response was far greater than expected, and overwhelmingly in favor of Nixon. The RNC received more than one hundred and sixty thousand telegrams, and switchboards were jammed as viewers phoned state and local Republican offices. My mother had been one of the letter writers. A staunch Republican, she would have cheered his victory in 1968.

My encounter with Checkers was the first time I had met any member of the Nixon family. That was soon to change when I married Dianne, who joined the vice president's staff the following year. But for now, I was enjoying my time with Checkers. Settling down with the bone between his front paws, Checkers had no idea of how he had changed the course of American history.

Notes

1. Handwritten note, property of the author. Published in: James C. Humes, *Nixon's Ten Commandments of Leadership and Negotiation: His Guiding Principles of Statecraft* (New York: Scribner, 1997), 13–171.

2. "Watergate" refers to the break-in at the Watergate Hotel in Washington, DC, in which papers were stolen from Democratic National Committee headquarters. The ensuing Watergate 'scandal,' if not precisely fake news, represented a gross exaggeration in terms of its relative importance to President Nixon's achievements. Watergate's power to take down a president was only possible in an age when the biased media ruled public opinion unchallenged—a state of tyranny that the Internet has swept away.

3. James C. Humes, *Instant Eloquence: A Lazy Man's Guide to Public Speaking* (New York: Harper & Row, 1973), 50.

4. A. E. Housman, "XXIII," in *A Shropshire Lad* (Mineola, New York: Dover Publications, Inc., 1990), 16.

5. John F. Kennedy, "Inaugural Address," January 20, 1961. Online by Gerhard Peters and John T. Woolley, *The American Presidency Project*, http://www.presidency.ucsb.edu/ws/?pid=8032, accessed April 27, 2018.

6. John F. Kennedy, "Speech of Senator John F. Kennedy, Houston Coliseum, Houston, TX," September 12, 1960, online by Gerhard Peters and John T. Woolley, *The American Presidency Project*, http://www.presidency.ucsb.edu/ws/?pid=25772, accessed May 3, 2018.

7. John F. Kennedy, "Inaugural Address," January 20, 1961, online by Gerhard Peters and John T. Woolley, *The American Presidency Project*. http://www.presidency.ucsb.edu/ws/?pid=8032, accessed April 27, 2018.

Chapter Two

Capitol Hill

Everett McKinley Dirksen: Senator from Illinois and Republican Minority Leader

Dirksen almost seemed like a cartoon caricature of that political buffoon on the Fred Allen radio show in the 1940s: Senator Beauregard Claghorn. But Dirksen's shaggy mane of gray hair and basso profundo voice masked a shrewd politician who could count votes as well as LBJ, his adversary in the 1960s. The press liked him because his rococo oratory was so over the top it poked fun at itself. Defending his expediency, he said that he had always been guided by one principle—flex-i-bil-i-ty. Named for McKinley, the Republican president martyred at the turn of the century, Dirksen gained prominence in the 1930s with his distinctive style of speechmaking.

Dirksen nominated Senator Bob Taft at the first Republican National Convention I watched on TV, Chicago's in 1952: Mr. Re-pub-li-can, Mr. Sen-a-tor, Mr. A-mer-i-can, Bob Taft, as he described him, lengthening out each syllable. At the convention, he had pointed to Governor Dewey and said that twice before, he had led us down the vale of defeat. He was known for charming the GOP women each year, not least because of his interest in horticulture. Dirksen campaigned tirelessly to make the marigold America's national flower: a favorite in his own garden. In 1972, his wife Louella published a biography of her colorful husband: *The Honorable Mr. Marigold: My Life with Everett Dirksen.*

I met Dirksen in 1969, when he sometimes breakfasted with us White House staffers before going up to have coffee with President Nixon. On one occasion, there was a controversial vote looming in the Senate. We asked how he would vote. Drawling in his throaty whisper, he confided that when he had to position himself on a vote that would win him enemies, no matter how he voted, he always waited until the very last minute and then voted on the losing side. This was because, as he told me, the winners forget, but the losers . . . never.

Bob Dole: Senator from Kansas and Republican Presidential Nominee

I first met Bob Dole in 1969; he had been elected to the Senate the previous year. Our friendship was based on our mutual admiration for President Nixon, who had finally captured the White House. At Nixon's death in 1994, Dole said that Nixon was the giant figure on the American stage in the latter half of the twentieth century. Dole shared with Nixon a lack of social adroitness. But, like Reagan, he used his sardonic humor as armor for deflecting intimacy. As a presidential candidate, he was a bust. By 1988, Vice President Bush knew more people by name in Kansas than Dole did.

For Dole's campaign, I had used a poignant closing anecdote about his fellow Kansan, Ike.

> At early dawn, just before crossing the Rhine in the spring of 1944, a glint of light was sighted. The observer of the spark approached the young G.I., who was nervously puffing a cigarette. "Are you nervous, soldier?" was the query. "Yes," the boy nodded affirmatively. "Well," replied his questioner, "let's both walk along the river together and we'll draw strength from each other." The private didn't know until later that the arm around his shoulder was that of Supreme Allied Commander Dwight David Eisenhower. [1]

Dole—who had suffered a grievous war injury—thought the anecdote too corny.

In 1976 I went out to the GOP convention in Kansas City. Dole had to deliver a keynote address, and I drafted a stem-winder with this cutting refrain about the Democratic nominee's inconsistencies, "And Jimmy Carter only says 'Trust me.'" Amazingly, the man with the reputation of being a partisan slasher rejected it, and instead delivered the usual Chamber of Commerce banalities.

Dole may have lacked charisma, but he had character and courage, which his war record proved. Just before we went to Kansas City, I bet him that he would be selected as VP for Ford. I didn't quite believe it myself. But he never forgot my prediction after he was chosen. (Ford told me Dole was the only one Reagan consented to.)

We knew Elizabeth Dole before she married Bob in 1975, because she worked for our Philadelphia friend, Virginia Knauer, who headed Nixon's Office of Consumer Affairs. In November 1980, I stayed with her seventy-nine-year-old mother, Mary Ella Hanford, in Salisbury, North Carolina. Elizabeth never concealed her ambition to marry up, and we introduced her to Sir John Wedgwood's son, Oliver. Both Bob and Elizabeth could be harsh with underlings. Bob was the finer person. He ranks with Bob Taft and Lyndon Johnson as one of the greatest legislative leaders.

John McCain: Senator from Arizona and Republican Presidential Nominee

Politicians have more than their share of faults: dissimulation, pandering at the cost of principle, flexibility of belief. But as a class, politicians are the most amiable and gregarious of people. If a man is not a "people person," then politics is the wrong profession for him. John McCain was an exception. Being a war hero, he must never have had to learn people skills. He had no use for small talk, and didn't hide the fact.

On one occasion, we were both speakers on the old Williamsburg Yacht, which is hired out by trade organizations. Later, he and I were both scheduled to speak at Mount Vernon. Since I had had dinner with his mother, Roberta, at her Connecticut Avenue apartment a few weeks before, I approached him. He brusquely dismissed me, and snapped that he was not interested in talking. So we sat side by side on the stern of the yacht for forty-five minutes. Even after I spoke, he did not acknowledge me.

Yet his mother is the most gracious of ladies. Daughter of an admiral and married to an admiral, she is a U.S. Navy person. She bonded with Pat Nixon when the Nixons first came to Washington, and was hurt when Pat's daughter Julie endorsed Obama in 2008.

Some gave John McCain slack for his sour temperament. Who would say what any of us would be like after a stint of torture in the Hanoi Hilton? I applaud him for his clear vision in foreign and defense policy. He was a true statesman.

Barry Goldwater: Senator from Arizona and Republican Presidential Nominee

Barry Goldwater was every inch the lantern-jawed, sun-bronzed rancher of the Southwest. I had a long talk with him once, when I hitched a ride back with him on a plane to DC from Williamsport, where he had come to address the Williamsport Jaycees. Goldwater's disinterest in history and book reading did not inhibit him from spouting his opinions. He was harsh on Nixon, and told me that Nixon blew it when he compromised with Rockefeller at the convention and picked Lodge for VP. Goldwater felt that he could have carried a lot of the South for Nixon against LBJ, but that Nixon might also have had Kentucky Senator Thruston Morton, who would have fared much better than the napping Lodge.

Goldwater spoke caustically of Eisenhower's dime store New Deal—an expansion of FDR's public works programs. He also attacked the UN as an institution that was purportedly helping to preserve peace. (He was right on that!) But compared to Nixon, he was too simplistic, shallow, and clichéd in his answers.

He was interested to learn that Churchill, in 1957, denounced the UN as congenitally deformed (because of the Soviet veto), and called the organization impotent and feckless. Yet he was critical of Churchill's giveaway at Yalta—to him the fact that the Soviets already had troops in Eastern Europe was no rationale.

All in all, Barry Goldwater was bold but not bright, rugged in looks, but not realistic in views. A politician whose time had not yet come—a good thing for the country! He was not ready to be president.

At his death it was said that in his 1964 campaign, he turned his back on the two Republicans who had been loyal to him, Nixon and Reagan.

Hugh D. Scott: Senator from Pennsylvania

Hugh Scott could have moved back to Renaissance Italy without much of an adjustment. I once wrote that he might eye his Chinese *objets d'art* all morning while considering what poison to use on a Medician rival that evening. An aide of his called me to criticize me for that statement, but when I saw Scott in person, he said he had enjoyed it. Urbane and learned, he had a wife and an adopted daughter in Chestnut Hill, where he visited on weekends.

Bill Murphy, Scott's man in Harrisburg, who was an aide to Scranton—some said his "spy"—once told me that Senator Scott believed I was the one man who could succeed him. He was trying to draw me into his orbit. At one point, he promised me a preferment and backing, and in 1967 I told Nixon about it. Nixon wryly asked me whether Scott had written down this promise, and if so, whether it had been notarized.

In 1964—the Goldwater year—he was up for re-election against a popular Democrat, Genevieve Blatt. To garner Jewish votes, he issued a telegram asking for police protection for some supposed assassination threats by Arabs. Thanks in part to these cloak-and-dagger tactics, Scott eked out a victory.

Because of possible scandals, he didn't run in '76. He wanted a post to Taiwan, but he was afraid of hearings that would investigate some shady payoffs and investments. Scott always wore his Society of Cincinnati rosette on his lapel button, showing his pride in his patrician ancestry. He was descended from Zachary Taylor. I once gave him, as a birthday gift, a letter from Taylor framed with his picture.

Arlen Specter: Republican and
Democratic Senator from Pennsylvania

"I can add colors to the chameleon, / Change shapes with Proteus for advantages, / And set the murderous Machiavel to school."[2]

Richard III's lines on his political expediency could just as well describe Arlen Specter. He was a Democrat from 1961 to 1965, a Republican from 1965 until 2009, and then a Democrat until he left office in 2011. He started his career as a Democratic lawyer on the Warren Commission, then morphed into a Republican, serving as Philadelphia district attorney and U.S. senator. But Specter defied easy pigeonholing. He was a Philadelphian whose roots were in a small town in Kansas (Russell, where Bob Dole was from). He was a Republican whose voting record was liberal. He was a proud Jew, but displayed a photo in his office that showed him shaking hands with Saddam Hussein.

If he was not likeable, Specter was undoubtedly respected for his brains. A wag told me: "When they operated on his brain to extract a tumor, someone said that they could take out half his brain, but he would still be the brainiest guy in the Senate." I always had a cordial relationship with him, because he respected my advice.

On occasion, I was with Specter when a friend asked him to support a certain piece of legislation. Specter smiled smugly, and told us that he had already done so: He had introduced it the previous week. When the visitor left, I told him about the time someone visited President Eisenhower to urge a certain proposal. Ike nodded interestedly, took some notes, and promised to do so. Eisenhower didn't inform his visitor that he already had taken steps along those lines, because he preferred to appear as a listener and ready to take counsel. Specter didn't comment on my pointed anecdote.

Specter was always a liberal, but became a Republican because the Democratic machine in Philadelphia had no place for him. Finally, in 2009, when he realized that he couldn't win a GOP primary, he became a Democrat. Despite backing from the state Democratic organization, in 2010 he lost to Joe Sestak in that party's Pennsylvania primary. It was a pathetic end to a brilliant career.

He was the longest-serving senator in Pennsylvania history (1981–2011). To survive, expediency became his policy. His reversals of position in switching from Democrat to Republican and back to Democrat would have given a snake a backache.

Yet if his labor and tax positions varied according to party, he was consistently strong for civil rights, a champion of minorities. To his credit, he held one other opinion that never changed: As one who was counsel for the Warren Commission, he continued to aver that communist Lee Harvey Oswald was the single assassin of John Kennedy, and no right-wing association was ever attached to the shooting. That Arlen was brilliant there is no doubt. His fault was that he had to let everyone know it.

Edward Kennedy: Senator from Massachusetts

I had dinner with the Massachusetts senator just once. It was early in 1970— half a year after Chappaquiddick. My friend Bob Smith, the chief counsel for Senator Sam Ervin's Judiciary Committee, had invited me for dinner at Ristorante Italiano on New York Avenue near the Capitol. Then he called me and asked if he could bring along Rick Duran, Ted Kennedy's legislative counsel. Later, upon his request, I agreed that Rick could bring along his own boss.

I was a Nixon partisan and nothing predisposed me to like the late president's kid brother. But I found myself enjoying his company. This did not surprise me. His grandfather, John Francis "Honey Fitz" Fitzgerald, was a likeable rogue of a bartender. I was surprised by Kennedy's knowledge of the issues and his study of history. But his lack of discretion with respect to other matters told me that he was not really serious about ever running for president. Shortly afterwards, I sent a memorandum to the Nixon White House saying as much. But in 1976, when he challenged Carter in the primary, I was proved wrong. Ted thought that the Kennedy mystique could prevail against anything. He too was wrong.

Sam Ervin: Senator from North Carolina

Sam Ervin mastered the role of Bible-quoting country folk philosopher. He was a bit of a poseur in that regard, but he knew his constitutional law. We met in 1969 through Bob Smith, his aide and chief counsel for the Senate Judiciary Committee. He remembered my father from Harvard Law School, but mostly, we shared a love of our Scots-Irish heritage and the works of William Shakespeare. He told me his practice of tossing out a biblical quote each day in the hearings, a gimmick he'd learned from his trial practice days, where he'd look through the Bible just before going into the courtroom for an apt bit of wisdom. I later would copy that trick.

His daughter attended George Washington Law School with me. Ervin despised the man she eventually married. Each time we met, he would ask me to tell him Churchill's story about Count Ciano. The count had married Mussolini's daughter. When Churchill's son-in-law Vic Oliver visited Chartwell with his wife Sarah Churchill, Oliver asked Churchill who was the greatest statesman. He said "Benito Mussolini." Astonished, Oliver asked why. The great man rumbled that "Il Duce" had been the only statesman with the courage to have his son-in-law executed.

I invited Sam to be guest speaker at the Philadelphia Bar Association in 1971. He loved my introduction, in which I paraded the paradoxes within his character: Constitutionalist, states righter, military patriot, critic of Vietnam, etc.

When the Watergate scandal broke, the country curmudgeon became a national folk hero through television. Chief Counsel Bob Smith had predicted to me in 1969 that the Judiciary Committee would one day recommend Nixon's impeachment.

This senator, who opposed civil rights and the Equal Rights Amendment, would have been labeled racist and sexist today. But since Nixon was the bête noire of the media establishment, such opinions of Ervin were muted by the roar of public acclaim.

Sam Nunn: Senator from Georgia

Sam Nunn was every Republican's favorite Democrat. He had no use for the McGovernite wing: In 1972, he supported Senator Henry M. "Scoop" Jackson. On one occasion, he and Republican Senator Pete Domenici asked me to do my one-man Churchill play at Wolf Trap—a theater in Virginia outside Washington—to raise money for the Henry M. Jackson Foundation, named in honor of Scoop.

It is worth noting that in the 1980s, it was not unusual for close friendships to exist across the aisles of Congress, such as Sam Nunn's with Pete Domenici, Ted Kennedy's with Orrin Hatch, or Joe Clark's with Hugh Scott. Now both parties have moved to the extreme, making such relationships rare.

Later, Sam invited me down to Warm Springs, Georgia, where FDR bathed in the healing waters in hopes of getting relief from paralysis. FDR's wife Eleanor never accompanied him to Warm Springs, even though her nursing had probably saved his life during his initial, crippling illness. Still, Roosevelt found his stays there therapeutic: In fact, on April 12, 1945, his long-time friend Lucy Mercer Rutherfurd was with him when he died. At Roosevelt's "Little White House" in Warm Springs, which is maintained as a museum, I rode in FDR's special open-topped car, with its hand-operated accelerator and brakes.

Sam was a protégé of Congressman Carl Vinson, for years the chairman of the House Armed Services Committee. Like his mentor, Sam felt he had a mandate to maintain a strong military. Because he was so strongly identified as a hawk, Sam thought he would never be accepted by the McGovern left of his party. He made the mistake of opposing Bush on Desert Storm, thinking he might thus win the affections of the McGovernite doves. Sam told me that his greatest regret was voting no on Reagan's Supreme Court nominee Robert Bork, and yes on George H. W. Bush's Supreme Count Justice Clarence

Thomas. He later wrote the Foreword for my book, *My Fellow Americans: Presidential Addresses That Shaped History.*

Jesse Helms: Senator from North Carolina

For liberals and lefties, Senator Jesse Helms was a latter-day Hitler. It was as though he personified the red-necked, gun-toting, Bible-quoting Yahoos they hated and feared. I liked him. For one thing, he loved me. When he was interviewed and asked to name his favorite book, he always said, "The Good Book." "Well, next to that," they would press him, and he would tell them he liked my biography of Churchill. My daughter Mary, who was on the staff of *The Harvard Crimson* campus newspaper at the time, asked me never to repeat this information, because if someone on the *Crimson* found out that Jesse Helms was a fan of her father's, she would be thrown off.

When I first called on Helms, he had a photographer shoot both of us. His wife, he said, wanted an inscribed photo from me. Helms's office was lined with political cartoons showing him as a mustachioed Hitler, proving that he could laugh at himself. Nixon was his favorite president. In the same month Nixon won forty-nine states in a landslide—November 1972—Helms was elected to the Senate. As chairman of the Senate Foreign Relations Committee, he once hosted a lunch for all the Democrats and Republicans on the committee, with the British ambassador and myself as the featured guests.

In every election, Jesse was the underdog in the polls—and he always won. It seems that a lot of those polled didn't want to admit they were voting for Jesse. Afterward, the farmers and laborers who loved him would say: "Old Jesse always says what he thinks." And they were right: He filibustered against naming Dr. Martin Luther King's birthday as a holiday.

In the fall of 1990, during another tight election, Jesse asked me to give my Churchill talk at a campaign event. I said no, because the date (October 20) coincided with my daughter Mary's wedding. When I went to lend my support at a rally the following week, Jesse arrived late, with Roosevelt Grier—the black footballer and one-time friend of the Kennedys—running interference. The crowd of rednecks chanted, "We want Jesse!" Outside the hall, women who looked like a Russian weight-lifting team battled the Jesse supporters. Finally, Jesse hushed his fans by saying that James Humes was a liberty-loving patriot and a great American statesman; and, furthermore, that I should be ambassador to Malta. They cheered, and Jesse went on to say that as head of the Foreign Relations Committee, he would have to hold his nose and vote for some effete striped-pants cookie pusher to be a diplomat, but if they didn't choose his friend Humes, he would sit on his hands.

When James Baker heard this aired live on C-Span, I was called to the State Department. Baker looked at me and asked me if I really wanted Jesse to carry out his threat. When I shrugged "no," I probably lost my ambassadorship with that frank admission.

Ernest "Fritz" Hollings: Senator from South Carolina

I can still hear Fritz Hollings's deep South Carolina drawl on the phone, asking me to come down to his office and talk history with him. The history he wanted to talk about with me was not so much American history as English. We would argue about Jesse Helms. He saw him as Snopes, the redneck stereotype from Faulkner. I said I admired both of them—as a reflection of their constituents, of real life, not the plastic politicians so often found in Congress. Like a Saltonstall from Massachusetts, or a Javits from New York's Lower East Side, they had the texture and fiber of their respective constituencies. Today we see too many one-dimensional anchorman types, guided by the latest polls and focus groups.

Hollings, like our seventh vice president, John C. Calhoun, sprang out of the Carolina soil, and he was proud to occupy Calhoun's Senate seat. The only vice president ever to resign out of principle, Hollings declared. (That was before Agnew.) He was fascinated by the story of Thomas Cooper, the attorney who became president of the University of South Carolina at Charleston, but was forced to resign in 1833 because of his liberal religious views. Cooper once sat on the same Pennsylvania court my father did.

Hollings supported 1985's Balanced Budget Act. I gave him this anecdote to use on the Senate floor: As Prime Minister William Pitt said to Edmund Burke, "This country is safe to the Day of Judgment." Burke replied: "It's not the Day of Judgment that frightens me, it's the Day of 'No' Judgment."

I relished sipping bourbon with Hollings in his Senate office.

Malcolm Wallop: Senator from Wyoming

In England, Malcolm Wallop could have been a baronial lord like his grandfather, tending his estate while hunting and fishing on his own lands. Instead, he was a U.S. senator enjoying the same activities in Wyoming. In either place, he would have been a "Tory" in politics and conservative in his principles.

I met Wallop in 1992, at a conservative conference in Vail, Colorado, that had been organized by a friend and fellow Republican partisan, Ann Bishop. The senator and I were both to appear as speakers, along with Delaware politician Pete du Pont, and Wallop introduced me to the audience. I had flown out to Vail with him, and on our trip he told me that his grandfather, Oliver Henry Wallop, was the only person in history to have served in both the House of Lords and Wyoming's House of Representatives. In 1925, on the death of his elder brother, State Representative Wallop became the

Eighth Earl of Portsmouth. They were cousins of the future Queen of England (and the late Queen Mother, Elizabeth Bowes-Lyon).

Malcolm Wallop served in both the Wyoming House of Representatives and the state senate, where he formed close friendships with Alan Simpson, later a U.S. senator, and Vice President Dick Cheney. An unprepossessing figure, with rimless glasses and a matter-of-fact speaking voice, he bonded with me based on our mutual love of Churchill, and was pleased when I gave him a signed copy of my book. Outspoken in his right-wing beliefs, and outrageously politically incorrect, he could not help but win one's admiration. A fervent Reaganite, he supported his fellow Yalie George H. W. Bush in 1988. He was an anti-communist, strong on defense, and an economic libertarian: a foe of estate and gift taxes. He avidly supported Reagan's Strategic Defense Initiative, better known as "Star Wars."

Roman Hruska: Senator from Nebraska

The press corps in Washington gave him this sobriquet: "the Noble Roman." But this was in reference to Roman Hruska's character, rather than any Italian ancestry. With his broad face, set on a square build, and smooth gray hair that had once been blond, Senator Roman Hruska manifested his Polish and prairie roots. One of the Senate's most outspoken conservatives throughout the sixties and seventies, he remained loyal to President Nixon, unswayed by the attacks that led to history's most famous impeachment and resignation.

I met him in April 1994 through his former Senate aide, Wally Johnson, with whom I was staying to make an appearance before the Omaha English-Speaking Union. When Johnson picked me up at the airport, he told me the news that President Nixon had died. I told him I was going to attend the funeral, which Johnson had to skip because of his law business. He and his wife had become friends with Julie Nixon Eisenhower and her husband David in the early years of the Nixon White House. Later, Johnson had taken a post in the Justice Department. He then suggested that we drive to Lincoln to call on his former boss, retired Senator Hruska. I told him that Dianne and I had got to know his daughter, Jan—a tall, leggy, athletic blonde—when she was a member of the DC Young Republicans.

When we got there, and relayed the solemn news, Hruska shook his head in sadness at the death of Richard Nixon. Nixon, in Hruska's opinion, was the best President there ever was. He didn't care about Watergate! He never wanted Nixon to resign, and felt that there were enough votes to stop conviction on an impeachment charge. Like much of the world, Hruska felt that Nixon was a genius at foreign policy.

Wally asked Hruska to tell me what he had said to reporters about needing a little more mediocrity. The press had laughed at Senator Hruska's rationale for supporting Nixon's nomination of Judge G. Harrold Carswell for Supreme Court justice. Nixon's first choice, the brilliant jurist Clement Haynesworth, was turned down. Nixon wanted to stiff the Democrats by sending them another southern judge, and while Carswell had not the stature of Haynesworth, Nixon hoped to consolidate his pro-South credentials by appointing him. When Democratic senators and the press said he was clearly "mediocre," Senator Hruska blurted out the case for mediocrity.

Hruska told me that he was just echoing what House Speaker Sam Rayburn said to LBJ about the Harvard grads and PhDs in the JFK White House: He just wished some of them had run for sheriff once. Hruska had the heart of the proud American conservative who is disdainful of the Ivy League East. He said that it was Harvard intellectual types like Robert McNamara and McGeorge Bundy who had got us into the mess in Vietnam, but went on to say that by the time Nixon left office, there were no American boys fighting in Asia—that was his Nixon Doctrine.

Hruska himself was no intellectual, and proud of it. He represented Middle America and the solid values that are its backbone.

Larry Pressler: Senator from South Dakota

I met Larry Pressler in 1990 at a seminar retreat in Shepherdstown, West Virginia, that was organized by the Republican senators. I was scheduled to deliver my talk on "The Language of Leadership: Churchill's Five Principles of Political Persuasion." He was much impressed by my experiences as a White House speechwriter who had known every Republican president since Eisenhower, a historian who had once met Winston Churchill, and a ghostwriter who had penned a speech for Margaret Thatcher and assisted former President Ford with his memoirs, *A Time to Heal.*

He called my room late at night and invited me over for a glass of wine. I took the elevator up to his room. He took a small bottle of cabernet from the bar cabinet, and asked me if his choice would be all right, admitting that he knew nothing about wine. I smiled and said, "Neither do I."

Pressler stood in awe of someone who had actually talked to Winston Churchill. I was nonplussed. In my own eyes, I was hardly more than a well-traveled political junkie. He sought my counsel. He told me that he didn't know what he was doing in Washington as a senator. He spent all day on the phone raising money, when his aides weren't shuffling him around to various committee meetings.

Pressler, in his late forties, had a bland, even-featured Teutonic face, perhaps inherited from his forebears, who came from Germany in the late nineteenth century to carve out a homestead farm on the windswept prairies. His smooth good looks might have made him the ideal choice for a South Dakota TV-station weatherman. Pressler told me that he had been the golden boy of his small high school. Good grades in high school had won him a partial scholarship to the University of South Dakota. Larry was as friendly and as eager to be liked and appreciated as a puppy-dog.

We discussed the future of our party. When I asked Larry about his Republican philosophy, he answered with a trite maxim attributed to Lincoln: We should only do for the people what they can't do for themselves. I suppose I had expected more from a former Rhodes scholar who had grown up in the home of Mount Rushmore, where Lincoln stares out soulfully.

To be fair, Pressler had a likeable boyish winsomeness, without a shred of arrogance or pride of office that so many politicians manifest. Notably, he was the first Vietnam veteran elected to the U.S. Senate, and the only one of nine senators who flatly refused a bribe from undercover agents in the FBI's 1980 Abscam sting operation. And he was sincere in his need for help. He told me that he was just playing a role—U.S. senator—a prize to be paraded at county fairs. A Rhodes scholar, now U.S. senator. (Cecil Rhodes had set up the award like the U.S. Senate, two for each state. Although it has been modified slightly since, the fact is that it is a lot easier to be selected as a Rhodes Scholar from South Dakota or Arkansas than to be chosen in New York or Pennsylvania.)

Under the program named for Cecil Rhodes, scholars attend Oxford University in England. Larry told me that between dining at the High Table and meeting with tutors who sported the upper-class accents of Eton or Harrow, the ivied halls of Oxford enclosed an alien world. He had read PPE (Politics, Philosophy, and Economics) but got little from it, as he told me, except some good American friends.

Washington he found almost as exotic. On the floor, aides behind him whispered in his ear how to vote, and then he returned to his office where his AA (administrative assistant) gave him a list of money-people to call.

Pressler confided to me that he didn't know who he really was, or like what he was doing. But everyone around him wanted him to run again. The people back home—as when he ran the first time—showed him polls and surveys that said he was the one who most reflected South Dakotans, and the one to whom they would trust their aspirations and hopes. Yet, as he told me, he didn't even know what he believed. They told him it didn't matter; that whatever the people believe, they feel you believe it as well. Finally, he asked me—as someone who had met Churchill: What would Churchill do?

I replied: "He'd do what's right for the country and South Dakota. He'd put aside what's popular." Larry sighed, and said that his wife wanted him to run again. Mrs. Pressler was doing well selling real estate because of her husband's connections. There was nothing back in South Dakota for her.

The next thing I knew, Larry Pressler was running for president. It was obviously an impossible venture. But resigning his seat was one way to escape Washington. He lost to Ronald Reagan in the 1980 Republican primary.

Kenneth Keating: Senator from New York

If you asked Central Casting to find a U.S. senator-type for a movie, he would have looked like Ken Keating—dignified, silver-haired, and slender. But if you looked beneath his statesmanlike surface, you could glimpse a bit of a ruddy-cheeked Irish leprechaun. At times, he revealed an impish sense of humor. I worked as his legislative assistant in 1958, when he ran for U.S. senator and won, at the same time Nelson Rockefeller defeated Averell Harriman by a landslide in New York. A friend of Nixon's in the old Chowder and Marching Club in 1946, he refused to take sides in 1960.

In 1962 he raised the alarm on Soviet missile bases in Cuba. President Kennedy repeatedly shrugged off his advice, and never forgave Keating for his correct warning.

Alongside LBJ's overwhelming 1964 victory over Goldwater in the wake of Kennedy's assassination, Robert Kennedy took Keating's Senate seat. Yet RFK ran a million behind LBJ in this New York State win. In 1965, I invited Keating to speak in Williamsport at the Junior Chamber of Commerce Man of the Year dinner. He gave a funny, self-deprecating speech, and chatted with me in his room at the Lycoming Hotel. I saw him again in 1969, when John Humes was appointed ambassador to Austria. Keating was appointed ambassador to India at the same time; in 1973, he was made ambassador to Israel.

Later still, I lunched with him at The Brook, just before he died. His daughter had married a fraternity brother of my brother Graham.

Here is a bit of wisdom he imparted to me: People are generally conservative, but liberal when it comes to specifics. He also told me that even though he was a staunch supporter of civil rights, it never brought him black votes. A superb politician with an eye for the gimmicky PR move, he once proposed to have both FDR and Ike sculpted on Mount Rushmore.

Joe McCarthy: Senator from Wisconsin

The low Castilian-accented voice told me of an amigo that I must meet. It belonged to the diminutive New Mexico Senator Dennis Chavez. In December 1955, we were at a coming-out party for the senator's granddaughter Bunny Miller at the home of his daughter, Ymelda Dixon, the second wife of Washington journalist George Dixon. I was called "Jamie," but Bunny insisted on changing it to "Jaime."

I followed the senator to a corner where a dark-jowled figure sat clutching a glass of bourbon. He rose from his chair, grabbed my hand, and slurred his name: Joe McCarthy. I shook it before I grasped whom, exactly, I was meeting. When I did, I thought of Lady Macbeth's line from Shakespeare's Scottish play: "All the perfumes of Arabia will not sweeten this little hand."[3] McCarthy was the arch-villain of the fifties—the only politician to give a word to the dictionary. Today, "McCarthyism" remains a pejorative that describes reckless persecution or witch-hunting.

When I was a student at Stowe—the English prep school where I first met Churchill—McCarthy was pictured as some sort of American Hitler, leading a mass movement. My years at Williams following the year at Stowe only sharpened this view. For academics, he was a bête noire, personifying what was worst about Republican America. President Eisenhower, who deliberately ignored McCarthy, was castigated for not engaging him personally and directly. But Ike was right. He let him die from his own excesses.

McCarthy up close was not the stuff of a charismatic leader. He reminded me of Alice Longworth's words about Warren Harding: not a bad man, just a slob. Yet McCarthy had not the distinguished looks of a Harding. He looked like a disheveled bartender who had got into the booze. The media lumped him with Nixon, who had little use for him, and the feeling was reciprocated. Actually, it was the Kennedys who were palsy with him. He was the god-father of Kathleen, Robert F. Kennedy's daughter, and Bobby got his job as a Senate counsel through McCarthy. It was the press who made McCarthy a national figure by headlining his charges, and then they orchestrated his defeat. The resulting victim was anti-communism. Without doubt, there were high-ranking communists in our government. But this drunken pathetic figure, painted as the demon of the right, was the wrong person to champion the anti-communist cause.

George Smathers: Senator from Florida

One day in November 1993, former Missouri Congressman Jimmy Symington called and asked me to join him and ex-Senator George Smathers at the Metropolitan Club in Washington. It was George's eightieth birthday. I happily agreed, and took the Metroliner down to DC, where I would spend the night at the club. Smathers was an admirer of Churchill, and Symington wanted me to treat him to some of Churchill's best anecdotes and quotes, delivered in my "British Bulldog" accent. For my part, I had been told countless choice anecdotes about Smathers from the 1950 Florida primary campaign against Claude Pepper. To scandalize his constituents, Smathers would refer to the sixty-year-old Pepper as a sexagenarian whose sister was a thespian, in wicked Greenwich Village, and remind them that Pepper had engaged in matriculation at Harvard.

I found myself fascinated by the lean, soft-drawling Floridian, who was now a lobbyist. Having served as an usher at John Kennedy's wedding, he ingratiated himself into Lyndon Johnson's coterie. Later, when Nixon was elected, he introduced Nixon to Bebe Rebozo, a son of Cuban immigrants who became a millionaire banker and one of Nixon's most loyal friends.

Smathers told us about the trip he took with Nixon and the freshman congressman Kennedy to Paris in 1947. They were part of a fact-finding committee led by Representative Christian Herter on the effects of the Marshall Plan. Smathers told me that they let Nixon do all the writing of the report in the hotel at night while the rest of them did the reveling. He said that they respected Nixon for his hard work and brains, but that he wasn't a barrel of fun: He wanted to be one of the guys, but he wasn't. John Kennedy would play tricks on Nixon. He'd tell what was supposed to be a dirty story: A guy went into this bar and asked for cigarettes, and said, "Can I have a pack of Camels?" "No," said the bartender, "but you can have a Lucky." Then, Smathers continued, everyone would laugh like hell, with Nixon joining in because he didn't want to admit he didn't get it. So Kennedy and Smathers would be laughing at Nixon's 'laughing,' rather than at the phony joke.

I thought the anecdote said a lot about JFK as well as Nixon.

Dan Flood: Representative from Pennsylvania

Dan Flood looked like the leading man in a Victorian stage play, and in fact, he had studied acting in his youth. He had a waxed blond handlebar moustache, flowing golden hair, and a stentorian voice. He even drew attention away from his equally striking, flame-haired wife, Catherine, who wore purple lipstick and sported six-inch fingernails. Flood was a beloved hero to his constituents, and he had some heroes of his own: the astronauts. In 1969, when he learned that Michael Collins was available to deliver talks, he had the town fathers invite Collins to a dinner in Wilkes-Barre, in honor of Flood.

Flood was the major power on the U.S. House Appropriations Committee. He was disappointed when Collins, despite our urgings, refused at the last moment. I was sent as a poor substitute, and I met Flood and his wife at the airport where our private jet landed. He was suffering from throat cancer, as I learned later. His lunch was vegetable soup, laced with vodka. If there was anything to the allegations against him for fraud and corruption, Flood's modest frame house and Spartan lifestyle belied it.

When I told him I was from Williamsport, he asked me if I was related to Sam Humes. I confirmed that he happened to be my father. Flood told me that he had lost to him once in a civil case, in which he represented the plaintiff, who had been injured by a train. In his closing, Flood used words from Shakespeare's *King Lear*: "Is wretchedness deprived that benefit . . . ?"[4] And my father answered: "The learned counsel quoted from Shakespeare's *Lear*. Yet his misplaced facts should have made him read further in that same play: 'Mend your speech a little / Lest you may mar your fortunes.'"[5]

Flood told me solemnly that he was a Shakespeare buff, and had once used that quote himself.

Hamilton Fish III: Representative from New York

Representative Hamilton Fish III made an unforgettable impression. Over six feet tall in stature, he had the husky build of a former College Football All-American, and a voice stentorian in volume. He was irrepressible in his opinions and prejudices. Fish was seated beside me at several dinners hosted by two Anglo-American fraternal societies, the Pilgrims and the Ends of the Earth. He told me the three things he was most proud of: being on Walter Camp's first All-American football team (from Harvard), being a co-founder of Pennsylvania's first American Legion post, and serving as FDR's congressman (the Republican representing Hyde Park).

Every time I'd see him, he'd ask me to deliver FDR's catchphrase from 1940, and I would oblige him by saying: "I still remember he is one of that historic trio that has consistently voted against the relief of agriculture— Martin, Barton, and Fish." I'd imitate FDR, and then Fish would rise from his seat with arms raised. He was then in his late nineties.

Fish's grandfather, Hamilton Fish I, was secretary of state for Ulysses S. Grant. His young grandson, although he had not been a Rough Rider, was given the uniform and made an honorary one when the elder Fish served as secretary to Governor Theodore Roosevelt.

When he learned that I was from Williamsport, Fish told me some of the history of their American Legion post. It was named for Williamsport native Garrett Cochran (whose grandson and namesake was my classmate at Cochran School). Fish and Legion officer Teddy Roosevelt Jr. were deadlocked on a choice of names for the post. Cochran had died in 1918 on a ship in a French harbor, pleading that he didn't want to be buried in France. In honor of the homesick Williamsport soldier, the post was designated Garrett Cochran American Legion Post #1.

When FDR roared out the names of his trio of "reactionaries," Joe Martin was the Republican House Leader. Bruce Fairchild Barton, an adman turned congressman, had written a biography of Jesus, *The Man Nobody Knows,* which depicted Christ as a master salesman. After Barton left office, fellow Congressman Fish would remain FDR's bête noire.

Fish went to visit my daughter Mary when she was an undergraduate at Harvard. Having gone co-ed since the congressman's day, the university had housed her in Fish's old dormitory. Fish died in 1991 at the age of 102, as the oldest living American to have served in Congress. Whenever I visited Anderson House, headquarters of the Society of the Cincinnati in Washington, I stayed in the room named for Hamilton Fish.

Notes

1. James C. Humes, *Instant Eloquence: A Lazy Man's Guide to Public Speaking* (New York: Harper & Row, 1973), 231.

2. William Shakespeare, *The True Tragedy of Richard Duke of York and the Good King Henry the Sixth*, in *The Oxford Shakespeare, Second Edition,* edited by John Jowett, William Montgomery, Gary Taylor, and Stanley Wells (Oxford, UK: Oxford University Press, 2005), 109.

3. William Shakespeare, *The Tragedy of Macbeth*, in *The Oxford Shakespeare, Second Edition*, edited by John Jowett, William Montgomery, Gary Taylor, and Stanley Wells (Oxford, UK: Oxford University Press, 2005), 990.

4. William Shakespeare, *The Tragedy of King Lear*, in *The Oxford Shakespeare, Second Edition*, edited by John Jowett, William Montgomery, Gary Taylor, and Stanley Wells (Oxford, UK: Oxford University Press, 2005), 1176.

5. Shakespeare, *The Tragedy of King Lear*, in *The Oxford Shakespeare, Second Edition*, 1155.

Chapter Three

State House

Mark Hatfield: Governor and Senator from Oregon

In 1960, the recently elected governor of Oregon was the pinup boy of Republican moderates. Vice President Nixon asked Hatfield to nominate him at the convention that year. A budding speechwriter at the time, I will never forget Hatfield's alliterative closing, in which he described how Vice President Nixon had fought communism from Caracas to the Kremlin, as a pilgrim for peace and a pioneer for progress.

In 1964, I invited Hatfield to be speaker at the Jaycees Man of the Year banquet in Williamsport. It was a time when moderates had misgivings about the front-runner, Goldwater, and because Hatfield was scheduled to be the keynoter at the 1964 Republican Convention in San Francisco, he was constrained from making any endorsement.

My wife and I invited Hatfield to dinner at our house. As a Pennsylvania legislator, I was worried. I argued that Goldwater would lose Pennsylvania and drag me to defeat. There was some talk that Pennsylvania Governor Scranton, a favorite son of our state, would make an announcement. Hatfield was discouraging; the young governor declared that Goldwater just about had it locked up.

Hatfield always looked like he had just walked out of a Brooks Brothers fitting room: white shirt, red striped tie, and dark blue suit. While having dinner with us, he had a call from "Youth for Christ" in Williamsport. I said, "The governor is busy." When I told him who it was, he asked me to call them back. They came to the house, and Hatfield told them, to my amazement, that he had heard the call from Christ in 1952, and decided afterwards to enter politics. It was surprising to see and hear this handsome moderate Republican speaking as a "born-again." But it was not a pose; it was his true conviction.

Jim Duff: Governor and Senator from Pennsylvania

Standing over six feet tall, and weighing more than two hundred pounds, Jim Duff was known as "Big Red," but his red hair had thinned by the time I met him. A Pennsylvania attorney general who had been appointed by Governor Edward Martin in 1943, Jim Duff succeeded his fellow Washington County resident and friend to the governorship in 1947.

Pennsylvania governors were limited to one term, and the state GOP—the Joe Grundy–Mason Owlett organization—were in control of the governor's selection. Duff, backed by the truckers, turned against the machine, which included the Pennsylvania Railroad. In 1948, the conservative GOP organization untypically supported the moderate Dewey—supposedly a sure thing—but against all expectations, Dewey lost to Truman. Duff, reluctantly carrying the old "Bull Moose" banner that year, went for Taft. In 1950, Pennsylvania witnessed an epic Republican primary fight—Duff for senator and Judge John Fine for governor ran against the organization, which backed Jay Cooke and John Kunkel, both of whom lost.

In 1951, Senator Duff was an early backer of Ike. That same year, Senators Henry Cabot Lodge Jr. and Richard Nixon accompanied Duff to Paris for the signing of the Treaty Establishing the European Coal and Steel Community (Treaty of Paris), which set the stage for the European Union. In 1967, when Nixon was preparing for another try at the presidency, I traveled to Duff's farm, and helped persuade him and former Governor Fine to endorse Nixon.

Duff greeted us warmly, accompanied by his wife Jean and their Chesapeake retriever. He spoke glowingly of my father, and I remembered that our mutual friend, Gladys McKay (a confidante of my mother's) once told me that my father was being groomed to be governor.

Duff gave us a puppy to take home, and we named her "Miss Duff."

William Scranton: Governor of Pennsylvania

Bill Scranton was my favorite governor, and I was his favorite Republican state legislator. The forty-two-year-old congressman was elected governor in 1962, and he swept me along to victory. Having just turned twenty-eight, I was the youngest state legislator on record, as he liked to point out. When his unpopular increase in the sales tax was being debated, I rallied the wavering GOP caucus with lines from Shakespeare's *Macbeth*: "If it were done when 'tis done, then 'twere well / It were done quickly."[1] Later, he had me appointed to the Shakespeare Quadricentennial Commission, along with novelists Pearl Buck and Conrad Richter, and the renowned artist Andrew Wyeth. Often, he would call me in for a tête-à-tête. I learned that his mother, Marjorie Warren Scranton—a member of the Republican National Committee—

adored my father and had worked on his behalf for higher state office. In 1963, Scranton sent me as his personal representative to the Young Republicans convention in San Francisco to use my influence in blocking a Goldwater takeover. When I went on an English-Speaking Union tour of Britain, Scranton had me report on the new British Prime Minister, Alec Douglas-Home, whom he knew.

Scranton was a Hotchkiss-and-Yale-educated scion of the city named for his family. A moribund Pennsylvania Republican Party drafted him because they needed a winner. The business community had sought relief from an oppressive unemployment compensation law, but the Pennsylvania General Assembly passed the Unemployment Compensation Reform bill in 1964 by one vote. In the course of debate over this contentious bill, a Republican legislator from Johnstown had his life threatened, and the Pennsylvania State Police came in to patrol the House. Union protesters picketed my home in Williamsport. The Democrats in Lycoming County offered to support me if I voted against the bill; I refused.

In June 1964, Scranton announced for the presidency to stop Goldwater, and some of the legislators went to Gettysburg to enlist the help of former president Eisenhower. It was too late. But I went to San Francisco for the 1964 Republican National Convention to support Scranton's failing cause. If Goldwater had given the vice president's slot to Scranton instead of Representative William E. Miller of New York, Goldwater wouldn't have won, but it would have saved many legislators, like myself, in Pennsylvania. Scranton, a popular governor, called Republican legislators "Boss" instead of by name, possibly because he had so many names to remember. But not me; he always called me "Jamie." It may have been because his mother had been such a booster of my father.

Late in 1973, Scranton called me to ask me to talk to Nixon about replacing Agnew; I did, but to no avail. In February 1976, when President Ford appointed him as his ambassador to the United Nations, Scranton invited me to celebrate with him at the Waldorf Astoria.

Tom Kean: Governor of New Jersey

I first met Tom Kean in 1964, at the Republican National Convention in San Francisco. I was then a Pennsylvania state legislator, and he was the head of Students for Scranton. We gathered in the "Scranton for President" suite at the St. Francis Hotel, named for the hosting city's Catholic patron. Kean always likes to remind me that I was writing postcards back to Democrats in my legislative district, because I knew I would need every Democrat's vote if Goldwater were to be nominated.

The next time I saw Kean, he was a New Jersey state legislator, readying himself to run for governor. He had already lost a GOP primary for Congress to Millicent Fenwick. But in 1977, he ran against Democrat Jim Florio and won. Despite Reagan's recession in 1981, he won again that year by a narrow margin. I wrote his inaugural address, and afterwards, his brother told me that it was a good speech, but the best was the end, which he knew that Kean himself had written. I nodded, even though he was wrong. In the Philadelphia Free Library, I had found the handwritten prayer Kean's ancestor William Livingston had written after his election as the first governor of New Jersey. Chancellor Livingston had written a prayer to read before the legislature, and Kean didn't want to use it. He didn't like mentioning an ancestor. I told him he had to. In the end, this resonant prayer was used to conclude his address.

I also wrote his second inaugural speech, and then his keynote address to the GOP convention in 1988. In an allusion to the Democrats' weak color reproduction of our flag, he said: "We reject pastel colors and pastel principles!"—to the roar of the crowd.

My daughter Mary, during her summer vacation from Harvard in 1985, wrote some speeches for Governor Kean. In response, he inscribed a photo to her as "A block off the old chip." Kean once told me that the only person who talked more than I did was Bill Clinton. But unlike most politicians, Kean is considerate and has no ego problem. If a "pictionary" had an apt image to illustrate *noblesse oblige*, it would surely be a portrait of Tom Kean.

Pete and Elise du Pont: Governor and First Lady of Delaware

When I first met Pete du Pont in 1969, he was riding the train with me from Washington to Delaware—but he would have looked more at home astride a white horse. Patrician Pete was like a prince. As tall and handsome as the fabled royalty of yore, he seemed ready to tilt his lance against rival aspirants in medieval contests of courage and stamina—those tests and trials befitting a peer of the realm. And he turned his regal bearing and sense of *noblesse oblige* to real politicking. His ascent from state representative (1969–70) to congressman (1971–77) to governor of Delaware (1977–85) seemed almost ordained.

If you placed Pierre Samuel du Pont IV back in the Middle Ages, he would fit right in with the other royals from the Holy Roman Empire, which, as Voltaire opined, was neither holy, Roman, nor an empire. Picture Pierre du Pont as the Duke of Delaware. As a Prince of Principalities. While most of the ducal heads of state were German in language and lineage, there were a few Francophones in the centuries-old league. The du Ponts and their forebears were among them, asserting their own pretentions of pomp and ceremony as were accorded to fellow league members. Protocols and rituals of royal etiquette had to be observed in welcoming kings and queens to

Aachen, Prague, or Wetzlar. Any breach was not just a slight, but an assault on the visiting nation's sovereignty.

When Governor du Pont filed for the New Hampshire Primary in 1988, Delaware was among the least populous U.S. states, as well as the second smallest. It may have been diminutive in size, but not in stature: Delaware is a moneybox, a corporate tax haven that also boasts some of the most lax banking regulations in America, with no cap on the interest that financial institutions can levy on loans or charge accounts. Half of America's credit card issuers, and more than half its Fortune 500 companies—including, of course, DowDuPont—are incorporated in the tiny Principality of Delaware, "America's Luxembourg."

Of all the presidential candidates who threw down the gauntlet in 1988, Pete du Pont was the most principled Republican, more so than Reagan or his successor George H. W. Bush. He was also the only pure laissez-faire conservative in the pack. But not everyone appreciated the fact that this scion of one of the richest families in America felt an obligation to enter the fray. In Delaware—named for *Baron* de la Warre—Governor du Pont was seen almost as royal, or at least, as a grand cavalier. To New Hampshire's unromantic Yankees, however, he was simply another "also ran." After finishing next-to-last in the Granite State primary, he went home to write for *The Wall Street Journal*, practice law, and administer a series of conservative think tanks.

Prince Pete's lady fair—the former Elise Ravenel Wood—may have struck one as a Duchess of Delaware, but in her own eyes she was a simple milkmaid, a beneficiary of Wawa Dairy Farm, the company founded by her ancestor George Wood, which later grew into the popular chain of convenience stores. True, their marriage was a merger of the bluest blue bloods of the Chesapeake, but Elise never had any airs about this. She was, as the Spanish would say, *simpatico.* She was caring, but in the role of candidate's wife, she was not comfortable. She was neither combative nor acrimonious, to the point where even her political foes called her sweet. Being a mother was not just a role to her, but real, and this maternal instinct was manifested in her personal contacts with others. She was that rarity in politics, a woman devoid of ego, and disdainful of self-puffery. (Her own venture into the lists—an attempt to unseat the Democratic incumbent, U.S. Representative Tom Carper, in 1984—was not successful.)

In our many meetings, she was the listener rather than the talker, and she took pride in her dashing husband. If she expressed admiration for his political successes, she would quietly deflect any mention of self. No vainglory animated her personality. Almost uniquely among people in political life, she could laugh at herself. But don't poke fun at her husband; he was ever the handsome prince she wed.

Note

1. William Shakespeare, *The Tragedy of Macbeth*, in *The Oxford Shakespeare, Second Edition*, edited by John Jowett, William Montgomery, Gary Taylor, and Stanley Wells (Oxford, UK: Oxford University Press, 2005), 975.

Chapter Four

State Department

Henry Kissinger: Nixon's Secretary of State

A member of the National Security Council once told me that Kissinger is Nixon writ large: more brilliant, more driven, and more insecure.

There were other differences. Kissinger could flash charm and impart the witty anecdote for reporters to use. But he lacked Nixon's personal compassion for the White House staff, and was ruthless in pursuit of his own personal agenda. He seemed to have agreed with Harry Truman's adage: If you want a friend in this world, get a dog. While he was Jewish by background, the German-born Heinz Alfred Kissinger might have been Prussian if given the choice. Nixon's historic hero was Disraeli, but Kissinger's was Bismarck. He claims credit today for Nixon's China initiative, but initially he was adamantly opposed to it. In December 1959—nine years before he met Kissinger—Vice President Nixon told me that someday he was going to China. Kissinger was a Europeanist, playing soccer on the shores of the North Sea tributary in Berlin. Nixon was a Pacificist, playing football by the Pacific and serving on a destroyer on its seas in World War II.

I had reason to personally dislike him. In 1969, I wrote a memo to President Nixon, urging him to host a White House dinner for Andrew Wyeth (I had served on a Pennsylvania Arts Council with him, and knew he voted for Nixon in 1960). Kissinger deleted my name, added his own, and tried to block me from being invited to this dinner.

I do not demur from the opinion that he is an accomplished diplomat and was a formidable secretary of state, but as a person he could also be petulant and petty. Kissinger, as well as Nixon, felt insecure within the eastern prep school establishment. But if Nixon shrank from it, Kissinger embraced the type.

The one-time high-school nerd loved to play the role of bachelor swinger in the White House, and relished escorting actresses and models to Washington soirées. In 1974, the pudgy Kissinger married a tall, slender blonde WASP: the former Nancy Maginnes, who had served as an aide to Nelson Rockefeller.

Zbigniew Brzezinski: Carter's National Security Advisor

"Zbig," as I knew him, was Carter's advisor on national security. Like his predecessor Henry Kissinger, he was a foreign-born academic with expertise in the Soviet Union, and spoke English with a Central European accent. Like Kissinger, he manifested erudition with flashes of wit. But unlike Nixon's guru, Carter's guide in foreign policy was gracious with people like myself, an attentive listener, and an engaging personality. Taller than Kissinger, with sandy thinning hair, he had an arresting face. His eyes were narrow, but they engaged you with intensity.

In 1979, Zbig and I met at the Hotel Jefferson in St. Louis, with communications coach Granville Toogood, his tennis partner in Newport. Zbig wanted to see me at dinner. He had been told that I had written President Ford's second Iron Curtain speech at Fulton in 1979, where Ford warned that free legislative chambers throughout Europe could have their lights turned off if Carter didn't rally them. The son of a Polish diplomat stationed in Germany, Zbig had spent his earliest years watching the Nazis rise to power, and later saw his native Poland disappear behind the Iron Curtain. Over Secretary of State Cyrus Vance's objections, he urged Carter to warn France and Italy of the danger of electing communist pluralities that would destroy NATO.

Ford said that all presidents from Truman to himself had taken a stand against the communists. And Zbig convinced Carter that so-called "communism with a heart" was a fraudulent façade. Carter then did speak out, and the communist parties were defeated in Europe. Brezinski was both charming and cogent in his conversation. It came as no surprise that Carter warmed to his friend Zbig as to no other of his top advisors.

James A. Baker III: Bush's Secretary of State

I've known Jim Baker for more than seven decades; he was my student advisor at the Hill School in 1947. He was loyal to Hill School, as was I: Three generations of James Bakers went there. Jim was in my brother Sam's class. At Hill, he was not a football star, but he was the head cheerleader for football. After that, our paths never crossed for almost three decades. In 1972, he probably became aware of my political activities through notes in the *Hill School Bulletin.* Four years later, in the summer of 1976, he hired me to be a White House consultant for Ford in the campaign against Reagan. He once told me that I had imaginative talents in language that needed to find their niche in public service.

Baker incidentally called his first son "Jamie," and always reminded me of it. Every time he saw me, he asked me whether I was losing weight. I wasn't, but I never objected; tact is the chief asset of the diplomat.

As secretary of state, Baker shepherded U.S. foreign policy at the end of the Cold War, as well as during the first Gulf War, Operation Desert Storm. The writer and foreign policy expert Harvey Sicherman, who worked under Alexander Haig, George Shultz, and Jim Baker, once told me that even though Baker may have lacked the vision and purpose of other secretaries of state, just give him a problem in finding agreement between adversaries and he would fix it. Baker evokes Shakespeare's lines from *Henry V*: "Turn him to any cause of policy, / The Gordian knot of it he will unloose."[1]

Baker knew that I had written speeches for George H. W. Bush, and in 1991, he promised me an ambassadorship to Malta or some other nice place if Bush won. Alas, he didn't. His inscription in the Hill School yearbook for 1949 describes him thus: "He was as smooth as alabaster." Smoothness is not necessarily a liability for a diplomat or statesman, but he wasn't glib or oily. Unlike so many politicians, he expressed a sincerity that was not skin deep.

Baker's ability as a statesman was first proven during Desert Storm, when he persuaded the United Nations to endorse the invasion to save Kuwait after it had been invaded and occupied by Saddam Hussein. All the Arab states— with the exception of Iraq—joined in supporting the United States. At the point when he retired from the public arena, Baker enjoyed the respect of allies and adversaries alike.

George Kennan: Ambassador and Cold Warrior ("Mr. X")

The former ambassador to the USSR and Yugoslavia was known as Mr. X. In 1947, he was the not-so-anonymous writer of articles that helped shape Cold War diplomacy against the Soviets following World War II. Kennan was both a realist and an idealist. A hardheaded diplomat, he could be quixotic in his pursuit for peace. He was the author of the "containment" approach towards the Russians, arguing against direct confrontation. He opposed Dean Acheson and Harry Truman's NATO and Point 4 doctrine: American support for nations under threat by communism, and technical assistance for developing countries. Yet his prescription for strength and patience was what America's foreign policy would follow. And his prediction—that eventually the Soviet system was destined to implode—would prove true.

I met him in 1977, at a small dinner given by the former ambassador to Austria, my cousin John Humes. Cocktails in John's private apartment at the

Hotel Carlyle in New York were followed by a dinner downstairs. John arranged for the limousine that drove the elder statesman to Manhattan from Princeton; Kennan was seventy-three at the time. (He would die in 2005 at the age of 101.) The intimacy of that small dinner allowed for frank conversation. Kennan, a Democrat, confessed to both Walter Annenberg and John Humes that he grew to admire Nixon, who had appointed both men to be ambassadors. He felt that Nixon was the most skillful of presidents in foreign policy since Roosevelt in World War II. Further remarks conveyed a disenchantment with Roosevelt, a dislike of Dulles, and disappointment with Kennedy.

Henry Cabot Lodge Jr.: Senator from Massachusetts and Johnson's Ambassador to Vietnam

Lodge was a prime example of what good breeding and a good tailor can do for a man. He was tall and slender, with a strong chin, patrician looks, and a stentorian voice. He was not a brilliant statesman like his grandfather and namesake. But, like his grandfather, he was no isolationist. His internationalism made him a foe of Taft and an early supporter of General Eisenhower. Senator John Kennedy defeated Lodge in 1952, despite Ike's landslide in Massachusetts. Later, President Eisenhower would appoint Lodge as our ambassador at the UN.

In 1960, Nixon named Lodge to be his running mate, as a substitute Rockefeller—in other words, a patrician WASP from the urban Northeast. The Goldwater conservatives grudgingly accepted him. In that campaign, Lodge flew to Williamsport, where I sat in the first row in front of the courthouse, and was introduced as assistant to Vice President Nixon. I was next to Lodge's wife, Eleanor Sears Lodge. She told me about her two sons: George Cabot Lodge, readying for his senatorial campaign against Ted Kennedy, and her younger son, Henry Sears Lodge, a doctor. She said the hardest thing for her husband to do was to usher Khrushchev around the United States the year before. Lodge gave a stirring stump speech, but repaired to the Lycoming Hotel for a nap afterwards, eschewing any schmoozing with local Republicans.

I next talked to Lodge in San Francisco, in 1964, when he held a press conference endorsing Scranton against Goldwater. I told him that they should not withhold support for Goldwater in general, but press for Scranton to be vice president. He frowned at the suggestion. That year, Lodge experienced a brief flurry of activity as a presidential candidate: He won as a write-in on the New Hampshire ballot, and returned from Vietnam, where he was LBJ's ambassador, to strengthen his failing candidacy. His Brahmin style far surpassed his substance, and it was Goldwater who won the nomination.

I had lunch with him at the Metropolitan Club in Washington in 1970, just after he had returned from his Vietnam post. Ever discreet, he was careful not to criticize President Nixon. He did offer the opinion that Nixon's fifty-state campaign in 1960 was ill considered.

Elliot Richardson: Nixon's Attorney General

Today, Elliot Richardson is best known as Nixon's attorney general during Watergate, who chose to resign rather than fire Special Prosecutor Archibald Cox. More than a decade earlier, Richardson had lost a race for Massachusetts attorney general to a fellow Republican who would come to be known for his anti-Nixon stance.

By birth, Richardson seemed destined for political stardom in Massachusetts. A graduate of Harvard College, editor of the *Harvard Law Review*, law clerk to Supreme Court Justice Felix Frankfurter, and then U.S. attorney for Massachusetts, he was endorsed by everyone in the elite GOP establishment—Saltonstall, Lodge, Herter—when he announced his candidacy for Massachusetts attorney general in 1962. Yet the Bay State native who shone at Harvard was beaten by a tenacious African-American prosecutor, a native of Washington who had gone to Howard University in DC, not Harvard University in Cambridge. His name was Ed Brooke.

Brooke was a former chairman of the Finance Commission of Boston, where he distinguished himself by uncovering citywide corruption. His shrewd mind and distinctive pale blue eyes lent credence to a rumor circulating in the city: that Brooke was a direct descendant of Thomas Jefferson. A moderate Republican in a Democratic state, Brooke would later become the first African American popularly elected to the U.S. Senate.

In the campaign to defeat his Brahmin rival, Brooke had sent off a "secret eyes-only" memorandum that said the only way they could win would be if Richardson didn't get out to small GOP groups across the state. This document made its way to Richardson, who took the bait and campaigned throughout Massachusetts. He would recite his brilliant resumé and explain why he deserved to be attorney general.

But with a simple slogan, "Proudly for Brooke"—which expressed pride in both American and black identity—Brooke won the day, his charm having beaten Richardson's aristocratic hauteur. He was the first African American to be elected attorney general of any state. Not to be daunted, Richardson ran again, and went on to serve as both Massachusetts attorney general and lieutenant governor under Republican Governor John Volpe. His next stop was Washington, DC, where he served as Nixon's under-secretary of state—the first of four Cabinet positions in that administration. He led the Department of Health, Education, and Welfare, then served as secretary of defense, and lastly, he became the nation's senior lawman. This was followed by a year's tenure as Gerald Ford's ambassador to the United Kingdom, and a subsequent year as secretary of commerce. No wonder Richardson's friends referred to him as "the former everything"!

Richardson possessed a wealth of knowledge on numerous topics, and enjoyed sharing it. In 1979 I was promoting my book, *How to Get Invited to the White House,* at a St. Louis TV station. Just before my appearance, the studio staff said, "I'm sorry, Mr. Humes, we have to cancel you. Former Ambassador Richardson is here. He's talking about his book *Law of the Seas.*" I replied, "Fine, he's a friend of mine, but keep me nearby, because you're going to hear a giant click—a turn off of sets across the country if you keep him talking too long." After about eight minutes, Richardson was just beginning to hit his stride as his narrative approached the fourteenth century. The moderator waited for a break in the monologue before interjecting, "We have your friend here, James Humes, speaking on his new White House book."

I got to know Richardson when we both served on the board of the Pilgrims Society, and we often sat at the head table together at the Waldorf Astoria. One day I mistakenly grabbed for his water glass. He slapped my hand away, and I murmured my apologies. I later found out it was filled with vodka.

Walter Annenberg: Nixon's Ambassador to the United Kingdom

I first met Walter Annenberg at the U.S. Embassy in London in 1970. He projected a stiff dignity, but it was self-crafted, not innate. He carried scars—outside, the deformed ear, and inside, the jail sentence of his father, Moe Annenberg, a newspaper mogul who had once owned the *Philadelphia Inquirer* and the *Daily Racing Form.* As a Republican whose papers launched attacks on Roosevelt's New Deal, Moe fell afoul of FDR, who told Treasury Secretary Henry Morgenthau that he wanted Moe Annenberg for dinner. Moe was prosecuted for tax evasion by FDR's Justice Department, fined eight million dollars, and sentenced to prison, where he died. This made his son fiercely anti-FDR and an equally staunch Republican.

As was common at the time, the younger Annenberg was looked down upon by the WASP establishment in Philadelphia, and despite his GOP loyalty and credentials, the Union League of Philadelphia rejected his application for membership. Later, when Nixon had appointed him ambassador to the United Kingdom, Annenberg was asked to join. A proud man, he refused, and would never take a step inside this club, even when invited to speak.

In 1970, Annenberg contributed $950,000 of his own money to a makeover of Winfield House, the ambassadorial residence in London, which was renovated under the guidance of his wife Leonore (later President Reagan's chief of protocol). When *The New York Times* interviewed him about it, he used too big a word for them—"refurbishment"—and was mocked by the left-leaning paper. Nevertheless, Annenberg was a respected envoy, and made friends with the Queen, enjoying greater popularity than the WASP Elliot Richardson, whom Ford appointed to replace him. Like Nixon, Annenberg made the most of his insecurities, which propelled him to rise as a publishing mogul—periodicals such as *TV Guide* and *Seventeen* earned him a fortune. By appointing him to the premier ambassadorship (and social pinnacle), Nixon was sticking it to the eastern establishment.

Walter and Leonore Annenberg loved fine art and beautiful objects. When Annenberg visited his fellow ambassador John Humes in Austria, he was impressed with John's collection of Steuben glass sculptures. On returning to London, he wired the company to say that he had just seen John Humes's collection of Steuben glass, and requested that they duplicate it and send it to him. While Annenberg was a man of great insecurities, who never forgot a slight, he donated a lifetime total of more than two billion dollars to various charities.

The Annenbergs enjoyed hosting friends at Sunnylands, their Palm Springs estate. I last saw Walter Annenberg there in March 1994, when I was invited for the weekend along with General Colin Powell. Though he entertained the Reagans more than twenty times at Sunnylands, Richard Nixon remained his favorite president. Nixon's daughter, Julie Nixon Eisenhower, came to Philadelphia to deliver Annenberg's eulogy in 2002.

Madeleine Albright: Clinton's UN Ambassador and Secretary of State

It has been written that a gentleman is one who never does anything intentionally rude to a lady. By that definition, I might rationalize my intentionally rude behavior toward a former secretary of state. It was in 2002, when I had been invited to speak at the Lotos Club in New York. This private gentleman's club (which now admits women) was named for Lord Tennyson's "The Lotos-Eaters," a poem that was popular at the time of its founding in 1870. Mark Twain, an early member of the Lotos Club along with both Gilbert and Sullivan, once called it the "Ace of Clubs." I was probably among the least famous of the former invitees, who had included Robert Frost and Ernest Hemingway. A caricature of each honored speaker was made and hung—mine, as I later heard, is hanging in the third floor john.

The night before the dinner, I was taken out to eat by the club president—a physician—at the Four Seasons in midtown Manhattan. As I ascended the elevator from the lobby to meet my host, I saw that Clinton's former Madam Secretary was the only other rider. An urge of naughtiness overcame me. Smiling broadly at her, I said, "I so much admire your work in diplomacy and your articulate advocacy for freedom." She beamed, and then I added, "Ambassador Kirkpatrick." Albright frowned in disgust. I pretended that I was one of those clueless types that recognized her as a noted woman, a TV talking head who was often called on to discuss foreign policy.

It was worth it just for the look on her face. I learned later that she was on her way to meet a group where she was to talk about her book, *Madam Secretary*. The former Marie Jana Korbelova owed her appointment as the first woman secretary of state to her fellow Wellesley graduate, Hillary Clinton. My wife Dianne was a couple of years ahead of Albright at Wellesley, and as a political science major, she had shared some of the same professors. Albright had been serving as Clinton's UN ambassador—a role with much prestige but little or no policy making. When Warren Christopher left the State Department, Hillary insisted on Albright's appointment to satisfy her feminist backers.

Although her father was a Holocaust survivor, Albright did not always embrace her Jewish heritage. It was understandable that her father, the Czech diplomat Josef Korbel, changed his religious affiliation to Catholicism in the 1930s, when Nazi influence surged in the republic bordering Germany. Later, he would escape to Britain, then to America. (Interestingly, he was a professor to Albright's later successor, Condoleeza Rice.) When Albright was appointed to the secretary of state post in 1996, public scrutiny was more intense than it had been when she was named UN ambassador three years earlier. She said at the time that her religion was Episcopalian, having converted from Catholicism at the time of her marriage, and that she was surprised by the discovery of her father's heritage.

Even if Albright's denial of Jewish heritage is understandable, what I cannot understand is her actual record as secretary, when she had dealings with the twenty-first century's premier murder and torture regime, that of North Korea. In October 1994, President Bill Clinton reached an agreement with the North Korean leadership to offer them aid if they would temporarily cease their nuclear program. In 2000, following a trip to Pyongyang in connection with U.S. easing of trade restrictions, Albright declared that North Korea was no longer a rogue state. But the Korean dictatorship reneged on the deal, and secretly continued their nuclear development and testing. Two decades later, the terrifying results—missiles lobbed over Japan, and a false report of incoming North Korean warheads over Hawaii in January 2018—posed a serious global threat.

Even more surprisingly for a Holocaust survivor, in a "60 Minutes" interview in May 1996, Albright characterized the deaths of five hundred thousand Iraqi children due to Clinton-era sanctions as having been worth it in realizing the administration's goals. Later, Osama bin Laden made use of this atrocity by filming recruitment videos showing Iraqi babies near death from malnourishment and lack of medicine.

William Rogers: Eisenhower's Attorney General and Nixon's Secretary of State

William Rogers had blue eyes that engaged you in friendly warmth. A Japanese diplomat once said to me he was "Sapporo" (the name of a popular beer, but in Japanese it means "generally unflappable, likeable"). To the Nixon girls, Julie and Tricia, he was known as "Uncle Bill."

I first met him at a Nixon White House Christmas party, but really talked to him for the first time at the swearing-in of John Humes as ambassador to Austria. I told Rogers that he was only the second secretary of state who had also served as attorney general. Later, I gave him a letter by the first such Cabinet member, Edmund Randolph, the attorney general who replaced Jefferson when he resigned during Washington's second term.

When President Nixon was at a loss as to a choice for secretary of state, he called on New York Governor Thomas Dewey, who turned him down. But Dewey recommended William Rogers, who had succeeded Herbert Brownell as Eisenhower's attorney general. Rogers, like Brownell, had been a Dewey protégé. When Nixon protested that Rogers didn't know foreign affairs, Dewey replied that Rogers didn't need that type of experience, because Nixon would be secretary of state. At Nixon's request, Rogers had assisted the House Un-American Activities Committee in nailing Alger Hiss—a Red spy working in the U.S. State Department—on a perjury charge, when Hiss denied he was involved in Soviet espionage. After Nixon's 1960 defeat, they became estranged, but when Nixon called on Rogers to fill the secretary of state's post, he readily agreed. Following this appointment, the two became alienated again, because Rogers could not take command of foreign policy at the State Department due to Nixon's hands-on diplomatic style through his advisor Henry Kissinger.

Rogers had agreed with State's consensus, and that of academia, that any entrée to China could only be achieved after the Vietnam conflict was over. For this reason, Nixon was forced to bypass the State Department in his secret negotiations with Chinese Premier Zhou Enlai. Kissinger supported this "cold shoulder treatment" for the State Department, even if he had at first strenuously opposed the Nixon initiative to open negotiations with China.

Nevertheless, Rogers came to the opening of the Nixon Library in 1990. I later met his daughter, Dale Rogers Marshall (who was at the time academic dean of Wellesley College, but later president of Wheaton College), at my daughter Mary's Harvard graduation in 1985. Marshall's daughter Jessica was in the same class as Mary. Dale Marshall told me that Rogers never forgave Kissinger for his humiliating treatment at Beijing in 1972, where Rogers was excluded from private meetings between Nixon, Mao Zedong, and Zhou Enlai. And he never overcame his bitterness when Kissinger succeeded him in 1973.

Michael Collins: Astronaut and Nixon's Assistant Secretary of State for Public Affairs

Michael Collins is the first genuine hero I ever met. He had the innate humility and modesty that you usually see on screen, in characters played by Jimmy Stewart or Gary Cooper. Collins was the Apollo 11 astronaut who never stepped on the moon, but stayed in the Apollo command module while his crewmates descended in the lunar module to carry out their mission. Collins told me that fellow astronauts Neil Armstrong and Buzz Aldrin never expected to return alive.

In 1969, President Nixon appointed him to be assistant secretary of state in public affairs. His role was to advocate the Nixon Doctrine in speeches throughout the country—arms but no more armies in Asia. This was in fulfillment of Nixon's campaign promise to end the war in Vietnam. To gradually withdraw from military involvement in the Asian conflict, Nixon initiated troop withdrawals each month he was in office—in contrast to both Kennedy and Johnson, who had favored escalation. I was sent to the State Department from the White House to assist Collins with those speeches.

The hardest speech I ever drafted was to be delivered to the Flat Earth Society in Cleveland. The audience didn't believe that America had ever visited the moon, and as proof, they argued that the flag in pictures of the landing was hanging straight out whereas the moon has no wind. Collins patiently told them that the astronauts had it pinned up. As assistant secretary, Collins was micromanaged by the governing bureaucrats in the State Department, a restriction he did not enjoy. After a year, he left to become the first director of the National Air and Space Museum.

Collins had a poet's ear, and could have written an eloquent talk on his own. In 1974, he published *Carrying the Fire: An Astronaut's Journeys*, which was written without assistance and got great reviews. Collins campaigned for Nixon in 1972, and was devastated by Watergate. He had admired Nixon and felt he had been let down.

John Humes: Ambassador to Austria

John Humes was my distant cousin, and he was also one of my closest friends. He had played an active role in managing the New York World's Fair in 1964, and had some run-ins with Governor Nelson Rockefeller—later a contender for the presidency. John early declared for Nixon, and contributed heavily to his presidential campaign. When Nixon was elected, John thought he was slated for the embassy in Belgium, especially since French was a second language for him. But when Nixon telephoned John Eisenhower and asked him to go to Brussels, I informed John Humes, and said that Austria was available. John's German was not as fluent as his French, but he was amenable to offering his services to America in the Alpine nation. He served as ambassador to Austria for two presidents—Nixon and Ford—from 1969 to 1975.

John Humes was the son of Augustine Humes, a lawyer and director of IBM. He had traveled widely, and knew that the Austrians were impressed with show and style. He therefore decided to ship his yacht *Scoop* to Vienna, so that he might entertain Austrian politicians and diplomats on overnight excursions down the Danube.

John had been educated at St. Paul's and Princeton, but he was no playboy. When America entered World War II, he volunteered for the army in his second year of college, not waiting for either his degree or a commission. He relished his years as a private, and would shine his own shoes until his dying day.

During the war, he was sent to London. His family had friends there, and through them he met one Mary Churchill. After a dinner with the young lady, John suggested having a drink somewhere. Mary countered that they should go back to her place, because her father had the best whiskey in London. Her "place" turned out to be 10 Downing Street! There they were, in the study, snuggling up after a couple of drinks, when Churchill walked in. As John told me later, "No battlefield hand-to-hand encounter with a Nazi would have scared me more." But Churchill—having noticed John' uniform—quietly closed the study door, saying that a private's business should remain private.

John's charm and humor captivated the Austrians. It was said they never had a more popular envoy. He had an ability to fix his attention on a guest and make him think he was the most important man in the world. At a presentation or ceremony, he would make his audience believe that he'd rather be there than anywhere else in the world. It was not his eloquence that won them over, but his sincere empathy for others, whatever their rank or station, whether they were a prince with a castle or a farmer from the Tyrolean countryside.

When I was first working in the White House and then at the State Department, my wife and I made three visits to John and his wife in Austria. John and Jean (a former New York surgeon) were delightful and fun hosts. The embassy staff had entertained presidents and prime ministers. One night after dinner, John offered me a cigar with my brandy, saying, "Shortly after I arrived, my chief of staff delivered this alarming news: 'Ambassador, we have discovered, in the basement, cases of Havanas. What shall we do with this contraband?'" (America had no formal relationship with Cuba, and the discovery of such a gift might have proved embarrassing to an American diplomat.)

John delivered an answer worthy of the wisest statesmen: "Burn them. Slowly . . . one by one."

President Nixon also paid John a visit in April 1970, when he was in Vienna for the Strategic Arms Limitation Talks with the Soviet Union. The night before the summit commenced, President Nixon and John dined together. Nixon complained that *The New York Times* and the *Washington Post* were ripping him for his recent passage of the Anti-Ballistic Missile Act. Editorials had declared that this legislation sent the wrong signal to the Soviets, if the SALT treaty was America's ultimate goal. But Nixon insisted that the Ivy League types had it wrong, and that the Anti-Ballistic Missile Act would strengthen our hand.

John Humes responded, "Excuse me, Mr. President, it's the 'Poison Ivy League.'" The President laughed uproariously, knowing that John had gone to Princeton. (And the president was right. We had stronger negotiating strength, and in May 1972, the Soviets did sign the treaty.)

The SALT talks were a sober business in serious times. Each day the Americans, British, French, and Italians would meet in a room on the top floor of the American Embassy, which looked like a chicken coop because of all the wires around it. It was protected against surveillance. One day, the alarm was set off, and everyone had to strip off their clothes. It had been triggered by a British diplomat who was found to have a wiring device in one of his shoes. The bug had been inserted by a local shoe repairman who was in the pay of the Soviets.

These were critical days in the Cold War, and we were fortunate to have envoys like John Humes. He died in 1985, but I still keep in touch with his family. His life's legacy includes the John P. Humes Japanese Stroll Garden in Mill Neck, New York, a seven-acre garden and teahouse that are open to the public. John conceived the idea for this garden during the time he spent in Japan as a lawyer for Mitsubishi. Frequently described as a hidden gem, the Japanese Stroll Garden commemorates America's strong cultural and economic ties to a former adversary that is now a friend.

Note

1. William Shakespeare, *The Life of Henry the Fifth*, in *The Oxford Shakespeare, Second Edition*, edited by John Jowett, William Montgomery, Gary Taylor, and Stanley Wells (Oxford, UK: Oxford University Press, 2005), 597.

Chapter Five

City Hall

Thacher Longstreth: Philadelphia Politician

Thacher Longstreth was "bigger than life" in terms of his six-foot-six stature, but inside that oversized frame was a little boy. He was a political innocent: naive, credulous, trusting, and passionate as a teenager in his fanatical loyalties to Princeton, basketball, the Republican Party, and Philadelphia.

The last two objects of his devotion are badly matched. Politically, the Quaker City has long been a bastion of Democratic machine politics, where the GOP aspirants find little scope for their ambitions.

Yet despite not winning the mayoralty, which he attempted twice (in 1955 and 1971), he dominated the Philadelphia political landscape like no other politician. And such leading Democrats as Mayor Richardson Dilworth, Mayor and Governor Ed Rendell, and even Police Chief and Mayor Frank Rizzo would agree with this assessment.

Among the eccentricities of the lovable Thach were his teetotaling abstinence, and his daily hitchhiking of rides from his home in Chestnut Hill to Center City, never wearing an overcoat even in freezing weather. (When he was a teenager, the hand-me-down overcoats he got from his father only reached his elbows, so he declined to wear them.)

His father had lost all his money in the 1929 crash, but thanks to financial assistance from the Pew family (founders of Sun Oil, now Sunoco), his family managed to send him to Haverford School and then to Princeton. Coming out of Princeton just after World War II, during which he served in the U.S. Navy, Thach joined the N. W. Ayer advertising company in Philadelphia. He handled the account for Tastykake, a line of snack cakes made by the Tasty Baking Company, and made it *the* food for Philadelphians. Later, it would become a culinary symbol of Philadelphia, just like the cheese-steak and soft pretzel. Thacher's indefatigable enthusiasm had manifested its effect.

I met him through my brother Graham when we were campaigning for Nixon in Philadelphia during 1960's contest with John Kennedy. Thach was a fan of Nixon—a fellow navy man—and had the vice president make a speech for him during the race for mayor in 1955.

He was ever loyal to his friends. In October 1961, he came to address the Lycoming County Young Republicans. Although I was at George Washington Law School that night, Thach knew from Graham that I intended to run for state representative against the Republican incumbent, "Doc" Whittaker. With Whittaker at the head table alongside him, Thach called on the audience to support James Humes, saying I was the young blood the Party needed. An angry Whittaker retorted that if 'Longstretch' thought he could tell Williamsporters what they should do, he had another think coming.

In 1966, two years after my defeat in the anti-Goldwater landslide debacle of 1964, Thach offered me a job as legislative counsel to the Greater Philadelphia Chamber of Commerce. A year later, in 1967, I would be appointed executive director of the Philadelphia Bar Association. At the same time, Thach would be elected councilman at-large for Philadelphia. If I became a spokesman for the organized Bar, Thach was the most dynamic voice for business and the Republican Party. In those days, as I would walk with him after a lunch together, he would be hailed by friends from all walks of life. Longstreth came from abolitionist forebears, and was particularly loved by the black community. A lifelong, ninth-generation Quaker, he was fond of preaching, and I sometimes substituted for him at a church pulpit when he had another engagement. It is a sad epitaph to his active-cause career that he died confined to a wheelchair.

Frank Rizzo: Philadelphia Mayor and Police Commissioner

Frank Rizzo was one of the few mayors outside of New York to achieve international fame. In Britain, I was told, Queen Elizabeth was fascinated after meeting him during the 1976 Bicentennial celebrations in Philadelphia. Rizzo was a squarely built hunk with slicked down black hair. He was perceived as a nemesis to liberals and blacks, yet the black policemen worshipped him. Women from South and Northeast Philadelphia squealed like groupies whenever he approached them, as police chief and later as mayor.

Rizzo wasn't handsome in the movie-star sense, but he manifested more macho masculinity than any Hollywood star. If "Law and Order" were to be symbolized by any one personality in the dictionary, it would be Rizzo. The *Philadelphia Inquirer* would often feature a picture of him in black tie with a billy club tucked into his cummerbund. On one such black-tie evening, he left the party wielding that club to stop an armed robbery that was taking place on the street outside.

I got to know him when I was director of the Philadelphia Bar Association and he was police chief. It was a time of urban rioting. In 1967, I organized the Police Station Observer project in anticipation of riots that were predicted to take place that summer. Under the auspices of the project, African-American lawyers would sit at police stations from 11:00 p.m. to 4:00 a.m. to monitor any trouble. I take pride in the fact that Philadelphia did not suffer from riots that summer, unlike New York, Washington, and Detroit. Afterwards, the Junior Chamber of Commerce named me Man of the Year.

Rizzo knew I was a friend of his hero Richard Nixon. When presidential candidate Nixon visited Philadelphia, the one person he wanted to greet him was Frank Rizzo. But in the tony Chestnut Hill section of Philadelphia, where he resided only a few houses away from me, he was treated as a pariah by the old WASP families.

Rizzo would often invite me over to regale his visiting policemen with Churchill stories. He told me he first met Nixon when he was vice president, and had volunteered to be Nixon's local police-security officer at an appearance in Philadelphia. He bonded with Nixon, and they corresponded over the years. In his office, Rizzo displayed a signed picture of Vice President Nixon facing the Venezuelan mobs who attacked his motorcade when he was there on a state visit in 1958.

Chapter Six

Buckingham Palace

Her Majesty Queen Elizabeth II: Queen of the United Kingdom of Great Britain and Northern Ireland and of Her Other Realms and Territories, Head of the Commonwealth, Defender of the Faith, and Supreme Governor of the Church of England

I was first aware of Princess Elizabeth, the little daughter of King George VI and Queen Elizabeth, when I was age five in 1939. Next to the study (off the master bedroom) in our Williamsport house, there was a 'secret' room—with no lights—where my brothers and I used a flashlight to read old magazines. The room had a sliding door through which one could crawl. There were old copies of *National Geographic* and *The Illustrated London News,* with stories about the British royal family. Our mother was a great fan of both princesses (Elizabeth and Margaret) even before King Edward VIII abdicated, moving them up in line as heirs to the throne, and into the forefront of world news. Their mother, Elizabeth Bowes-Lyon, was the daughter of a Scottish earl, and our mother—a Graham—was proud of her own Scottish heritage. She told us: "It's about time to bring some Scottish blood into that German background." Mother was a year younger than Queen Elizabeth, whose second child, Margaret, was born the same month as my brother Sam in 1930.

The next time Princess Elizabeth burst into public awareness, she was Queen. Prime Minister Churchill greeted her when she flew home to England from Kenya in February 1952, upon the death of her father. I was at Stowe as an exchange student later that year. At Christmastime, my housemate, Nick Luddington, invited me to Sandringham House in Norfolk—the new Queen's private country estate. His father, a retired brigadier, was steward: the manager of this royal manor, and he confided to me that I might have a peep at the royals. Mrs. Luddington asked me whether I had a black tie. On Boxing

Day, which is the day after Christmas, the Queen was hosting a private reception for her cousin, Princess Alexandra, who was celebrating her sixteenth birthday, and they needed extra young men at the dance.

At one point, an equerry said I should dance with Her Majesty. I felt left-footed and tongue-tied. She was twenty-six, I was eighteen. She was five-foot-two, and I towered a foot above her at six-foot-two. She had a radiant "English rose" complexion, and a figure Jane Russell might have envied. I focused on the ceiling. I couldn't look down. It was like looking at the cleavage of the Virgin Mary. She was, after all, the head of the Church of England. I might be taken to the Tower! She asked me how I liked the English Christmas. "Fine," was my terse answer. Did I miss my family? "Yes," was my monosyllabic reply. She was unfailingly gracious and kind, but that was part and parcel of her regal presence. She was every inch a Queen.

Forty-five years later, in 1997, when Brian Lamb interviewed me on C-Span about *Confessions of a White House Ghostwriter*, he asked me if I remembered the song they were playing when I was dancing with the Queen. I could never forget it. It was the Jo Stafford classic, "You Belong to Me"— about traveling the world to see the sights—which was just what I was trying to avoid.

Sir Edward Heath, the former prime minister, gave me his views on Queen Elizabeth when he hosted me for lunch in his London townhouse. Significantly, he pointed out that she had history tutors that would top those of any university, beginning with Winston Churchill, and including Anthony Eden, Alec Douglas-Home, and Harold Macmillan. Heath learned to seek her advice and respect her counsel.

After Churchill first met the eldest daughter of the Duke of York (later George VI) in 1929, he wrote to his wife that the young lady had remarkable presence and poise. Churchill would ever be a hero to Elizabeth, but remarkably, a man she particularly admired in history is our own George Washington, her distant relative. When she visited Williamsburg, Virginia in 1957 and attended the parish church, she was escorted to the Royal Pew where the Royal Governors had formerly been seated. But she declined, preferring to sit where George Washington sat.

Her Royal Highness Princess Margaret: Countess of Snowdon

Queen Elizabeth may have looked like that older, sweet and wholesome girl in your high school class, the one you'd love to introduce to your mother. But her sister, Princess Margaret, was glamorous—sexy, and radiating a bit of naughty excitement.

I danced with her, too, on that Boxing Day, December 26, 1952, at the birthday reception for their cousin Princess Alexandra. But Margaret couldn't hide the boredom in her eyes. She didn't have to be gracious, like the Queen, to this American visitor.

My hair was an American crew cut, which, to the British, resembled the cropped style one saw on their convicts. I had not the looks or charm to compensate for the awkward fact that I was about a foot taller than Margaret. But once I had danced with the Queen, I was urged to dance with others. After all, that was the reason I had been invited. As a young man visiting my Stowe schoolmate, the son of Brigadier Luddington, steward of Sandringham, I was simply an extra young male to fill out the dance floor.

I danced with Princess Alexandra, the birthday honoree, who is still the most beautiful of the royals. I had an instant crush on her. Another young lady I danced with was the daughter of a neighboring lord, the Lady Frances Fermoy. (Years later I found out that she was the mother of Princess Diana. She was the same age as Princess Alexandra—sixteen—but much more sophisticated.)

To be fair to Princess Margaret, she had been denied her only real love: Group Captain Peter Townsend. He had been an aide to her father, King George VI, and after the war, Margaret and the R.A.F. hero (who was married at the time) fell in love. Following Townsend's divorce, Churchill dispatched this unsuitable match for a princess to Belgium, where he served as an attaché. In our sometimes more humane twenty-first century, the House of Commons would have given their reluctant consent to such a marriage by the monarch's younger sister.

But at the time, Margaret was not a happy twenty-two-year old. And she was looking for an exciting older man—if not of the military world, then perhaps someone artistic. That should have been the end of any association with Princess Margaret for me or my family. But there would be a denouement.

In February 2002, my oldest grandchild Caroline attended a birthday party for Arthur Chatto, a classmate in her pre-school—Miss Marley's—near Sloane Square. She found herself the only girl among eight boys. An old woman, frail and unsteady on her feet, addressed her: Wasn't Caroline a fortunate young lady to be surrounded by eight handsome young men? My granddaughter shyly nodded.

The woman looking older than her seventy-two years was Princess Margaret. She had risen from her sick bed to attend her grandson Arthur's birthday party. Two days later, she was dead.

I met Arthur's mother—Lady Sarah Chatto—just once, at a school function of my granddaughter's. In her white T-shirt and jeans, Lady Sarah was just another school mother. Eschewing fashion or the famous, Sarah concentrates on being a good parent. Later, Lord Anthony St. John, a close friend of Queen Elizabeth's, confided to me that Lady Sarah was the favorite of the Queen—perhaps more than any of her own children.

I wrote a letter to Lady Sarah saying that I had once danced with her mother. I spoke of her charisma, which could light up any room, and as a biographer of Shakespeare, I ended with this line from *Romeo and Juliet*, "O! she doth teach the torches to burn bright."[1]

Afterward, Lady Sarah hand-wrote a reply to me, saying it was the most poignant and beautiful letter she had received on her mother's death. She also sent me a signed photograph of her grandfather, George VI, in full regalia.

His Royal Highness Prince Charles: Prince of Wales and Duke of Cornwall

I met the Prince of Wales only once, in 1986 at a Birmingham soccer stadium. I was on an ESU speaking tour, and was staying with Michael Cadbury, head of the famous chocolate firm. One evening Michael told me that the cook would get my dinner that night, because he was headed out to a rock concert. I was incredulous. "You, going to a rock concert, Michael?" But he was serious: He had to attend, because he was head of the Royal Trust, and it was a benefit concert whose proceeds were going to that organization.

I went to this concert, and sat with Cadbury. At one point the Prince of Wales and Princess Diana went down to shake hands with the screaming rock group. Charles soon left Diana and came over to where we were seated. He was wearing a yellow waistcoat, green trousers, and a tweed jacket.

Cadbury introduced me, and explained that I was on a speaking tour for the ESU. No response from Charles. Cadbury repeated himself, only a bit louder; Charles was silent. Then, embarrassed for me, Cadbury addressed Charles for the third time, shouting my name at the prince.

Charles replied that he was dreadfully sorry, but he could not hear Michael at first—and then he took out his earplugs. "That's fine," I replied, "I wish I had some." Clearly, Charles didn't share the same musical tastes as his wife, who was enjoying herself talking to the band members. He may come off as a pedagogical prig to some, but to me, he was charming and courteous. He was especially interested that I had gone to Stowe, and he talked knowledgeably about Lancelot "Capability" Brown, the landscape architect for the renowned English preparatory school. I regret that I never met Camilla Parker-Bowles, Charles's inamorata whom he later married.

Anne, Princess Royal: Daughter of Elizabeth II

For many years, the second child of Queen Elizabeth was dubbed "the royal sourpuss." Her photos at exhibitions, fairs, or other appearances always seemed to catch her in a pout, which did nothing to make the least comely of the royal children more attractive. Some said her sulkiness was due to the early breakup of her marriage to a fellow equestrian, Captain Mark Phillips.

She was, however, the favorite of her father, the Duke of Edinburgh, and the special bond between the two might have affected her relationships with men.

I met Princess Anne in 1982, when she was the honored guest at an English-Speaking Union event in Denver. I had planned to bring my daughters, Mary and Rachel, to meet the princess, but a dinner dance opening the Gertrude Vanderbilt Whitney estate in Long Island was their preferred choice of entertainment that night. (They would be paired at the table with Carter Cooper and his brother, Anderson Cooper, children of Gloria Vanderbilt.)

Seated next to Princess Anne at dinner, for I was to introduce her, I tried to make conversation to my clearly uninterested dinner partner. "Zara" was the name of their daughter. In my mind, I could only think of a sign over a shop in Soho that said: "Madame Zara Reads Fortunes for All Distressed." But I told her that I thought Zara was an interesting name. The princess responded that it was an ancient way to spell Sarah.

It was the time of the Falklands War, and Prime Minister Thatcher had decided to defend England's remote South Atlantic outpost against an invasion by Argentina. Before I went into my remarks about Anne, I said, "First of all, I think it appropriate to toast her gallant brother, Prince Andrew, who is piloting planes to guard the Royal Marines . . . . " The chairman interrupted, saying, "The English-Speaking Union does not enter the realm of politics." Anne nodded vigorously. But I was, after all, speaking to a group that is meant to foster relations among English-speaking people. I was giving my Churchill talk, which is replete with humorous Churchill anecdotes. But their laughter never got off the ground once they saw the princess maintain a stony face at the head table.

Middle age has brought to Anne, if not beauty, a certain dignity and presence. My friend Jamie Dugdale, Lord Crathorne, was formerly the Lord Lieutenant of North Yorkshire, who must be present when royals visit. He was, in effect, the ceremonial head of the shire, a royal deputy of the Queen. He tells me that Princess Anne, like the Queen, is knowledgeable and well briefed. He also says that she is always gracious, and takes a genuine interest in the home crafts, flower shows, or medal-giving ceremonies, and that she is now popular and receives an enthusiastic reception wherever she goes.

His Royal Highness, The Prince Philip:
Duke of Edinburgh and Consort of Elizabeth II

In March of 1953, I met the Queen's consort at a tea hosted by the ESU for some of their exchange scholars at schools within short rail distance of London. It was held on Charles Street in Mayfair, where the ESU has its headquarters.

I had sighted him off in the distance at a dance for Princess Alexandra the day after Christmas, but I hadn't actually met him. We were coached on how to address him: first saying, "Your Royal Highness," and afterwards, "Sir."

I had come down from Stowe, wearing a gray flannel suit topped with a Royal Stewart tartan tie. Around the corner from Berkley Square there was a Cockney bootblack on the Piccadilly, a bald, grizzled ex-navy tar. I explained whom I was seeing, and he refused payment, telling me: "I once served on a ship with the lieutenant. Give a salute to the skipper for me."

My shoes at mirror polish, my tie neatly knotted, I arrived at the tea. The British are bemused by Americans sporting ties, scarves, or waistcoats in plaid, items which at that time were often purchased at Scotch House, once a tourist mecca in London. I had chosen Royal Stewart because Philip is, after all, the Duke of Edinburgh (and Royal Stewart is the Queen's personal tartan).

Philip, military slim and elegant in British Navy garb, looked taller than his five-foot-ten-inch stature. He is polite and gracious, but betrays little enjoyment for these ceremonial duties.

He looked at my tie, and asked me why Americans like to proclaim their Scotch background.

I had a schoolteacher mother who drilled into me that "Scottish" or "Scots" is the adjective, not "Scotch." So I answered, "My heritage is Scottish. Scotch is the drink." Philip replied that I could be right, but that he ventured to say more scotch flowed in American veins than Scottish heritage.

My meeting was the cause of a pejorative nickname back at school. I had to talk about the royal engagement the past Tuesday to the school assembly. Americans don't use the long U in conversation, much to the merriment of our English cousins. We pronounce duke to rhyme with kook, not cuke, and the second day of the week comes out as Toosday. (Even in American dictionaries, the correct pronunciation is Tews-day.) So the moniker the Brits gave me was "The Doook of Tooosday." I spoke only of *Prince* Philip after that.

Ernest Simpson: Second Husband of Wallis Simpson, Duchess of Windsor

Ernest Simpson is a footnote to history. He was the former husband of "that woman"—to quote Churchill—whose marriage to King Edward VIII almost toppled the British monarchy. I met him for a Sunday lunch in April 1953. I had mentioned to Howard Lund, father of my Stowe friend, Richard, that my father was once a schoolmate of Simpson's. Lund was a commercial fleet owner, and he and Simpson, who was a marine insurance broker, were professional acquaintances. Lund contacted Simpson and I was given his number to call. I did, and I was told to come to Simpson's-on-the-Strand, a traditional English restaurant that had opened its doors in 1828. He later said the *maître d'* always jokingly treated him as if there was some family connection with the elegant dining establishment.

Ernest Simpson was a dark, mustached, handsome man in his middle fifties—every inch an Englishman, with his Coldstream Guards tie and Savile Row suit. He said he remembered my father as a large boy, but hardly knew him because he was three years older (if only two classes ahead of him) at the Hill School during World War I. He vaguely recalled, as he told me, that my father was not from Philadelphia or New York, but from somewhere in upstate Pennsylvania.

At this point in his life, Simpson was widowed. In 1937, following his divorce, he had married Wallis's best and oldest friend, Mary Kirk Raffray from Baltimore. The two friends had been classmates at Oldfields, a girls' boarding school in Maryland. (When I spoke there in 1991, the headmaster showed me a plaque that gave her years of attendance as 1912–1915.) The divorce was relatively amicable; rumors circulated that Wallis even encouraged the match.

Simpson asked me about my time as an exchange student at Stowe. He confessed that he was a would-be architect, and that when he and his wife Mary lived in Buckinghamshire, they often drove to see Stowe. I agreed with him when he told me that the architect Vanbrugh, not to mention Capability Brown, the landscape architect, had made it a small Buckingham Palace.

Simpson, if stiff, was polite and gracious. He was more interested in my time at Stowe than his time at Hill School, which he didn't enjoy. With some trepidation, I brought up the quotation under his yearbook graduation picture, which had proved to be eerily correct: "Someday I shall dine in the presence of the King." *The New York Herald-Tribune* had a sidebar story on this topic at the time of the abdication. Simpson frowned when I mentioned it, and confided that his English accent was the cause of great teasing, because schoolboys can be great bullies.

His Anglophile passions did not make him popular in an American prep school. He was a monarchist to the core, and later loved the Queen—if not her royal grandmother, Queen Mary. He asked me whether I was happy with the newly elected President Eisenhower, and told me that he was happy with the people's choice, too. Some of his friends, he said, liked Adlai Stevenson, but not those at his club.

Interestingly, it has since come out that his father's name was originally Ernest Louis Solomon, and that he had Anglicized it to Simpson. This New Yorker of Jewish background had founded the international ship-broking firm of Simpson, Spence, and Young. In the 1930s, any Germans who conducted business with Ernest Simpson would have found this shocking, and he would surely have lost their patronage.

Note

1. William Shakespeare, *The Most Excellent and Lamentable Tragedy of Romeo and Juliet*, in *The Oxford Shakespeare, Second Edition*, edited by John Jowett, William Montgomery, Gary Taylor, and Stanley Wells (Oxford, UK: Oxford University Press, 2005), 377.

Chapter Seven

Parliament

Sir Winston Churchill: Prime Minister

Ever since I can remember, Churchill was my great hero. My mother had me listen to his radio broadcasts in 1940, on the nursery radio just off our ship-themed, port-holed bedroom with its built-in bunk beds. I was not yet six, and I could hardly understand his lisped growl. I do remember, however, hoping he would win office again in 1951. Mother had predicted his selection as "Man of the Century" before *TIME* magazine confirmed it in January 1950.

I first saw Churchill in person from the Strangers' Gallery in the House of Commons, early in 1953. I was disappointed in the slumped figure seated on the front bench. When he rose for a few words, I was reminded of the actor Charles Laughton, who had won an Oscar for playing King Henry VIII.

I would later shake hands with him on May 29, 1953 at the Mansion House—the lord mayor's residence—where he was hosting a luncheon for Commonwealth Prime Ministers attending the coronation of Elizabeth II. When I was introduced, I said I was interested in government. He told me to study history, because in history lie all the secrets of statecraft.

For me, Churchill was the "Man of the Millennium," as Edward R. Murrow called him: the only man who ever predicted the course of history, made history, and then set it down on paper. I later wrote a book on his prophecies, *Churchill: The Prophetic Statesman* (2012). At age fifteen, in 1889, Churchill predicted a world war in 1914, with trenches and as many as ten thousand casualties in a day. He would also prophesy the rise of the Nazi menace, the Iron Curtain of the Soviet Union, the European Economic Community, and many other events, such as the creation of a super-bomb.

On my honeymoon in 1957, I heard him speak to the American Bar Association in London. He said that the UN was a feckless organization, maimed by a congenital deformity: giving veto power to the Soviets. He had high praise for Richard Nixon, noting that no one he had ever met was more qualified, in terms of knowledge and preparation, to speak on behalf of the American government.

Churchill was a Renaissance man: soldier, statesman, author, historian, pilot, inventor, and painter—a polymath, like our own Benjamin Franklin. The last time I saw him was in 1959, after he had visited Eisenhower in Gettysburg. It was also the last time Churchill stood on American soil—a cold, rainy afternoon in May at Andrews Air Force Base. Slowly, one step at a time, Churchill mounted the airplane ramp. The rain stopped as the Man of the Millennium raised his hand with fingers in a V, bid farewell to the land of his mother, and asked God's blessing for all those present in wishing them goodnight.

But I can never forget our first handshake at the Mansion House. He looked bigger than life. It was as if I was meeting Napoleon, Alexander the Great, or Julius Caesar. I was shaking hands with history.

Anthony Eden: Earl of Avon and Prime Minister

Dianne and I had lunch at Anthony Eden's home near Salisbury in 1970—a dozen years after the single term he served as prime minister. He may have personified distinguished ministerial elegance, but he was also a classic example of the brilliant number-two man who was a failure as number one. Fifteen years as Churchill's deputy had not taught him everything: The former foreign secretary who said that peace must always come first was not very good at waging war.

Churchill once admitted to some misgivings about his successor, and pinpointed what would be Eden's downfall: He thought of Britain as an equal partner with the United States. Not a junior partner, but a peer, given Britain's seniority on the world stage. When Egyptian President Gamal Abdel Nasser seized the Suez Canal, an oil-shipment route vital to Europe, Eden assumed that America would go along with the military intervention planned by Israel, France, and Britain. Instead, he was pressured into declaring a cease-fire after only twenty-three miles of the canal had been secured. Following his Suez failure, Eden blamed Dulles for manipulating a weak Eisenhower, who sandbagged Britain with a series of diplomatic and financial maneuvers. As Churchill later said, without U.S. concurrence, Britain should never have intervened militarily—but once it did, Eden shouldn't have stood on the diving board allowing opposition to develop. He should have jumped.

Eden's wife Clarissa, who was Churchill's niece, told me that the Nile had flooded their living room, in a manner of speaking, and that she had ended up tending the garden when she craved the excitement of politics. She went on to say that her mere two years as spouse of the prime minister stood in contrast to the experience of Anthony's first wife, who, conversely, hated politics and loved gardening. I told Eden that my mother worshipped Churchill, but Anthony Eden could have put his shoes under my wife's bed any day. He laughed delightedly.

I presented Eden with a letter written by his kinsman, Colonial Governor Charles Eden of North Carolina. In this letter, Governor Eden wrote that he loved the New World more than England, and cited a resolution from the state legislature declaring that Eden, in North Carolina, meant freedom. (The town of Edenton, North Carolina, was named in honor of this ancestor on his death in 1722.) Eden told us that nothing presented to him had ever meant more. At the time of our visit, Eden was Conservative Party leader in the House of Lords on foreign policy, which included oversight of Britain's role in European unification. He told me that while he voted with his head for entry into the European Economic Community, his heart would always remain with America and the North American alliance. I reminded him of how I first met him on the steps of the Capitol in 1952. I had said, "God save the Queen." In response, Eden had expressed his wish that God would always bless America.

Sir Alec Douglas-Home: Prime Minister and Foreign Secretary

Lord Home served as chieftain of the Home, Hume, and Humes Clan. Our family grew up with an awareness that this Scottish peer was the head of our clan. His name had originally been Hume. Lord Home's brother Henry told us it was spelled with a macron over the long vowel so it wouldn't be pronounced "Hoom." Careless reading and transcription closed the macron over the u and made it an "o," resulting in "Home."

My wife and I expected to see Lord Home in 1957 at The Hirsel, the family seat in the Scottish Borders, when his mother, the Dowager Countess of Home, held a little reception after our wedding. But he was busy making a speech and presentation, as secretary of state for Scotland and a member of Harold Macmillan's Cabinet. Later, Lord Home would be selected as Macmillan's foreign secretary. A photo of Home with Neville Chamberlain at Munich makes him look like a gawky, chinless teenager. But Home's wimpy effete looks belied a flinty resolve. Foes misinterpreted his *noblesse oblige* manners and courtesy to their regret and sorrow. As foreign secretary under Heath, he ordered all spies in London operating under cover of diplomats to be out at the end of the day—an unprecedented move in a Western democracy.

When I sat with him in the House of Lords dining room in 1991, the eighty-nine-year-old peer modestly shrugged off this historic act: He told me he was the only one who actually had a steel spine. (It had been implanted as a result of scoliosis.)

Dianne and I first met Lord Home in London in April 1970, and he was gracious to us. He and his wife hosted us at Carleton House, the foreign secretary's residence. Afterwards, Lady Home took us to a children's bookstore to buy books for our daughters Mary and Rachel. But I first heard Home deliver a speech in 1963, at a Conservative conference in Blackpool. At the time, the retiring Macmillan was trying to maneuver Home into the prime ministership, sidestepping a fight between Lord Hailsham and R. A. B. ("Rab") Butler. Home was everyone's second choice, and at first, the press scorned this earl. Britain was tired of the Conservative aristocratic image: Churchill, Eden, Macmillan. But Home was selected for the one-year replacement slot, and he almost won the following election against Harold Wilson. Despite an aura of disenchantment with peers in the nation's highest elective office, people began to prize the virtue of this gentleman–statesman. For a short time, he ennobled the name of politician, as one who placed principles above popularity.

Labour leader Harold Wilson once asked Lord Home how his status as the thirteenth Earl qualified him to be prime minister. Lord Home shot back that it was no more of an asset than being the thirteenth Mr. Wilson.

Sir Edward Heath: Prime Minister

Silver-haired Edward Heath may have looked a bit like a statesman, but he did not have the personality of one. Like Nixon, he was an introvert in an extrovert's profession, but unlike Nixon, he didn't try to be friendly or sociable. When I met him in 1998, the former prime minister was the longest-serving parliamentarian. My friend Dr. Jarvis Ryals and I were guests for tea in his Belgravia town house. He was gracious, but he still came off as stiff.

British politics do not accommodate the electioneering one sees in America. It is accepted that Reagan, the populist movie star, could never have risen to be prime minister, just as the forbidding and formidable Margaret Thatcher could not have been elected president. But it is hard to imagine Ted Heath being selected as even a congressional candidate.

Heath was the only Conservative prime minister between Alec Douglas-Home and Margaret Thatcher. Although some might compare the two shy, hard-working men in terms of their detailed mastery of issues, Heath was not drawn to Nixon. He told me that although he respected Nixon for his grasp of foreign affairs, he thought his knowledge of economics limited. It should be added that although Macmillan, like Churchill, Douglas-Home, and Thatcher, was pro-American, Heath was not. He thought of himself as a European. He did not hide his animus for Harold Wilson, the man who replaced him. But he never mentioned Thatcher in the course of our conversation. When I asked him to name the greatest prime minister after Churchill, he paused for a long time before selecting Douglas-Home. He said that Reagan was a clueless entertainer, and that his adversary Wilson had never been impeded by principle.

Heath never married, and like many distinguished bachelors, he became the subject of imaginative gossip. But for all his formality, we found him to be a courteous and gracious host.

Margaret Thatcher: Baroness Thatcher, Prime Minister

I did not like Thatcher. She was not a likeable person. She commanded respect, but did not invite affection. In American politics, she could not have been elected president, but then again, Reagan the TV cowboy could not have become prime minister under Britain's parliamentary system. With eleven years to her credit, the late Baroness Thatcher still reigns, not only as the first woman to win the UK's highest elective office, but also as the twentieth century's longest-serving British Prime Minister.

My first encounter with Margaret Thatcher took place in the summer of 1975. In February of that year, she had been elected head of the Conservative Party upon the rejection of Edward Heath. Ministers in Heath's Cabinet who were vying to succeed him cast their votes for her, hoping to knock Heath out, secretly confident that a woman couldn't make it. Yet enough did vote for her that she won a plurality.

Thatcher now headed the Conservative Party as opposition leader—the equivalent of our minority leaders in the House and Senate. The ruling Labour Party was unpopular, but its leader, Prime Minister Jim Callaghan, was a more congenial personality than Thatcher—the friendly neighborhood pub keeper versus the blond-helmeted "Iron Lady" of British politics.

The Conservative Party asked me to draft a speech for Thatcher. The idea, they said, was to give her a softer portrait, taking the harsh edge off "Thatcher the Milk Snatcher," a nickname she had earned by cutting the provision of free milk in schools. I was supposed to cast her as a wife and mother of two who was as familiar with the shopping market as the Common Market—someone who could quote the price of "nappies" (diapers) as well as anyone.

She met me for lunch. Her handshake was as icy as her greeting, and she asked me whether I had ever read *The Road to Serfdom* by Friedrich von Hayek. "Yes," I stuttered. (This landmark work by the British–Austrian economist warns against the dangers of centralized economic planning.) Thatcher snapped that she thought this unlikely, and tore up my speech. It seems that the Conservative Party writers in the central office were afraid to draft such a talk. So they retained me. I was paid, but Thatcher never forgave me. Nevertheless, I rate her as one of the great leaders of the twentieth century. When she stood up to Argentina in the remote Falkland Islands—and won—she made Britain proud again. She, along with President Reagan and Pope John Paul II, brought down the Soviet Union.

In the Cabinet, she presided over ten men like a nanny with ten school-boys. When she came in with her oversized handbag, they almost shivered in expectation. When she left to take a call, the oversized bag (left in the middle of the table) rendered them mute. Turning a deaf ear to criticism, she cut welfare, slashed regulations, gave public-housing tenants the right to buy their homes, and privatized many industries, transforming Britain into the most prosperous nation in Europe. Naturally, the British media had a field day mocking Thatcher, whose indelible personality and mannerisms lent themselves to parody.

Following her reluctant and tearful resignation in 1990—which she characterized as being forced out—Thatcher continued to serve in the House of Commons until 1992, and was active for the next two decades as a consultant, public speaker, and author. When I gave her a copy of *The Wit & Wisdom of Ronald Reagan* in October 2008, this frail lady praised him as having won the Cold War without firing a shot. And Margaret Thatcher certainly helped!

David Cameron: Prime Minister

On March 4 of 2015, my wife and I attended the Anglican confirmation of my grandson James in the College Chapel at Eton. There were thirty pupils to be confirmed that day, each of whom had invited family members and god-parents. For this reason, seating in the chapel—where rows of pews face each other in the nave across the central aisle—was tight. Because I walk with a cane, the usher showed our family group (my wife Dianne, my daughter Mary and her husband Cecil, their three other children, and Cecil's parents) to the front-row pew towards the back of the chapel.

Gazing at the members of the congregation opposite me, I soon recognized the distinctive brunette fringe of Samantha Cameron, the wife of the prime minister. Seated in the pew in front of "Sam Cam" was someone who looked, at first glance, like a slimmer version of her husband. I recalled how television cameras add pounds to public figures, and decided that it really was David Cameron. I later found out that they were both godparents of two of the confirmands, and so they were seated in different pews with the boys' families.

The service required a lot of standing up and sitting down—a huge effort for me. To my dismay, in a moment of reverential silence, my cane (which was propped precariously against the edge of the pew) slipped and clattered onto the stone floor of the chapel. All eyes turned my way. Before I could begin to collect my thoughts, much less the cane, an energetic figure in the pew opposite had leapt to his feet, bounded across the aisle, and placed the cane back in my hand. "Thank you, prime minister" were my whispered words of gratitude.

At forty-nine, Cameron was thirty-two years my junior and well into middle age. But with his boyish-looking, rosy-cheeked face, he could almost have passed for one of the youngsters attending the service. From an aristocratic Scots lineage, and a descendent of William IV, Cameron took steps to mask his background. Raised in Berkshire, one of the "home counties" surrounding London, and educated at Eton and Oxford, Cameron was only too well aware of the public-school caricature Labourites had made of his predecessor Sir Alec Douglas-Home—the last prime minister to have bestrode "the playing fields of Eton." And so he restyled himself as a new kind of conservative, despite the fact that the Home County gentry from whom he wished to distance himself favored him as one of their own. Yet on that confirmation day, his good breeding and manners showed. Cameron's father suffered from a long-term illness that confined him to a wheelchair or made him walk with a cane for most of his adult life. I can't help but think I reminded him of his Scottish father, Ian Donald Cameron, who had died in 2010.

When the time came for communion, the bishop personally served me. During the "peace," the part of the Anglican service when congregants greet each other, Cameron came over to shake my hand. I told him he was the fourth Conservative prime minister I had met, starting with Churchill in 1953. I also divulged that the late Sir Alec Douglas-Home had been the head of my Scottish clan, to which he responded that Douglas-Home was his second-favorite Conservative prime minister.

My friend Jonathan Aitken knew Cameron's parliamentary secretary quite well. And so, he made arrangements to have a copy of my book, *Churchill: The Prophetic Statesman*, delivered to the prime minister's office. I was delighted when, less than two months later, the results of the general election gave Cameron a landslide victory, even though pundits had rated him unlikely to command a majority in the House of Commons. As in the United States and Israel, pollsters and political experts had underestimated the conservative vote. In the end, the undecideds voted overwhelmingly for Cameron and the Conservatives. But the following summer, Cameron bowed to the will of the British people in their landmark "Brexit" vote, which determined, by the slimmest of margins, that Britain would leave the European Union. He resigned in July of 2016.

Robert Hankey, Second Baron Hankey: British Ambassador to Sweden

I first met the second Lord Hankey in 1959. A neighbor of Howard and Eileen Lund (my "adoptive parents" in Cowden, Kent, during my year as an exchange student at Stowe), "Robin" Hankey had been invited for a game of bridge. He was a lanky, spare-framed man with thinning brown hair. Just under five-foot-ten, the recently widowed Hankey spoke with a crisp, melodious voice. The Lunds would later tell me he was the leading tenor in the choir at St. Mary Magdalene Church. He played bridge, in the language of the U.S. Supreme Court, "with all deliberate speed." He was graciously uncritical of his inexperienced partner. His interest was piqued when he learned that my wife Dianne worked in the West Wing of the White House, near Eisenhower's secret office. He was generous in his praise of Eisenhower, and told me that he couldn't understand how Ike had managed to get along with Monty, seeing as the egotistical British Field Marshall Bernard Montgomery could be most tiresome. Ike was a hero to the British for his leadership during the war, and later, in building the North Atlantic Treaty Organization.

If Hankey had little regard for Field Marshall Montgomery, he was even less a fan of John Foster "Massive Retaliation" Dulles. His poor opinion of Ike's secretary of state was shared by his father. The First Lord Hankey was a civil servant who rose to prominence under Arthur Balfour, the former head of the Conservative Party, who in 1916 served as foreign secretary of the wartime coalition. Serving as Cabinet secretary from 1916 to 1938, the archmandarin Maurice Hankey was credited for winning World War I due to his role in screening all documents before they reached the prime minister and the Cabinet, thereby saving valuable time. At Versailles, the elder Hankey was irked by young Dulles, a recent Princeton graduate serving as an assistant to his uncle, Robert Lansing, Wilson's secretary of state. Dulles was a staunch Presbyterian who truly believed he was a member of God's elect, and many people found him insufferable.

The younger Hankey had a gift for languages. He could speak German, French, Italian, Polish, Romanian, Persian, and Arabic. His last posting was as ambassador to Sweden. During a conversation with me in between bridge deals, he manifested a grudging respect for Gamal Abdel Nasser, the instigator of Britain's ill-fated military venture in the Middle East, when the Egyptian leader attempted to nationalize the Suez Canal. Not an outspoken man, he made comments on the Suez crisis that were as spare as his frame. He questioned me as to the future of the Arab statesman, as well as American politics. I remember him as a courteous listener with crinkly, twinkling eyes.

Tony Benn (Viscount Stansgate): Member of Parliament, Cabinet Minister, and Labour Party Chairman

Benn was the British version of our limousine liberal, the prep school and Ivy League scion of the upper-class privileged who advocate the egalitarian policies of the left while enjoying the lifestyle of the rich. His type dates to the founders of the Democratic Party. Thomas Jefferson, for example, while attended by slaves, would proclaim his support for the French Revolution—

which was good for cleaning out the aristocrats—as he sipped the best French claret. American author Tom Wolfe made fun of the modern Manhattan version, who cheered the Mau-Mau while wearing jewels mined by exploited blacks in South Africa.

I had lunch with Tony Benn in October 1963 on a train from London to Bristol, the southwest seaport city that was home to his constituency. The son of Viscount Stansgate, Lord Anthony Wedgwood-Benn was a radical in the Labour Party, currently in opposition to the Conservatives who had ruled since 1951. But when his ailing father died, Benn—as a peer—would no longer be able to serve in the House of Commons.

Under a parliamentary act written by Benn (he gave me a copy from his briefcase), the Earl of Home had just given up his title to become Alec Douglas-Home. Benn told me that Home actually didn't have to give up his earldom. That, he explained, was a Scottish title. Not all Scottish peers were made British peers in 1707, and Home held his seat in the House of Lords as Lord Dunglas. (Years later, Sir Alec told me that this was true, but that the public would never have understood it.)

Tony Benn had a *bonhomie* and looks that somewhat recalled the young Franklin Roosevelt. Though an aristocrat by lineage, he did not support the monarchy. He said it was *panem et circenses*, adding that no one studies Latin in America.

"Bread and circuses," I answered.

Benn nodded in agreement, and went on to say that the Royals were Britain's bit of Hollywood to divert the working classes.

Benn's economic policies were anti-capitalist, although his lavish lifestyle depended on the earnings of his Vassar-educated wife—heiress to a New England manufacturer. The advantage for these champagne socialists, as the *London Express* likes to call them, is that unlike in America, they do not have to reside in the working-class districts they represent. The Central Labour Committee in London can recommend them the way English bishops assign priests.

So, the future Viscount Stansgate ceased to be Lord Wedgwood-Benn, and assumed the more proletarian moniker Tony Benn. "Just-call-me Tony" generously treated me to a two-wine lunch—a white for the fish, and then a Bordeaux for the pheasant course. His hero was FDR. He believed that Truman should not have dropped the bomb, but was right in dismissing MacArthur. He felt that Eisenhower was wrong in executing the Rosenbergs. Kennedy he liked, but preferred Stevenson. (Our luncheon took place a month before JFK's assassination.)

I was beguiled by his charm if not the causes he championed: During his forty-seven years in Parliament, these included socialism, unilateral nuclear disarmament, and abolishing the monarchy.

John Profumo: Fifth Baron Profumo, British Defense Minister, and Commander of the British Empire

In May 1963, I was doing a series of speeches as a guest of the ESU in England. One city where I appeared was Stratford-on-Avon—the birthplace of William Shakespeare. I was introduced by its MP, John Profumo, who was then secretary of state for war in the Macmillan government. At the time, rumors of scandal were swirling about him. Profumo had slept with Christine Keeler, a model and topless showgirl who was at the same time having a dalliance with a Russian naval attaché and intelligence officer, Yevgeny Ivanov. On the floor of the House of Commons, Profumo had denied the relationship, as a matter of personal honor. What mattered was not the affair, but the inamorata herself. Did their pillow talk include defense secrets that she could have shared with her Russian lover?

The tall, darkly handsome Profumo cut a striking figure, as he introduced me using a line from Shakespeare, "Small cheer and great welcome makes a merry feast."[1] His beautiful wife, the actress Valerie Hobson, whispered the source: *Comedy of Errors*. I had seen Valerie in the films *Great Expectations* (as Estella) and *Kind Hearts and Coronets* (as Edith D'Ascoyne).

Eton and Oxford educated, Profumo had swarthy looks that could have been due to his distant Italian forebear. He closed his talk by referring to the lord mayor's office as the mayoralty. It sounded enough like "morality" to trigger a nervous laugh from some of the women. A week later, Profumo had to resign for lying to his fellow members of the House of Commons. The lurid details spilling out from various orgy participants rocked the Macmillan government. The British Prime Minister, already stricken with a stomach illness, also left office, and Alec Douglas-Home succeeded him.

The disgraced Profumo entered into East London social work, continuing to live on his fortune. He served as a volunteer cleaner, but later as a fund-raiser, for Toynbee Hall, a charity for the benefit of East Enders in need. In 1975, with his loyal wife Valerie standing beside him, he was made a Commander of the British Empire by Queen Elizabeth.

Sir Hugh Wontner: Hotelier and Lord Mayor of London

Hugh Wontner was the premier hotelier in London. He chaired the Savoy Group of Hotels, which, in addition to the Savoy, included the Ritz, the Connaught, and Claridge's. I first met him at Holywich House in Kent, at Gillian Lund's twenty-first birthday party. He was Gillian's godfather and a good friend of shipping magnate Howard Lund. It was July 1953, not long after the coronation of the young Queen Elizabeth II. It had been a busy time for him. Mansion House, the official residence of the lord mayor, had been the site of the Commonwealth Prime Ministers' luncheon hosted by Churchill and the lord mayor. (I had attended the preliminary reception, which was where I first met Churchill.)

He told me that when Churchill was defeated, Wontner knew he had no home, and so he gave Churchill his suite at Claridge's. He said at the time he thought that Churchill was through and would never return to office. But he did, in 1951. Then, in June 1953, Churchill suffered a severe stroke right after the coronation. (Amazingly, he would recover and deliver an hour-long speech at the Conservative Party Conference that fall.)

In 1972, I saw Wontner again in the lobby of the Savoy, and re-introduced myself. A bluff man with a ruddy face, he continued his story, and went on to explain that Churchill had asked to be moved out of Wontner's luxury suite at Claridge's. As Hugh told me, Churchill said he had a problem with the room's high balcony. Wontner drew a deep breath before concluding his story: In the days following his crushing defeat, Churchill had told him that the balcony gave him suicidal thoughts.

Randolph Churchill: Son of Winston Churchill

In 1964, Sir Winston's only son went to the hospital for a possible growth of cancer. The surgeons reported later that the tumor removed from his lung was benign. On hearing this news, the acerbic writer Evelyn Waugh is said to have jibed that the doctors had cut out the only part of Randolph that wasn't malignant. But when I met Randolph in Blackpool in October 1963, he was an amiable teddy bear—not a grizzly bear.

He had missed my dinner appointment, but I caught him outside on the pier, drinking beer and eating prawns. He wore a big "Q" badge for Quintin Hogg, who, as Lord Hailsham, had resigned his peerage to enter the campaign for prime minister against Rab Butler. (But Alec Douglas-Home would be the surprise choice.)

It seemed that no one liked Randolph—including his mother, Clementine, who tried to separate father and son at Chartwell. Yet I found him to be fun and engaging. He insisted that his faults and failures were his own, not his father's, and that the right things he had done were all because of him. Winston Churchill was his inspiration; the mistakes were his own. Then he added that his greatest enemy was himself.

Perhaps his greatest legacy will be the first two volumes of his father's biography, and his having picked Sir Martin Gilbert, his researcher, to complete this work.

John Ambrose Cope, Lord Cope of Berkeley:
Conservative Party Politician

At the age of eighty-one, Lord Cope is among the most active peers in the House of Lords. When I first met him, he was a chartered accountant who was dating Hazel Osborne, daughter of right-wing Tory MP Sir Cecil Osborne. He was an aspiring young Conservative at the time. Later, he wooed Djemila Payne, who was from a wealthy family; her American mother had strong ties to Jerusalem. Djemila became his wife in 1969. Cope and I would meet from time to time, as he ascended successive stages to political success. While he did not prevail in his first race for Parliament, his persistence paid off four years later, in 1974, when he was elected MP for South Gloucestershire—a position he would hold for nine years. Shortly after he was defeated in 1970, he visited us in Washington.

In 1982 we dined with him at the House of Commons, right in the midst of the Falklands War. Riding a surge of patriotism, Thatcher had won popularity based on her resistance to Argentina, and Cope was made Her Majesty's officer of military payments while still an MP whip. On a subsequent visit to Cope's residence at 12 Downing Street, I asked him, "Did Wellington ever meet Nelson?" He replied that while he thought this was unlikely, each man had sat in this chamber, waiting for his paycheck.

In 1989, with the Northern Ireland dispute still rife with violence, Cope was made minister of state for the troubled province, a position he held for about sixteen months. He lost in the Labour landslide of 1997, but at the request of retiring Prime Minister John Major, who himself had turned down a peerage, Cope received his title that same year. As Lord Cope of Berkeley, he became deputy leader in the House of Lords. The following year, Dianne and I were in the visitor's gallery when he made constitutional history by thrice overturning a measure passed by the Commons, which had posed constitutional questions. This was the peer-purging House of Lords Act of 1999, introduced by Labour MP Margaret Beckett as a feature of openly socialist Prime Minister Tony Blair's efforts to 'reform' Parliament, in this case by cutting its number of inherited positions in half.

As an MP, Cope was a master of parliamentary procedure. Perhaps for this reason, a fellow parliamentarian once described him as a "safe pair of hands." He is that and more: a highly skilled and articulate politician, one who excels at listening to people and is never overbearing or arrogant in his interactions with others. This modesty and ability to work behind the scenes is the key to his success. If Jonathan Aitken was the speedy hare, Cope is the tortoise who won the race to a continuing top-leadership position.

Bessie Braddock: Member of Parliament from Liverpool

"Bessie Braddock" is hardly a household name in America. Yet she was the butt of one of the most popular anecdotes about Winston Churchill, even if she is sometimes misidentified.

A proud Liverpudlian, as she called herself, Bessie was a socialist who boasted decades-long representation of that industrial city on the Irish Sea. She was a firebrand and trade-union activist until her successful bid for Parliament in 1945. Before the emergence of the Beatles, Bessie was the city's most colorful personality, adored by her working-class constituency. But her popularity was not due to her looks: She was barely taller than she was wide, with a voice that screeched like nails on a blackboard. Several chins made her face as jolly as it was homely. She was, in brief, a character, who exploited class hatreds with her screeds against the top-hatted toffs smoking big fat cigars in their clubs while racking up dividends.

Because she was a local member of Parliament, she was chosen to introduce my talk on American federalism, given at Liverpool in 1963. I was visiting the pottery heir Sir John Wedgwood in Staffordshire, and we got into his Jaguar and zoomed up the six-lane highway from Birmingham to Liverpool at ninety miles an hour for our engagement at the city's grand old hotel, the Imperial.

Sitting next to me, Bessie confided that since we were both politicians, she knew that we would get along fine. (I was then a Pennsylvania state legislator.) She didn't like Eden or Macmillan, whom she thought were Etonian swells. But oddly, she adored Churchill, and told me that while she didn't like his politics, they enjoyed each other's company. This, she felt, was because he had no use for the intellectual types in the Labour Party—university dons who spout off their plans, but have no idea of how the working class lives.

Bessie described how she and Churchill would banter and tease each other. When she said he was nothing but a fascist pig, he replied that he loved pigs, and that they were the smartest of animals.

Bessie relished telling me of one confrontation with Winston after he had left 10 Downing Street in 1955. Infrequently, Churchill would make an appearance in the House of Commons, attend a bit of the debate, and then retire to the members' bar. One day the bell sounded for a vote, and the eighty-two-year-old Churchill clambered up unsteadily to register his "aye" or "nay." Turning one way was to vote for the motion, and to turn the other way was to vote against. There, Bessie collided with him, and pointed out to the former prime minister that he was not only drunk, but disgracefully drunk. He replied that while Bessie was not only ugly, she was disgracefully ugly, but he (on the other hand) would be sober the next morning. Bessie laughed uproariously as she delivered Churchill's punch line.

I think I was the first to tell this story to American audiences. Other raconteurs sometimes say it refers to Lady Nancy Astor—the first female MP to serve in the House of Commons—who was a frequent target and source of Churchill's jibes. (Lady Astor is said to have told Churchill that if he was her husband, she would put arsenic in his coffee. Churchill's reply was that if Lady Astor happened to be his wife, he would eagerly drink it.) But the elegant Nancy Astor was for many years the most beautiful woman in England.

Looking back on all the beautiful and intriguing women I've met in Britain—prime ministers and princesses—no face or personality registered more indelibly than Bessie Braddock's.

Antony Moynihan, Third Baron Moynihan: Liberal Whip in the House of Lords

Lord Moynihan's son Tony was drawn to me at Stowe because I was different—the only American, the one with the crew cut and the broad Yankee accent. Because of that accent, he tried to recruit me as the lead singer in his five-piece band. I couldn't even carry a tune in the shower. But we both enjoyed politics. He had issues with Churchill and the Conservatives—now back in office again—because he was a staunch Liberal like his father. The first Baron Moynihan was Tony's grandfather: an Australian by birth, and a socially prominent surgeon in Harley Street, whose patients had included King George V.

It was spring vacation in 1953, and Tony asked me to reserve two days for our get-together. The first would be at his mother's home. The former Lady Moynihan was recently divorced, and had a two-story flat in Pimlico. The three of us sat down to eat at the well-appointed table, the center of which, as I later found to my dismay, was actually a "dumb waiter" that conveyed courses from the kitchen below to the dining room above. (In the still hard-pressed Britain, right after the war, even a gentlewoman like ex-Lady Moynihan employed no servants other than the cook.)

In my sloppy adolescent years, I sometimes slipped off tight shoes while eating. Although I still can't figure out how it happened, when the inside section of the table rose from the kitchen with the dessert pudding on top of it, it my shoes were somehow on it as well! Tony laughed uproariously, quipping that this was a new twist on putting the shoe on the wrong foot. The former Lady Moynihan maintained a stoic composure as she kicked her son under the table. But Tony continued to dig at his shoeless and funny dinner guest by singing the song I had practiced crooning for his band: the Harry M. Woods standard "Side by Side."

My mumbling reaction that night did not prepare me for the speechless embarrassment on the following night, when Tony's father Lord Moynihan took our entire party to the Windmill. This was the oldest burlesque theater in London, and had stayed open during the Blitz. Lord Moynihan introduced me to Harry Pollitt, the head of the British Communist Party. What contributed to my unease was that on one side of me was a communist, and on the other was a comely and provocative young thing, the lord's new wife, garbed in a tight scarlet frock. My emotions were somewhat scrambled. There I was, at eighteen, viewing my first bare-breasted women, while sitting between a real live *communist* and a sexy peeress, almost young enough to be my date!

Pollitt, noting my awkwardness, tried to put me at ease by expressing his admiration for Adlai Stevenson's eloquence.

My conversation with the new Lady Moynihan, not more than seven years my elder, was not political. She was excited by the coming coronation in June. My sympathy went out to the first Lady Moynihan, who had missed the 1937 coronation because her father-in-law, the first Lord Moynihan, was still alive. Now she had been replaced by this young trophy wife.

A decade later, I was taking my bar exams in Philadelphia. When I finished the last day's test, I was wiped out, and I looked at the paper's movie section for a means of escape. To my surprise, the Trocadero—Philadelphia's burlesque house—was featuring "Lady Moynihan." It *couldn't* be the wife of my old school friend Tony. But it was—this Lady Moynihan was Tony's second wife, Shirin, an exotic dancer from Malaysia, and I met with them after her show. I remember her warm greeting: She called me "sweetie," and told me how nice it was to meet me. And I still harbor a regret that I didn't call up any of my grandmother's old friends in the Colonial Dames to invite them for dinner with Lord and Lady Moynihan.

Thomas Dugdale, First Baron Crathorne: Churchill's Cabinet Minister

When I was a teaching fellow at the Fels Institute of Government (part of the Wharton School at the University of Pennsylvania), I came across something called "The Crichel Down Precedent" in a book on public administration. This tenet is also called the Dugdale Rule in Britain, after Sir Thomas Dugdale, minister of agriculture in the second Churchill government. In 1954, Dugdale resigned as a point of principle when bureaucrats sold Crichel Down, a wooded tract purchased by the government during the war, to some local developers. This action bypassed the rightful owners and heirs to the land, who had been forced to sell in the first place. Dugdale had no knowledge of the transaction, and would have stopped the sale had he known about it, yet he resigned on principle because it happened on his watch. Dugdale became widely admired for this action: As captain of the ship, he felt that whatever his subordinates did was ultimately his responsibility. In the field of public administration, this act is widely cited.

In the end, the heirs to Crichel Down were allowed to buy it back from the government. Dugdale was later awarded the Crown's last hereditary barony, and became the first Baron of Crathorne. His son, the Honourable James Dugdale, became our close friend.

But in the mid-1930s, Lord Crathorne was PPS (parliamentary personal secretary) to Prime Minister Stanley Baldwin during the abdication crisis. Baldwin had the post office intercept letters from Wallis Simpson, the inamorata of King Edward VIII. I was shown these letters by Lady Crathorne. They engaged a handwriting expert to analyze them, and he concluded that the letter-writer was "shrewd, quick-witted, and superficially intelligent."

Jamie, who was closer to his mother than to his father, always thought she was the brains of the operation. She did write his speeches, but it was Lord Crathorne who wrote the first draft of the instrument for abdication. He later told me he was worried that King Edward would choose the third way besides quitting Wallis or quitting the throne: a morganatic marriage, in which the lady in question would gain no title with her marriage. (In that case, the former Mrs. Simpson would have become Mrs. Windsor, not Queen Wallis.) Baldwin told Lord Crathorne not to bring it up, and Edward did abdicate.

At my seventieth birthday party, which was celebrated at the House of Lords, Jamie Crathorne raised his glass in a toast to the Duchess of Windsor. To a surprised audience, he explained that Britain owed her gratitude for keeping a Hitler-sympathizing monarch off the throne.

Sir John Wedgwood: Polymath and Pottery Namesake

John Wedgwood was a polymath; a published economist, a yachtsman, a racing car driver, an intelligence agent in World War II, and one of my closest friends.

I first met him in 1963, when I was representing Governor Bill Scranton and delivering a talk about William Penn at the Buckingham State School, which was being renamed in honor of the Pennsylvania colony's founder. At this gathering, Wedgwood presented the headmaster with a jasperware cameo of Penn, and told him how his ancestor Josiah had admired the Quaker philosopher for his abolitionist principles.

Wedgwood tended to talk and write at a machine-gun pace. (As a result, his blue airmailed letters were an undecipherable scrawl.) He stayed with us in Philadelphia and Washington, and we, in turn, were often his guests in England. My wife and I visited him at his manor, White House, in Suffolk, at his mother's house in Staffordshire, and also at his town house in London, where the front hall displayed a huge portrait of the Wedgwood family, most of whom are on horseback, by the noted eighteenth-century horse painter Sir Charles Stubbs.

Back in the States, I was with Wedgwood when we were invited to George Washington's estate, Mount Vernon, by the Mount Vernon Ladies Association, which opened the property especially for us on the day after Thanksgiving. We had tea on Wedgwood china that Josiah Wedgwood had presented to the Washingtons. His descendant told the ladies how the estate had been built by George Washington's older half-brother Lawrence, and named after Admiral Lord Vernon—admiral of the fleet under whom Lawrence Washington had served. Admiral Vernon, as he told us, was responsible for the nickname "Limey" given to all Britons, after the slice of lime provided in a sailor's grog (rum plus tea) to prevent scurvy.

One of our most treasured possessions is the Wedgwood plate John Wedgwood had made for the moon landing. It depicts the lunar module, known as the LEM vehicle, which carried a plaque whose words I had helped write: "Here men from the planet earth first set foot upon the Moon, July 1969 A.D. We came in peace for all mankind." Signed in white ink on the back of the plate are the names John Wedgwood, Baronet; Michael Collins; and Neil Armstrong.

Jonathan Aitken: British Cabinet Minister

Jonathan Aitken was a privy councilor to Queen Elizabeth, a Cabinet minister to John Major, a noted biographer of Richard Nixon, a theologian, a journalist, and a talk show host. He was also a convicted felon.

Ever since he was Number One Boy at Eton, and then honors graduate at Oxford, he seemed destined for 10 Downing Street. Tall, handsome, charming, and witty, he was feared by the left as a Tory politician who combined the charm of Reagan and the skill of Thatcher.

When Aitken was writing his biography of Richard Nixon, the ex-president suggested I get together with the author to give him some input. We first met at the dedication of the Nixon Library in 1990, and we became instant friends. I set up some interviews, in which I discussed the time I had spent in the Nixon White House, and my impressions of the former president. *Nixon: A Life* was published early in 1993, and is considered a unique biography, given the author's unprecedented access to the former president and his personal archives.

In the mid-1990s, leftist media outlets such as *The Guardian* newspaper and Granada Television mounted a savage campaign against Aitken, claiming that as minister of defense, he took bribes from the Saudis. In the midst of this vilification campaign, Aitken told me that the only way he could become prime minister was to sue the *Guardian* and win. Aitken declared—under oath—that he had never taken a pound. But evidence was produced in the form of a hotel bill from the Ritz, which the Saudis had picked up. He lost his seat in the Labour landslide of 1997, and in 1999 he was sentenced to jail for perjury.

Jonathan studied theology while in prison. Always a devout Anglican, he founded a ministry for the incarcerated after his release (and wrote another biography, this time of Chuck Colson, another Christian apostle as well as a former convict).

In 2004, now divorced, he married Elizabeth Harris, the ex-wife of two actors, Richard Harris and Rex Harrison. My wife and I went to their wedding. At the reception, I sighted a black man sitting alone.

"Friend of the bride or groom?" I asked him.

"I'm Jonathan's friend," he replied.

"How do you know him?" I asked.

"We were soul mates." (At least that's what I thought he said.)

"Soul mates?" I queried.

"No, no, CELL mates!" was the answer. Jonathan relished telling this story.

Note

1. William Shakespeare, *The Comedy of Errors*, in *The Oxford Shakespeare, Second Edition* edited by John Jowett, William Montgomery, Gary Taylor, and Stanley Wells (Oxford, UK: Oxford University Press, 2005), 292.

Chapter Eight

Library

Carl Sandburg: Poet and Lincoln Biographer

Carl Sandburg called Lincoln's Gettysburg Address the great American poem, but this bard from Middle America may well be the great American poet. I had no way of knowing this when I met him, shortly before my fifth birthday. I just knew him from my mother's description as the one who knew the most about Abraham Lincoln. My mother had invited him to speak at the Williamsport Women's Club. When he arrived, she told him, "Mr. Sandburg, you can stay in the local hotel, or you can stay with us on the third floor—no breakfast. We'll leave coffee, juice, a sweet roll and the *New York Herald Tribune* at your door at any time you specify." He agreed. Then she added, "We're having an Italian night—spaghetti and wine with some of my girl-friends. You are *not* expected to come—but you can if you want."

He did come. He came down our living room stairs armed with his man-dolin, and sang bawdy songs to entertain my mother's friends—accompanied by his strumming.

Sandburg had a round saturnine face rimmed by short white hair combed forward. His shirt was open at the neck. I remember asking him whether he had lived in the "Silver War." The next afternoon, before his lecture, he told me stories about Lincoln as a boy: The future president begged and borrowed every book he could lay his hands on and read at night by candlelight. His father didn't allow him to read, but he did, with his stepmother's encourage-ment. When Sandburg departed the next day, he left me a copy of *Rootabaga Stories*, inscribed with his signature and a poem entitled "Jamie Boy."

> *Boy curious*
> *Climbs on lap*
> *With hungry ear*
> *Face agape*

To hear tales of Lincoln lad.

Sir Cedric Dickens: Great-Grandson of the Novelist

Sir Cedric looked more like Mr. Pickwick—the leading character in Dickens's first book—than his small-statured, black bearded, and saturnine great-grandfather. Like Mr. Pickwick, Cedric was a large, hearty, red-faced fellow, radiant with good cheer. Mr. Pickwick appeared in the story as an innkeeper's guest, but Sir Cedric was an actual tavern owner, of The Dickens Inn, located in Philadelphia. I first met him in 1987. Sir Cedric, as a part owner, was dividing his time between London and Philadelphia (which he found to be a most English city). He wanted me to speak at the Pickwick Club, a Philadelphia organization that met monthly, and where one went to hear entertaining speakers. I may have entertained Dickens with humor gleaned from the works of his forebear, but I did not impress my heavily lubricated audience, most of whom had known or heard of me only as a former White House speechwriter and raconteur of political anecdotes.

Despite the name of their club, these Pickwickians were bored by any meaningful explanation of *The Pickwick Papers*. Sir Cedric, on the other hand, liked my impersonations of Sam Weller, the Cockney manservant, and the bluff but merry Mr. Pickwick. Following my performance, he arranged to have me to do a reading of *A Christmas Carol* as part of a Yule-log-rolling ceremony at the British embassy in Washington.

On our Metroliner train ride to DC, Sir Cedric revealed a bit about himself and more about his celebrated ancestor. His grandfather was Sir Henry Dickens, who was unique among the famous author's children in that he went on to find success in life. Dickens had neglected Henry in favor of the oldest son, Charles, on whom he doted. Charles proved to be a failure in business, yet Henry would be knighted for his career in law.

Sir Cedric related how his grandfather had told him the story of Dickens's literary career, which began in 1836. His great-grandfather was engaged in writing his observations of English coaching life, which were to be illustrated by Robert Seymour. Soon Dickens inserted the character of Sam Weller, the Cockney handyman from *The Pickwick Papers*, into his tales of life on the road in England. At that point, the travelogue began to evolve into a tale by a budding novelist. The interaction between the shrewd servant, Weller, and the naive Mr. Pickwick had the makings of a plot.

Sir Cedric also told me of another astonishing revelation by his grandfather: Scrooge, the villain who finds redemption in *A Christmas Carol*, was actually the novelist himself. In 1843, Dickens had just returned from America. He faced a mountain of debt. Obsessed by the nightmare example of his bankrupt father, John Dickens, the author was resolved not to suffer a similar fate. So he rented a flat away from his family, to work on a Christmas book that his publisher had commissioned. Dickens closed himself off in the Spartan one-room second-floor dwelling, and wrote around the clock. If he fell asleep, a manservant he had hired for this purpose would pour a bucket of water on his face. Eventually, Cedric told me, his great-grandfather became the money-crazed curmudgeon he always despised—a misanthrope who avoided people, even his own family.

Just before Christmas Eve, Dickens penned the last page of his most beloved and best-known story—familiar to millions of Americans because of the many film versions shown at holiday time each year. (George C. Scott is the greatest American actor to have played this role, but Cedric's favorite Scrooge was Alastair Sim.)

Cedric relished his regular visits to America. He said that each time he landed at the Philadelphia airport, he felt an exhilaration comparable to the first sip of an icy martini.

But he went on to say that his great-grandfather's relationship with the United States was one of love–hate. The novelist first arrived on these shores in 1843, full of romanticized conceptions of the new republic, which had neither a monarchy nor a caste system. It offered opportunities to all. Yet his illusions were soon destroyed by the ugly fact of slavery, not to mention Americans' disgusting habit of chewing tobacco and spitting it out on the floor. There was economic mobility, to be sure, but money-grubbing merchants and land speculators had tainted it. The ever-resourceful Dickens depicted these New World mores and abuses in a novel based on his American experiences, *Martin Chuzzlewit.*

John Updike: Prize-Winning Novelist

John Updike was one of the great literary craftsmen of the last century. To me, his talents exceeded those of J. D. Salinger (Updike was much more prolific) and Saul Bellow (his descriptive prose is far superior). Updike's novel *Couples* (1962), a paean to suburban adultery that put him on the cover of *TIME* magazine, did as much to legitimize the 1960s' relaxation of morality as Jacqueline Susann's entire *oeuvre* or a dozen Woodstocks full of free-loving hippies.

I met him in Camp Hill (west of Harrisburg) in 1978, at a book signing for myself and other writers. At first, I refused the invitation because it meant driving 100 miles north from Philadelphia, but when I heard that Updike would also be signing books, I decided to go. The queue in front of Updike's signing table was long, whereas mine had only a few people. I waited in Updike's line to get a book inscribed for my brother Graham, who was the same age as Updike and a fervent fan of the bestselling novelist.

In the audience, there was only one woman under sixty. I sat next to her and found that she was Mrs. John Updike. I asked, "Are you the one who inspires the most sensuous sentences in the English language?" She said no, and told me that the credit must go to Updike's first wife, because she and John had been married for less than a year.

It turned out that her mother, a Camp Hill librarian, had organized the book signing. It was Updike's first visit to his mother-in-law's home in Camp Hill.

I told Updike that I had spent five years in Pottstown, fifteen miles from Shillington next to Reading, where he grew up. Updike guessed, correctly, that I had gone to the Hill School, but went on to say that his grounding in English at Shillington High School was superior because of his schoolteacher mother.

Later, I learned that his mother, Linda Grace Hoyer Updike, was a genius who had graduated from college at the age of nineteen. She published two novels, plus many short stories, some of which were printed in *The New Yorker.* Updike has often credited her example for inspiring his persistence in realizing his artistic aims to their fullest potential. Feminists who have criticized Updike's depiction of women in his highly sexualized works may wish to ponder the mother of America's late-twentieth-century literary lion, and decide whether she should be blamed or praised for her most enduring creation.

William F. Buckley Jr.: Writer and Editor

Bill Buckley was a polymath—a writer, former CIA agent, yachtsman, wine connoisseur, talk-show host, magazine editor, and organist. His trans-Atlantic accent, combined with exaggerated pronunciations and a compendious vocabulary, registered an indelible impression. Of his nine siblings, the brothers I have met (James and John) and his sister Trish Bozell didn't speak a bit like he did. It was Trish who agreed that I should write *The Wit & Wisdom of William F. Buckley Jr.* (Due to his son Christopher's objections, this book was never published.)

I talked with Buckley when he was a speaker at a formal dinner given for the authors of Regnery Publishing, a conservative imprint, in 2002. (Trish Buckley had been my editor for the Regnery title *Confessions of a White House Ghostwriter.*) When I told him my daughter Mary had been editor of *The Harvard Crimson,* he asked where she had gone to school before that. I said, "St. Paul's." He smiled approvingly, and asked where I went. I said, "Hill." He thought the Hill School second rate, and he told me so. He was right, when you compared my little school to St. Paul's, but he shouldn't have said it. He wrote commentary on two of my books—*Churchill: Speaker of the Century*, which he panned in *The National Review*, and *Eisenhower and Churchill: The Partnership That Saved the World*, which he praised (because I asked his sister, Trish, to have him give it a plug). The first book was actually my best—it was nominated for a Pulitzer Prize, and won the Athenaeum Award as best biography.

He was witty, yet at the same time haughty and dismissive of most people as stupid and inferior. And he was poor in political judgment. He denounced Churchill as an appeaser (of both Hitler and Stalin), and recommended John Gardner (LBJ's secretary of health, education, and welfare) to Nixon for vice president in 1968. He also wanted Ike to run as VP with Goldwater in 1964! But I liked his one rule for elections: Endorse the conservative with the best chance of winning.

Patricia "Trish" Buckley Bozell: Editor and Publisher

When Al Regnery called to tell me that Trish Bozell would be the editor for my autobiography, *Confessions of a White House Ghostwriter*, I was both delighted and daunted. To have a distaff version of a William F. Buckley word-stylist sneering at my prose was worrisome. Fortunately, Trish had her brother's brains but not his bite. Neither did she have his airs or his arrogance.

Bill's younger sister did have his wit and naughty impishness. She laughed at some of my encounters with the Kennedys as described in the book, and regaled me with the tricks Bill played on an Episcopal rector in Connecticut. She said she never regretted slapping the microphone away from radical feminist Ti-Grace Atkinson at Catholic University in 1971, due to an ill-informed and blasphemous tirade that was insulting to Catholics and all Christians. This physical courage worthy of a Templar was echoed in the intellectual courage Trish displayed in founding *Triumph: A Journal of Catholic Orthodoxy,* her defense of the Church and its traditions under siege from a secular world.

The tale I most relished was her description of touring European capitols in 1938–39 on the eve of World War II. Trish (going on twelve) and her sister (a year younger) knew that their father would ship them back to America if there was a war. Sure enough, their father pulled them both out of their English convent school and hired a Russian emigré to Paris, a man named Boris, to chauffeur them in a gorgeous Hispano-Suiza from Vienna to Rome to Paris and then to Madrid. The girls knew little about art and architecture, but Boris took them to Gothic and Romanesque cathedrals and to the galleries, and kept them peering at Raphaels and da Vincis in Italy until their feet ached and they begged for an ice cream treat.

Madrid would be a relief, because some family friends who were Spanish expatriates visiting from Mexico would take them for the day. They took Trish and her sister for tea at the Hotel Principe Pio, Madrid's grandest. Passing a cocktail bar, the girls could hear Boris's familiar Russian accent, and rushed over to give him a hug. Boris stood up, and then introduced them to his companion: His Majesty, the King of Spain. It seems the czarist Boris was the King's second cousin!

In editing my *Confessions*, Trish used a skillful scalpel, not a cleaver, on my prose. For some reason, she cut out a whole passage of my first day at an English public school, and I was inundated with a whole new glossary of Christian names to familiarize myself with, as pseudonyms for some of my schoolmates: Nigel, Clive, Algernon, Colin, Derek, Trevor, Liam. I had never heard them in America before, but Trish explained that in the intervening decades, Hollywood had made them more common.

She was critical of my penchant for name-dropping, and asked me if she could cut out some references to the famous. "Trish," I responded, "I've dropped so many names you will need an industrial vacuum cleaner!" (I thought the only way an autobiography by a nonentity like me could be published was if I crammed in as many names as I could.) She pared down my words with precision. I only wish someone else would have the same success, pain-free, with my weight.

After her brother Bill died, I called her and asked if she thought I should be the next one to write a book about him. Trish told me that I would be perfect for this undertaking. She thought that *The Wit & Wisdom of William F. Buckley* would definitely work. My "Wit and Wisdom" series already included *The Wit & Wisdom of Winston Churchill,* plus volumes on Benjamin Franklin, Abraham Lincoln, Ronald Reagan, and FDR. What better addition to the series than the arch-conservative pundit whose sister had been so kind and professional a colleague? But it was not to be.

Trish was one of the most scintillating women I ever encountered. She was a handsome, elegant lady, who had the regal presence of her brother without his predatory nose. I had dedicated my unpublished book about her brother to her, with these lines from Shakespeare: "A fine woman! a fair woman! a sweet woman! . . . O! the world hath not a sweeter creature."[1]

William Manchester: Churchill Biographer

William Manchester was just about the weirdest-looking human specimen I had ever seen. On top of a lanky, gangly, LBJ-like frame sat a face that looked like Truman Capote's. In September of 1983, Manchester and I were guests at an International Churchill Society meeting in Vancouver. On consecutive nights, we were to speak about our Churchill biographies. These were, respectively, *Visions of Glory,* the first volume of Manchester's trilogy *The Last Lion: Winston Spencer Churchill,* and my own book, *Churchill: Speaker of the Century*, which highlights the statesman's mastery of English and his genius as an orator.

In the Vancouver hotel's assembly room on the first night, my wife sat next to me on a raised platform. Seated beside Manchester was a research assistant, whom the author dwarfed. The beginning of the banquet saw the obligatory toasts to the Queen and President Reagan. Manchester sat on his hands during the toast to the U.S. president. Later, he explained to me that he didn't agree with Reagan politically. To me, for an American citizen to refuse to honor the president and his office, especially when outside the United States, amounts to treason at the misdemeanor level.

My biography explaining how Churchill mastered the art of speech as his staircase to power—even though it was nominated for a Pulitzer Prize—in no way matches the sweep and majesty of the Manchester book. Yet Manchester's biography as well as my own relied on Martin Gilbert's earlier works on Churchill as their principal source.

In a way, the moderate success of my book led to Manchester's writing his planned opus on Churchill. But when it was already in galleys and ready to be printed, *Churchill: Speaker of the Century* was rejected by Harper & Row. At the last minute, they had decided that a book on Churchill would not sell. This struck me as odd, because they had books on General George S. Patton and Alice Roosevelt Longworth scheduled to be released, and Churchill, as I told them, was a greater figure in America than either of them. Eventually, I was able to sell my book to a minor publisher, without any publicity, marketing apparatus, or staff to promote it. When it went to three editions before hardcover was extended to trade paperback—despite almost no newspaper mention—a nationally known and acclaimed biographer was selected to write a Churchill book. This was Manchester, who had already written hagiographic accounts of the Kennedys.

Unfortunately, that night in Vancouver, instead of delivering a talk on how he had tackled this mammoth writing project and the insights he had learned, Manchester chose to read excerpts from his Churchill book in a dry monotone. To read a speech is bad, but to read from a book is worse!

When illness prevented Manchester from finishing his Churchill opus, he passed the task along to Paul Reid, a friend who was a feature-writer for the *Palm Beach Post.* Reid finished it in 2012, garnering only mediocre reviews. It was better to have left it unfinished, like Beethoven's symphony.

Lord Jeffrey Archer: Author and Politician

To say that Jeffrey Archer had a checkered career is one way to describe his unusual ups and downs. The light squares on the checkerboard would highlight his successes: top-selling fiction writer, member of Parliament, deputy chairman of the Conservative Party, and peer in the House of Lords (recommended by British Prime Minister John Major). The darker squares would be: embezzler of charity funds, convicted perjurer, libel-case loser, expelled member of the Conservative Party, jailed convict.

I met Archer early in his career, in October 1977, when he was on an American book tour touting *Shall We Tell the President?* Although it was written by an author whose imaginative and creative talents I would come to envy, that first White House mystery was a dud. By happenstance, I was on the same Pittsburgh morning television show as Archer, as part of my own book-pushing foray for *How to Get Invited to the White House.*

While I was waiting for a taxi to take me fifteen miles east to the studio, I heard a man with an upper-class British accent. I turned around and talked to him briefly, but was dismissed. When a stretch limousine came to pick him up, he did not offer me a ride, even though I told him we were to be on the same TV program.

We met in the studio's green room (the waiting room), where he divulged that he had attended Wellington and Oxford. While technically correct, this was misleading. It was not the famous Wellington boarding school in Berkshire, but another one in Somerset. As for Oxford University, he was never registered there as an undergraduate student, although he did take a course at the university's Brasenose College.

Notwithstanding his resume puffing, there was no hiding his brains, charm, and clever wit. He could entertain and enthrall an audience.

The show was hosted by a Dr. Lynn Townsend, who had a degree in psychology. Dr. Townsend asked Archer why he, as an Englishman, had written a novel about American politics. (In this work of fiction, the FBI foils a plot to kill President Edward M. Kennedy; the revised 1986 edition of the book replaces Kennedy with a female president.)

Archer opined gratuitously that he had always found Americans woefully ignorant about their own history.

The host caught my look to the ceiling, and told Archer that I was a former White House speechwriter. He wondered if Archer would ask me some questions on American history.

Archer replied that he wouldn't think of it.

I retorted, "But I will quiz him about some facts in English history."

Archer smiled and told me to go ahead.

I asked him: "Who was the last monarch to veto an Act of Parliament?"

When he hesitated, and said that he would soon come up with the answer, I told him, "Queen Anne, with the Scottish Militia Bill. I'll ask an easier one. You know, Mr. Archer, we have father–son presidents in the Adams family, and the Pitts, William and Robert, are two in Britain, but who are the other British father and son?" Archer said he didn't think there were any.

"The Grenvilles," I said. "The first Lord Grenville of the Stamp Act, and the second, his son, in the Ministry of all the Talents."

While Archer was annoyed, the panel host was enjoying the sight of this posh-sounding Englishman being taken down a peg by an American.

I then said, "I apologize for my nit-picking pedantry, so I'll ask you an easy one. Who is the only British Prime Minister ever assassinated?" To American ears, that sounds easy, but the British have a hundred or so prime ministers to our forty or so presidents.

Archer expostulated that very few Englishmen would know the name, muttered something, and then strode from the studio. (The answer was Spencer Perceval, in 1812.)

This was a bit "over the top" for me, as my friend Jonathan Aitken later told me, but I don't regret it.

I had another connection with Archer, but I didn't know about it at the time. In 1963 I stayed in the house of Sir Cyril Osborn, MP for Louth, Lincolnshire, where he resided in Quorn, Leicestershire, and served as justice of the peace. We were both members of the Pilgrims Society and the ESU, and his daughter, Baroness Byford, is still a close friend. Sir Cyril was perhaps the most right-wing Tory. A law and order man, and an early opponent of mass immigration, he once said that rapists should be burnt at the stake. When he died in 1969, there was some competition to succeed him in Parliament. Jeffrey Archer, who did not even serve on any of the local Conservative committees, was in New York, but he flew back and then hired a private plane to journey on to the small town. A talented speaker, Archer wowed them with tough-on-crime sentiment that Osborn would have seconded. But after the election, he would stand against capital punishment, and urge more sympathetic treatment for juvenile offenders. If constancy was not part of his character, he did inspire loyalty. After a conviction for perjury ended his career, his talented wife Lady Mary remained loyal, as did Jonathan Aitken and many of his other friends.

Ezra Pound: Poet and Radical

It was Lincoln's Birthday 1958, a holiday weekend. Stanton Evans, editor of the right-wing polemic *Human Events*, had asked me whether I wanted to go with him the following week to see Ezra Pound at the insane asylum, St. Elizabeths, where Pound had been incarcerated since his arraignment for treason in 1945. Ursula Biddle, whose father was a close family friend of my mother and a staffer for Evans, had introduced me to him. He was an anti-John-Birch, pro-Joe-McCarthy conservative. His heroes were the late Senator Taft and General McArthur. He had nothing but contempt for Eisenhower. To Evans, Pound had been "jailed" for his beliefs by FDR.

Some weeks earlier, at the end of January, I'd had a poetry book signed by Robert Frost, who was appearing at a bookstore on G Street near the White House. Frost had been Eisenhower's guest at the White House, and was interceding for Pound at the time.

Evans and I went out on a bright February afternoon to see Pound. St. Elizabeths is seated on a hill over Washington on some four hundred acres, with wide lawns. The trees were still winter-bare.

Upon meeting him, I thought the seventy-three-year-old Pound looked every bit like a lunatic, with a shaggy beard, hair askew, and wild eyes. But the more we talked, the more I came to think that his eccentricity—an act he overplayed—was not madness. He got my name as Hume, his favorite philosopher, as he said. Pound offered us tea, and brought out a peanut-butter jar full of tea leaves. His wife Dorothy (his legal guardian, who made daily visits to Pound's comfortable quarters) took it and made the tea.

Evans asked the questions: Was Pound a fascist?

Never! He had never liked fascism!

Evans reminded Pound that he had liked Mussolini.

Well, yes, Pound admitted: but so had the Roosevelt-loving Churchill. Pound liked what Mussolini had done for Italy in the twenties.

Then Evans asked Pound about his radio broadcasts denouncing FDR. Pound felt that Roosevelt had deserved this, because (as he said), Roosevelt had trashed the Constitution and kissed Stalin's ass.

Evans asked him about McCarthy, and his quest to eradicate communists in America's halls of power. This seemed to trigger the poet, who believed that McCarthy's witchhunt paled beside what had been done to *him.* Moreover, he believed that Hollywood was full of communists. With this rant, Pound proved that he was his own worst enemy. He 'dissed' both T. S. Eliot and Frost, who were lobbying to get him out of St. Elizabeths. Evans mentioned that Hemingway had recently voiced the opinion that Pound should have won the Nobel Prize for literature in 1957 instead of him. But Pound's status as a government-certified lunatic had made that unlikely.

Pound proves that eccentricity does for a reputation what talent alone cannot.

Louis Auchincloss: Novelist of Manners

Louis Auchincloss published three-score volumes over as many years, spanning the last days of the elegant age he once knew, and ending with our own. He wasn't simply a novelist of manners, he was a novelist of money: old money, money so old it arrived on these shores as golden guilders in iron-bound chests. Like Jane Austen, he limned the upper classes and their mores with rare insight. But like John O'Hara or J. P. Marquand, he suffered critics who came from a different milieu and preferred the Saul Bellows, Norman Mailers, and J. D. Salingers of the publishing world. He was more a literary craftsman than any of those contemporaries. But he would never be honored with a Nobel like Bellow, or a Pulitzer like Mailer, or a dubious cult like Salinger (John Lennon's assassin was a rabid fan of *The Catcher in the Rye*).

Auchincloss and I were both members of the St. Nicholas Society, descendants of the original settlers of New Amsterdam. He spoke to us once about his 1964 bestseller, *The Rector of Justin*, whose hero is headmaster of a fictional private school that combines Groton and St. Paul's. It was nominated for a Pulitzer Prize and National Book Award, but lost in favor of Bellow's *Herzog* and Shirley Ann Grau's *The Keeper of the House*.

For just about every old New York family, Louis Auchincloss was either a relative or the lawyer who handled their trust and estate work. He was intimate with the faults and idiosyncrasies of Social Register families—the heavy drinking, the clubbiness, but also the sense of duty and *noblesse oblige.*

Auchincloss was an innate conservative who almost always voted Republican. While he was tempted to vote for his kin-by-marriage, John Kennedy, in 1960, he stayed with Nixon. Yet he voted against Goldwater in 1964, having been an enthusiast for Scranton, whom he knew at Yale.

I said to him, "You remind me of Edith Wharton." He replied that I was not the first to note this. He told me that he considered himself to be a novelist of manners, the greatest of whom was Jane Austen. But while there are dozens of movies and television shows based on the works of these two ladies—not to mention J. P. Marquand's—we have sadly neglected Louis Auchincloss. No more than two or three Auchincloss tales have been adapted for stage and screen. Hollywood, are you listening?

Christopher Robin Milne: Best Friend of Winnie-the-Pooh

In 1953, on Old Boy's Day—the English boarding-school equivalent of Alumni Day—an Old Stoic came back to Stowe to have a look at his sixth-form study. It was now my own room. On the wall over the desk, someone had scratched "Winnie-the-Pooh." Eyeing this inscription, Christopher Robin—the one-and-only Christopher Robin—frowned and turned to his wife. I listened in as he told Lesley Milne that he had not written it—needless to say. It was the work of some classmates who had been ragging him about the world's most famous teddy bear. He told us that it was a cause of lots of teasing in his young years, and that he hated his father for inventing Pooh.

Afterwards, the Milnes invited me to join them for the Stowe–Eton cricket match while they shared their tea and crumpets with me on a lawn blanket. (I found the game of cricket very boring: like slow-motion baseball.) Later, on that spring afternoon, they invited me to their home in East Sussex. After dinner, in the guest bedroom, they plopped a ragged old teddy bear on the pillows of the bed. I picked him up and cradled him in my arms.

Christopher Robin smiled approvingly, and told me that someday, I could tell my children that I had hugged the original Winnie-the-Pooh. The next morning, I breakfasted with them before driving back to Stowe, and Christopher Robin continued the story of how he met Pooh. The teddy bear was purchased from Harrods (London's best and greatest department store) and sent to him on his first birthday in 1921. It had been an odd choice of gift from his father, who was awkward with children, even though he wrote some of childhood's classic stories. In the 1920s, English parents hugged their dogs or patted their horses but not their children. Christopher Robin never ate meals with them; they dined downstairs, in black tie, while he ate in the nursery with his nanny.

A. A. Milne was a novelist, poet, and playwright who came late to children's fiction. A shy man, of intellectual bent (as Christopher told me), he was reticent with others, and uneasy with his own son. As middle age approached, in his forties, he somehow wanted to reach out to his only child. His vehicles were children's books, and his most endearing was *The Adventures of Winnie-the-Pooh*. Milne took the name "Winnie" from Winston Churchill in the twenties, his good friend before he became a hero. "Pooh" was Christopher Robin's baby-talk name for "bear."

In World War II, Christopher Robin had served in the R.A.F. as an engineer. During his service, and also as a young broker, he tried to live down the Pooh association.

I told him I had been enthralled when my mother read the Pooh books to me, particularly the two collections of Milne's poems for children, *When We Were Very Young* and *Now We Are Six*.

When I became the father of two girls, my daughters were far more impressed that I had hugged the original Winnie-the-Pooh than with my meeting Winston Churchill or dancing with the Queen.

Frances "Scottie" Fitzgerald: Daughter of F. Scott Fitzgerald

To promote my 1980 biography, *Churchill: Speaker of the Century,* I did a series of speeches across the country to chapters of the ESU. In Montgomery, Alabama, I stayed at the home of Frances Scott ("Scottie") Fitzgerald, the daughter and only child of the novelist F. Scott Fitzgerald and his wife Zelda. Though past her sixtieth birthday, she was still stunning and vivacious. When she was born, her father hailed her as a second Mary Pickford—meaning the blonde, blue-eyed screen ingénue who had married Douglas Fairbanks Sr.

Scottie and I had a mutual friend in Thacher Longstreth, the City Council member for whom I once worked in Philadelphia. Thacher was a close Princeton friend of her first husband, Jack Lanahan, whom she visited about every weekend when she was at Vassar. Later, she married Grove Smith, but she was divorced when I met her.

Before the dinner, I drank three diet colas. (I never drink alcohol before dinner speeches.) She commented that I reminded her of her father, who would down gallons of cola; as she explained, this is a habit with alcoholics, who often have a craving for something sweet. (She didn't mean me, of course.)

Later, at her home, I asked her what her childhood was like. She told me that to say they were a dysfunctional family was an understatement. "Daddy" was an alcoholic, and her mother was in and out of institutions. Growing up, Scottie was a spectator as a dazzling parade of authors and even some Hollywood types dropped in and out of where they were living—John Dos Passos, Sinclair Lewis, Gertrude Stein, and actress Helen Hayes. Her favorite was Edith Wharton. Ernest Hemingway, she said, was a looming figure in her father's life, but "Daddy" seemed to hold some ambivalent feelings about his literary rival.

She told me that as a child she was both cosseted and neglected—shunted around and passed off on a series of nannies and housekeepers. She then asked about my children. I replied that my oldest was at St. Paul's, an Episcopalian prep school in New Hampshire. She laughed, and told me that when her father was at Princeton and they asked where he came from, he said St. Paul. But Princetonians thought that this stylish and articulate young man meant the boarding school in Concord, New Hampshire, not the twin city of Minneapolis, Minnesota.

Scottie said that her father—author of *The Great Gatsby* and other novels depicting America's upper crust—was always socially insecure. Growing up in Minnesota, he was poor compared to the neighbors, who had mansions in St. Paul. Then he was poor compared to his wealthier classmates at Princeton. Even in *nouveau riche* Hollywood, he was daunted by the actors' splashy and lavish lifestyle.

Notwithstanding his alcoholic binges, she always adored her daddy.

If F. Scott Fitzgerald was not an aristocrat in background, at least he looked the part: "Clean favored, and imperially slim,"[2] as poet Edward Arlington Robinson described one of his "died-too-young" subjects, Richard Cory. Fitzgerald could have played a matinee idol in some of the movies he scripted in the late 1930s—most of which were rejected. He may have been the hero of a self-created tragedy. But his legacy included the daughter who was his most ardent supporter: a beautiful scion of the Jazz Age, a living testament to one of the most enduring true-life love stories in the world of literature.

Gloria Steinem: Feminist Writer

In 1997, on a Presidents' Day weekend in February, Dianne and I went to New York to visit our daughter and new granddaughter on East Ninety-Sixth Street. On that Monday, we dined in an Italian restaurant on Ninetieth and Madison. We sat with our backs to the wall. No one sat on our left, and so we couldn't help overhearing bits of the conversation two tables away from us, between a well-groomed sixtyish lady and an elegantly tweeded gentleman opposite her.

One comment by this lady echoed in my ears: She said that marriage was just not her thing, that her schooling didn't prepare her to be a mother and homemaker, and that she had needed a career.

I stole a closer look when I went outside to the men's room. It was Gloria Steinem, who had founded *Ms. Magazine* in 1972. Two decades later, she published *Revolution from Within*, which disdained marriage and childbearing as stifling. She had been one of the first adherents of Betty Friedan's book, *The Feminine Mystique*, published in 1961, and my brother's wife was one of their first disciples. She left my brother with their only son and went off to "find herself," which ended unhappily for the Vassar alumna. She never remarried or found the fulfilling career she had sought, and was left with regrets. He, on the other hand, remarried happily.

At the end of lunch, my wife and I went to the front entrance to retrieve our topcoats on that wintry day. Stopping beside her table, I said to her, "Ms. Steinem, I have always admired your years in public service to your country."

Having taken the bait, she simpered and thanked me for the compliment.

I went on to say: "I mean, of course, your only years in government service—in the CIA. William Buckley said you were a capable operative."

Ms. Steinem scowled in anger, and pointed out that she had been a co-founder of Women for Peace in Vietnam—and, of course, a liberal Democrat. She went on in this vein. True, she had been just like Julia Child, who graduated from Smith two years ahead of Steinem and worked, according to her memoirs, alongside her husband, who was also a CIA professional.

I was Steinem's contemporary: studying at Williams when she was at Smith in nearby Northampton, Massachusetts. A profile of her in the 1990s said that she rented a New York apartment, furnished. She never had those instinctive feminine urgings to nest, and make the apartment her own. This might have been the result of a troubled childhood, with a divorced and absent father and an often-institutionalized mother.

I always wondered at the optimism of those college women who believed you could be a super careerist, super wife, and super mom. My daughter, who was managing editor of *The Harvard Crimson*, then a graduate of Oxford, and later, of Yale law school, is a career mother of our four bright and happy grandchildren. As she once said to me, "I don't believe you can delegate the formative years of children to an au pair girl." But for too many women, full-time jobs and day-care are cruel necessities for those who would rather stay home with their families.

I agreed with former Vice President Quayle's controversial (at the time) attack on *Murphy Brown*, the television series about a single mother. Later, even the liberal *Atlantic Monthly* expressed second thoughts about the media attacks on Quayle for his criticism.

Curiously, in 2000 at age sixty-six, the professional feminist married David Bale, the father of actor Christian Bale. Presumably she found fulfillment as a wife, and as mother to her famous stepson. Her husband died in 2003, and I'm sure her apartment is filled with pictures and remembrances of this better-late-than-never marriage. I wish her well.

Notes

1. William Shakespeare, *The Tragedy of Othello, the Moor of Venice*, in *The Oxford Shakespeare, Second Edition*, edited by John Jowett, William Montgomery, Gary Taylor, and Stanley Wells (Oxford, UK: Oxford University Press, 2005), 897.

2. Edward Arlington Robinson, "Richard Cory," in *Edwin Arlington Robinson: Selected Poems,* edited by Robert Faggen (New York: Penguin Group, 1997), 9.

Chapter Nine

Hollywood

Sir John Gielgud: Shakespearean Actor

Sir John Gielgud was one of the supreme actors of the twentieth century. Although he did not generally perform chameleon roles like Sir Laurence Olivier or Sir Alec Guinness, he had a unique voice with a range and depth that resonated on stage. One could imagine that he sounded just like the man from Stratford. His great aunt, Ellen Terry, was one of the most acclaimed theater actresses of her day.

I met Gielgud in a bar on Pennsylvania Avenue in DC, on a Wednesday between matinee and evening performances in February 1977. This gracious gentleman—a descendant of Lithuanian nobility—seemed happy to share my companionship at the bar. Listening to his distinctive timbre, I said, "Thy voice is thunder," and he completed Shakespeare's line: "but thy looks are humble."[1] Gielgud quickly identified the source of this quote: It was the line spoken by George, Duke of Clarence, to the murderers sent to his prison cell by Richard the Third. And as Gielgud told me, he ought to have known, because he played Clarence and Olivier played Richard in Olivier's classic film version of the drama. When I called him the greatest living actor, he modestly deferred to Olivier and Sir Ralph Richardson. He shrugged off Richard Burton as having wasted his talent in movies. Late in his career, Gielgud performed roles in some Hollywood movies, for the money: Notably, he played the butler Hobson in the hit comedy *Arthur* (1981), for which he won an Oscar.

I told him about my schooling at Stowe. Gielgud knew the school very well. He had a manor house nearby in Buckinghamshire, and invited me to come for tea when I was back at Stowe. In one thing he would not yield to any other actor, and that was his knowledge of Shakespeare. His favorite play was *The Tempest,* in which he said Shakespeare's soul is manifested in the character of Prospero. Gielgud did the introduction to my Churchill tele-play, *Blood, Sweat and Tears,* which was produced by PBS in 1985, and wrote me a gracious letter inviting me, once more, to visit him. The last time I saw him was in 2000, in a one-man show he performed in Denver at the age of ninety-five.

Sir Richard Burton: Star of Stage and Screen

I first met Richard Burton in 1981, when BBC Radio interviewed both of us. He was asked what first attracted him to Elizabeth Taylor, and he replied that it was her eyes—her violet eyes. But later, after the interview, he whispered to me that his own eyes had actually been drawn a bit south of the forehead.

Burton was smallish, with a pockmarked face. But on stage his eyes and voice transfixed an audience. He had portrayed Churchill on BBC television in the 1970s and he was terrible. He left two impressions of Churchill—one as a drunk, and the other as a depressive beset by the statesman's "black dog" mood.

I told him that I had just published my Churchill biography, *Speaker of the Century*, and Burton talked about how Churchill attended a performance of *Hamlet* in 1953, with Burton in the title role. Churchill sat in the first row, and Burton could hear the echo of Churchill's growl repeating the same lines. Burton said he tried to step up his pace—Churchill did likewise. Then he slowed his delivery. Churchill again followed suit. Then he tried omitting lines, only to hear Churchill's roar of protest from the first row. At the end of the first act, his dresser told him, "I think the old man has left." Just as Burton heaved a sigh of relief, Churchill walked in and asked "Prince Ham-let" (meaning Burton) if he might use the lavatory.

Burton would conversationalize the lines of Shakespeare, whereas Giel-gud uttered them with Elizabethan majesty. His personal pursuits took prior-ity over his acting. I saw him one final time in 1984, when his last wife, Sally, accompanied him at the Ritz-Carlton bar on Piccadilly. He entertained us with some anecdotes about Dylan Thomas, a fellow Welshman. Unlike the great Welsh bard, Burton never let his innate genius flower into immor-tality.

Dame Olivia de Havilland: Film Legend

For three years, I was president of Kingstree Communications, a speech-coaching and speechwriting group. One day in 1979, our private plane picked up James Dugdale (now Lord Crathorne), Olivia de Havilland, and I at West-chester Airport in New York, to fly to Newport, Rhode Island, where we had our headquarters. During our week in Newport, Olivia was to give a lecture called "Women in Shakespeare," and the next night, I would deliver a talk on Churchill entitled "Never Give Up."

We both had to introduce each other. I said in her introduction: "Our speaker was christened Olivia de Havilland, born in the Isle of Jersey. Her rector father named her Olivia for his favorite character in *Twelfth Night*. Her uncle, Sir Geoffrey de Havilland, was the chairman of the makers of the de Havilland bombers that flattened Germany, and her French cousin, René Havilland, creates the beautiful Havilland china that graces our tables. As Melanie in *Gone with the Wind*, the tortured soul in *The Snake Pit*, or the old maid in *The Heiress*, for which she won the Academy Award, she manifested all the steel of Havilland motors and all the fragile beauty of Havilland china."

We watched a private screening of *The Adventures of Robin Hood*—the first Technicolor film about the English legend, in which Olivia had starred as Maid Marian. But the audience laughed at this classic as if it was "camp." Olivia reached for my hand, and told me that at the time, the release of this movie had been a serious event—it was the first Warner Brothers movie filmed in Technicolor, a milestone in the art of cinema. Afterwards, she had me walk her to her hotel room—to shake off an old suitor.

The next day, a reporter questioned her about a new book by Lawrence Higham, which alleged that Errol Flynn was gay. Olivia replied that if Errol was gay, he was the greatest actor who had ever trod the stage, as she knew from personal experience! In movies such as *Robin Hood* and *Captain Blood*, Olivia's heartfelt love scenes with the handsome Flynn seem to have been made in heaven.

Olivia told me that, contrary to conventional belief, she never sought the role of Scarlett in *Gone with the Wind*. She had always wanted the role of Melanie, and it suited her perfectly. Of candidate Ronald Reagan, she said that she hoped he would be elected president, and that if he was not: He had already played his greatest role in the Cold War, ferreting out communists in the Hollywood Actor's Union at the risk of threats against his life.

Cary Grant: Matinee Idol

Cary Grant was born Archibald Leach, the product of a working-class family in northern England. He became a matinee idol who appeared in many films, but he had only one role—the debonair, urbane gentleman. I had only one encounter with him: in 1984, after Grant had retired from Hollywood. They still wanted him, but he didn't want them. He was now a distinguished octogenarian with silver hair, but he didn't want to spoil the image of women fans who remembered him as the romantic lead for Ingrid Bergman, Katharine Hepburn, Joan Fontaine, Eva Marie Saint, Doris Day, and countless others.

So, he chose to enter the lecture circuit, and that's where I came in. We shared the same agent, Colston Leigh, who almost invented the profession of lecture agent. Then as now, the lecture circuit is predominantly audiences of clubwomen. Leigh, after seeing me do Churchill, had recruited me. Grant was about to do nationwide tours at a fee of fifteen thousand dollars per appearance, but the prospect of writing and delivering a talk unnerved him. Actors, except for Shakespeareans, are used to single lines, not monologues.

Ready to assist him in his new métier, I met him at the Hotel Carlyle in New York. My proposal was that he walk to the stage and say something like, "I feel so much at home with all you elegant women. Today, I'm going to tear up this speech they wrote for me and just answer some of your questions." As a former White House speechwriter, I'd had to anticipate questions for White House Q & A sessions. So, I just made up some that I thought likely:

"Who was your favorite leading lady?" His mother.

"What is your definition of style?" Anything Audrey Hepburn was wearing.

"What did you especially like about Hitchcock?" The fact that he always cast such elegant, cool blondes for his leading men to act with.

Some questions we couldn't anticipate, but Archibald Leach always found snappy, funny lines as the droll character that he invented, Cary Grant.

Gene Autry: Western Actor and Singer

The first Hollywood celebrity I ever met was the cowboy Gene Autry. Actually, the word "celebrity" was not used in those days to describe stars or great personages, and Autry wasn't really a cowboy. That is, he had never been a real cowhand. His country singing style got him his start, and cowboy films became his medium.

In February 1942, on a Friday night, my family drove our blue Lincoln Zephyr to Hershey, Pennsylvania—the chocolate capital of the world. We would stay overnight at the new Hershey Hotel, built during the 1930s in neo-Spanish style. One of the first resort hotels that was not built next to an ocean, it had, as I was delighted to note, soap made of cocoa butter.

My father, Judge Samuel Humes, was a rabid ice-hockey fan. Usually we'd drive back home to Williamsport after a game. But a snowy night made us stay over. In the hotel lobby, we saw a picture of Autry on his horse, Champion. My oldest brother, Sam, fancied himself a detective, because a police detective friend of my father's had given him a badge. On Saturday morning, by watching waiters and trays, Sam had discovered Autry's room. I said, "Why don't we knock on his door?" Sam replied: "No, Jamie, that isn't right. We'll have to wait in the lobby until he emerges."

I was seven at the time, and secretly composed a note: "Dear Mr. Autry, I am a seven-year-old boy. You are my favorite cowboy. Champion is my favorite horse. My older brother told me not to write to you, that you would not bother with someone little like me." Instead of "Jamie," I signed it "James Calhoun Humes," as I thought it sounded older, added my room number, and slipped it under his door. An hour later, the desk sent a message to James Calhoun Humes: "Come to my room at 3:30."

At the appointed time, off I went—without telling my brothers Sam and Graham. A big expansive man answered the door, and with a smile from ear to ear, he asked if I would like root beer or chocolate milk. I took the root beer, and so did Gene. He asked me what grade I was in, and what my father did. I proudly said, "First grade, and my dad is a judge." With a grin of approval, Gene replied that it was his job to capture the bad guys and take them to people like my father. My chest burst with pride when I showed Gene's autographed pictures to my brothers. They were green with jealousy.

Shirley MacLaine: Hollywood Actress

When I met Shirley MacLaine in Washington, she was zany, zaftig, and oozing with zest—a volcanic force. The meeting of this Nixon Republican and Hollywood lefty in September 1972 was bizarre. I had left the Nixon State Department, and had a job doing some lobbying in Philadelphia. One of my big clients was the Philadelphia National Bank, whose CEO was John Bunting, an up-from-the-ranks Philadelphian. He always said his college was Temple O, because when he said he went to Temple, the old-guard Philadelphians invariably said, "Oh."

John told me that he wanted to give a thousand dollars to the Nixon campaign. I told him, "You might as well drop it out the window for the effect it would have. People are giving a hundred thousand dollars to Nixon, the sure winner. Why not give a thousand dollars to McGovern—you'll be the only banker in the country giving to McGovern. I'll get an item printed in *Newsweek*'s 'Periscope' or Washington Wire that you'll be his secretary of the treasury."

Bunting protested that McGovern would never be elected. "True," I replied. "But you'll get great ink!"

I had a friend—Henry Kimmelman—a big fundraiser for McGovern, and he arranged a luncheon at Sans Souci for John and I with Gary Hart, who was running the McGovern campaign. There, at the Washington lunch with Hart, was Shirley, in white pants and a purplish paisley top. I had just seen Clint Eastwood's western, *Two Mules for Sister Sarah*. Never had a nun looked so sexy. When I was introduced as a former Nixon speechwriter, she looked at me with all the fascination a bird has for a snake at the zoo. I don't know what she was thinking, but I can guess: "Republican" comes just after reptile and just above repugnant in the dictionary.

But I was won over by Shirley's exuberance. She flirted with me, with abandon. She opined on everything from UFOs to the afterlife. She had sighted an alien spacecraft, and was Cleopatra in an earlier life! I bet her a lunch that Nixon would win. She never paid up.

She may have seemed crazy, but she was no shallow bimbo—she was a great actress and an author to boot. And I was glad to see her get a leading role in *Downton Abbey* in the fall of 2012. As Shakespeare wrote of his own Cleopatra: "Age cannot wither her, nor custom stale / Her infinite variety."[2]

Cole Porter: American Composer

When we were planning my daughter Mary's wedding in October 1990, the band conductor wanted to know what music she wished to hear during the reception. She said, "Anything by Noel Porter." The puzzled musician asked her: "Do you mean Noel Coward or Cole Porter?" Mary shrugged: "Whatever."

Both songwriters, one English, the other American, dominated the pop music world in the 1930s. Coward, a playwright and an actor, too, was the hit of British society. Porter, from Indiana, made himself over from a small-town country boy into the debonair idol of the cosmopolitan East, much like the working-class Archibald Leach morphed into the suave, witty Cary Grant.

Porter was "the tops"—as in "You're the Tops," the song that was repeatedly played at Mary's wedding reception. I met him once in Williamstown, Massachusetts, in the fall of 1954 when I was a college student. He was driving his buggy wagon down Spring Street, and I could see he wore a cap, green vest, and tweed jacket. At the light, I went up to him and said: "Mr. Porter, you're the tops."

He thanked me, and asked me if I was at Williams.

I nodded "yes." Mr. Porter wanted to know whether I had ever run across another horse and wagon driven by an old codger with galluses, a Mr. Prindle.

I nodded, and told him: "He's my uncle Clarence. He's from an old Williamstown family. He has a wooden leg. He lost it playing chicken with a train at a railroad crossing."

Porter asked me to tell Uncle Clarence that he had a bad leg, too, and drove off. (In 1937, Porter had been crippled in a horseback-riding accident.)

Years later, in December 1998, my daughter Mary and her husband Cecil were treating us to a night out in New York. I recounted the story about Porter to Bobby Short, who was playing the piano at the Carlyle Hotel on the Upper East Side, where he would entertain guests for thirty-five years. This handsome African American was a protégé of Porter's. A year later, I heard this same music while driving out of Pueblo, Colorado, on a jazz program broadcast from Colorado Springs. It brought back memories of the great Bobby Short, and a wonderful night out with my children, but also, a more distant recollection of the jaunty gentleman waving goodbye to me from his carriage with a cane. He was "the tops."

Orson Welles: Actor and Director

One night in Vienna, in the spring of 1970, my wife and I were seated with Ambassador John Humes and his wife Jean at a dinner table in the Sacher Hotel. Scanning the other diners, I sighted a gargantuan figure with a recognizable face.

I said: "John, isn't that Orson Welles?"

"No," John replied.

But then I asked the waiter, "Who's at that table?"

"Herr Welles," was the answer.

I walked over and introduced myself, saying: "I am presently a presidential speechwriter, but I gained my love of words and cadence by hearing your records, where you recited *Macbeth* and 'The Rime of the Ancient Mariner'—'water, water, every where . . . Nor any drop to drink.'"[3]

Welles's corpulence made me seem svelte by comparison. When I told him I wrote for Nixon, he frowned. His *basso profundo* pronounced "Nixon" with opprobrium. Looking at his young blonde dinner partner, who was evidently a would-be starlet, I told him I loved his film *The Third Man.* He grunted. I asked if Joseph Cotten was his favorite at the old Mercury Theater. Welles said that Cotten was the only matinee idol among them, but that he liked Ray Collins the best. I vaguely remembered Collins as Police Lieutenant Arthur Tragg on the *Perry Mason* TV series.

Later that night, John took us to the annual spring wine tasting in the Viennese woods. There on the terraced hills were long tables where oenophiles would sip the new white wine. At the table behind me, I could hear the familiar bass voice recite the closing words of Goethe's *Faust* in German. I looked in back of me, and I could see the golden-haired ingénue, listening in rapt attention. Welles recited the German verse from memory. Even though I could only interpret some of the words, his voice thrilled me. He closed with that last line, "Das Ewig-Weibliche / Zieht uns hinan"[4] (the eternally female draws us upward). The young woman was seduced by his magnificent voice. One sensed that the evening would end horizontally for them.

Vincent Price: Actor and Fashion Icon

Today Vincent Price is best known as the star of horror movies from the forties and fifties, but I found him to be that rarity from the film world—neither vulgar nor coarse. The son of a prosperous candy manufacturer in St. Louis, Missouri, he was an aristocrat with cultivated tastes in paintings and cuisine.

In 1980, Price and I were on the same TV talk show in Boston. He was promoting his cookbook, and I was pushing my biography *Churchill: Speaker of the Century*. Price, who had an English actress for a wife, was far more interested in discussing Churchill. He was thrilled by my renditions of Churchill's wartime speeches. He was not interested in talking about his movie career, except that it was fun doing the horror films. In his opinion, the best film he ever acted in was *Laura*, which he also thought was the best mystery ever to come out of Hollywood.

Price was fascinated when I told him how Churchill overcame his stutter and lisp. He particularly relished how Churchill used a deliberate stutter pause to give emphasis to certain words. Afterwards, he took me to lunch at his hotel, the Copley Plaza. He was the gourmet, and so I let him order for me: Dover sole, the best this side of the Atlantic. He was Savile Row elegant: Almost forty years later, I can remember exactly how he was dressed. He wore a Turnbull & Asser shirt with a spread collar, a regimental gold and blue tie, and gold cufflinks. His bespoke suit was navy blue, and double-breasted. As elegant as his unique voice, Vincent Price was ever the consummate gentleman.

Shirley Temple Black: Actress and Ambassador

Gerald Ford's new ambassador to Ghana did not look like the golden-tressed child star of the thirties, with the smile and laugh that melted hearts. I first met her in 1964, when she came to call on my office in the White House, and she was kind enough to sign some autographs for my daughters. She was not blonde, cute, and bubbly any more. She was a brunette, demure but elegant—as an ambassador should look. In fact, she reminded me of an older version of Julie Nixon Eisenhower. The Nixons and Fords were all fans of hers, as she was an avid follower of Congressman, Senator, Vice President, and then President Richard Nixon. That Ford appointed her to the country from which America imported the most cocoa beans somehow seemed appropriate: After all, she had once danced on the Good Ship Lollipop! Ghana would love her. She passed out Hershey bars for me to give to my daughters.

Having switched her venue from Hollywood films to children's television, Shirley found a new career in 1967, as a Republican candidate for office, and later, as a diplomat. Active in the Golden State's Republican

Party, she ran (unsuccessfully) for Representative J. Arthur Younger's old seat in 1967, following his death from leukemia. She worked hard for Bob Finch, who, as Lieutenant Governor, ran ahead of Reagan in the 1974 election in which Reagan beat Pat Brown. The Reagan people never forgot this fact, and would hold it against the former child actress. She despised the John Birchers who were the cause of Brown's defeating Nixon for governor in 1962. While she was a pro-choice feminist, she had no use for the feminist left, or the hard right of the Republican Party.

Following her tenure as his ambassador to Ghana, she was appointed Ford's chief of protocol. Throughout Watergate, she remained loyal to Nixon, and when California's Reagan challenged Ford in 1976, she stuck with Ford. During the Reagan years she was out of favor, but after the election of George H. W. Bush, whom she supported, he appointed her as America's ambassador to Czechoslovakia.

Shirley Temple Black was a top star for less than a dozen years, but a patriot all her life. As a child, she lifted Americans out of the despair of the Depression. In the course of her charitable and diplomatic missions, she witnessed both 1968's Prague Spring—where the bloodshed before her eyes confirmed her anti-communist views—and 1989's Velvet Revolution, when communism in Europe crashed and burned. What better face to represent America in the world's most challenging environments than one whose wholesome sincerity was never an act? She was truly America's best.

Brooke Shields: Actress and Model

The first time I saw Brooke Shields, I was stunned by how tall the long-stemmed brunette actually was. I shouldn't have been, because I knew her father, Frank Shields Jr., who stood more than six-foot-four. I was having drinks with Frank and his friend Jamie Niven (son of actor David) at The Brook club in New York. Frank, who incidentally was vice president of the club, said that "Brookie" (the young star of movies including *Pretty Baby, The Blue Lagoon,* and *Endless Love*) was with Bob Hope over at the Plaza. Hope had just returned from what would be his last visit to U.S. troops, in 1991, during Operation Desert Storm. Although he was close to ninety, and stumbled somewhat through his presentation, he was loud and clear in his praise of Brooke.

It's hard to imagine, but Frank may have been more handsome than Brooke was beautiful. His dark Gaelic looks would have put Tyrone Power to shame. He also had the Irish gift for storytelling, and could keep an audience spellbound. Curiously, Brooke Shields owed her name to her father's club. Her mother had the "e" added because she thought that such an elegant club should have an "e" at the end of its name.

Brooke's mother was the curvaceous hatcheck girl at a bar on Fifty-Fourth Street, down the block towards Lexington on the other side of The Brook. Frank Shields, with his Brook club pals, used to drop into the bar in search of female company. (At that time, The Brook's policy was no women allowed.) The comely attendant instantly caught Frank's eye. Her name was Theresia—Teri for short.

Not too long later, she announced that she was with child. Frank belonged to a Roman Catholic family; his mother was an Italian aristocrat who had married a handsome tennis star, a scion of one of the wealthiest families in New York. Frank Jr. married Teri quietly but then did not consummate the marriage, allowing for annulment. After the dissolution of this marriage, Frank wed one of his own circle, and lived in the North Shore of Long Island.

Left on her own, Brooke's mother became a determined stage mother, pushing her young child into modeling and acting roles. Brooke's father lost any real contact with his superstar daughter until she went to Princeton University. Now pursuing his investment career in New York, Frank could visit Princeton easily, since it was only several train stops away from the city.

Brooke's mother was at that reception for Bob Hope at the Plaza in 1991, and I was shocked by her appearance. Due to life's disappointments, or for some other reason, the comely bar hostess and cosmetic-counter girl was no more. But if Brooke's mother could no longer be considered *soigneé* by New York standards, she certainly had not neglected her daughter. Some may think of her as the quintessential stage mother, but if so, she was attentive to Brooke's education, having recognized her brains and talent as well as her looks early on. As for Brooke, she found in Frank Shields the dark and handsome prince charming of fairy tales. Unfortunately, he died too soon, but lived long enough to vicariously enjoy her acting fame.

After her father died, Brooke wed Wimbledon and U.S. Open ace Andre Agassiz. The marriage broke up before there was issue. Alas, with their combined genes, a son or daughter should have been a tennis star. But a more recent love has borne new life for the beautiful Brooke.

Douglas Fairbanks Jr.: Swashbuckler

I first met the film actor in 1953, when I was an ESU exchange student at Stowe School in England. Fairbanks, a staunch supporter of the ESU, had invited me to dinner at his London town house. With him were his daughter Daphne, and his wife Mary Lee, the former spouse of A&P Supermarkets heir Huntington Hartford. Fairbanks and his wife asked me questions about Stowe. I mentioned that my uncle George—my maternal grandmother's younger brother—was a lawyer who had done some of the legal work for the purchase of Pickfair—the storied twenty-five-room mansion where Douglas

Fairbanks Sr. and his wife, silent film-star Mary Pickford ("America's Sweetheart") had once entertained European and Hollywood royalty.

We next met three decades later at The Brook club in New York, dining together at the communal table. The younger Fairbanks often performed swashbuckling roles in the "talkies," just as his father had played swordsmen in the silents. But the son took greater pride in his real-life courage than in his cinematic derring-do. Ever dashing and charming, he modestly downplayed both his acting talents and his heroic record as a lieutenant commander in the U.S. Navy. For his highly dangerous work as one of the "Beach Jumpers," commandoes assigned to North Africa and France, Fairbanks received the navy's Legion of Merit, along with the Silver Star for valor in the Pacific. Half a dozen allied nations bestowed similar honors upon the real-life swashbuckler, including Britain (Distinguished Service Cross), France (Croix de Guerre and Legion d'Honneur), and Italy (War Cross for Military Valor). After the war, Fairbanks remained in the U.S. Naval Reserve, retiring at the rank of captain in 1954.

Still, as he told us at The Brook, his most discomfiting experience took place at Buckingham Palace, when he was given his "gong" by King George VI. The monarch was ailing at the time, and so Fairbanks knew he should be brief. He had also been instructed by the courtiers never to turn his back on the monarch. So, caught in a dilemma, presumably with the knowledge of the King, he backed slowly down the long hall towards the door, declaring ever more loudly that he would always cherish this honor.

Another time at The Brook, our conversation turned to religion, and Fairbanks told me that while he was an Episcopalian, he did not believe that there was a hell in the afterlife. He had already experienced that in this life, in his two-year marriage with Joan Crawford!

Fairbanks attended the engagement party for my daughter Mary at The Brook in 1997. In his toast, he took note of my daughter as managing editor of *The Harvard Crimson,* a star at Oxford in classics, as well as an editor of *The Yale Law Journal.* He told the guests that he hoped Mary would become president of the United States, or the mother of ten children.

On hearing his suggestion, Mary replied, "Mr. Fairbanks, thanks, but no thanks!"

Jane Wyman: Actress and First Wife of Ronald Reagan

I met Jane Wyman once, in 1981. We were in Buckhead, a tony suburb next to Atlanta where CNN had its first studio under former CEO Ted Turner. We were in the studio's green room, where Wyman was waiting to do some promotion for the TV-serial epic *Falcon Crest.* I was hyping my humorous volume, *How to Be a Very Important Person.* At that time, her former husband was president.

Clad in a blue dress, Wyman was elegant and poised, and somewhat taller than Reagan's second wife—the former Nancy Davis, also an actress. While we waited our turn in the green room, I asked her about her 1946 film *The Yearling*, the story of a boy who adopts a wild fawn. That year, her young co-star, Claude Jarman Jr., had come to Williamsport for a promotional tour, and stayed in the bunkroom with me. My mother had suggested this arrangement because my brothers were off at Hill School. I told her that Claude and I shared the same birth date, October 31, 1934.

She told me that while Claude was a sweet boy, she didn't think he liked acting. The young star had no experience prior to his selection for *The Yearling,* which was the result of a nationwide talent search by MGM. A few years later, he seemed to enjoy playing the son of John Wayne and Maureen O'Hara in *Rio Grande.* And Wyman's role in *The Yearling* was not the last time she played a devoted mother. Her favorite film, as she told me, was *Johnny Belinda*, for which she won an Oscar. For this part, in which Wyman played a victimized deaf–mute woman who conquers the odds to raise her son, she won an Academy Award without speaking a single word of dialogue.

Our conversation turned to President Reagan, who had told Wyman that I was a speechwriter for Nixon. Jane admitted that she was not into politics: That was Ronnie's thing. She liked Nixon, as she told me, and had voted for him, as she intended to vote for Ronnie: He was her children's father.

On the show, Wyman was asked how she felt about Reagan. She smiled, and said that of course she wished the best for her children's father. (Her two children with Reagan were Maureen, an actress and co-chair of the Republican National Committee, and Michael, a writer, talk show host, and Republican political strategist, who was adopted.) Always professional, and a team player, Wyman quickly switched the conversation to the new TV series. She was every inch a real lady, with no airs about her.

Marvin Hamlisch: Music Composer for the Cinema

I sat next to Marvin Hamlisch during a long dinner at the National Arts Club in New York, in September of 1993. We were both there to salute philanthropist Wendy Reves, the wife of Emery Reves, who had been a literary agent for Winston Churchill. In 1991, Hamlisch had written a symphony in honor of Wendy's pacifist husband—*Anatomy of Peace*—which had been performed that afternoon at Carnegie Hall.

I knew little about the multi-Oscar winner, but one of his compositions—the theme from 1973's Barbara Streisand vehicle *The Way We Were*—often ran through my head. Though only ten years younger than I, the fifty-year-old Hamlisch looked boyish. If he was addicted to the spotlight provided by

People magazine and talk show interviews, he displayed surprisingly little celebrity narcissism.

Hamlisch was enthusiastic about philanthropist Wendy and her generous heart. Of course, he should have been, since she had given him a handsome figure for writing the symphonic suite, via the Dallas Symphony Orchestra, which had commissioned it. His affection for her seemed entirely sincere, however. He had recently visited La Pausa, her Cap d'Antibes chalet on the Riviera, the house that the Duke of Westminster built for Coco Chanel. Wendy's husband had gifted it to the former model and one-time runner-up Miss Texas.

Churchill, in his octogenarian years, liked to spend time without his wife, who was no fan of Wendy Reves. He usually occupied himself by painting one of his seascapes, which he would give to his hosts. Wendy, who married Reves a few years before he died, became a millionaire widow with hundreds of Churchill paintings. (She gave one to Hamlisch.)

With me as fellow saluters of the voluptuous if aging Wendy were the French-born American fashion designer Pauline Trigère, who offered Wendy a creation named in her honor, and Timothy Sullivan, president of the College of William and Mary, to which she had donated a sizable gift. He presented her with a key to the main building on campus, whose design is credited to Christopher Wren. I read her my own Shakespearean sonnet, and she cried out that only her dear friend Winston could have done better.

In telling the audience how he had visited Wendy at La Pausa for four weeks, Hamlisch waxed poetic about her late husband: He had sat in his chair, he had slept in his bed. This was because he wanted to feel the man's very essence if he was to write this symphony to honor his crusade for peace. Given the book agent's Churchill connection, this cloying tribute to a pacifist was disquieting. He concluded with this praise of Wendy: While everyone knew his song, "One," there was only one Wendy in the world.

Later, Wendy wrote me a perfumed letter with pink script on her blue stationery, asking me to come to the Riviera to write her biography. I wrote back and asked for a twenty-five-thousand-dollar advance. I never got a reply.

I found Hamlisch to be without any airs or pretense. He wanted to hear about my books on Churchill. As a lyricist, he was fascinated with the reported acronym for Churchill's delivering a memorable line: CREAM (contrast, rhyme, echo/repetition, alliteration, metaphor).

All in all, having Marvin Hamlisch for my dinner partner that evening had made for a memorable event. It is possibly a testament to his skill as a composer that I had remembered the melody rather than the lyrics to "The Way We Were," or the fact that Barbara Streisand had sung it.

Eugene Ormandy: Conductor

Richard Nixon was a hero worshipper. Some of his heroes were sports idols like Ted Williams and Joe Louis (he once asked me to draft a letter to the dying boxer). Some were musicians, like pianist Van Cliburn, or, most notably, Eugene Ormandy, long-time conductor of the Philadelphia Orchestra. I was also a fan. My mother, who was tone deaf, nevertheless wanted her sons to have an appreciation of music. She bought a piano for me after our father died. Before my dad's death, every Sunday afternoon we would tune in on our living-room radio to hear Eugene Ormandy. It was Ormandy's emphasis on the strings that gave the Philadelphia Orchestra its unique, silky resonance.

When they were doing a tribute to Ormandy in Philadelphia on the occasion of the orchestra's seventieth anniversary, in 1970, Nixon signaled his intention to be invited. By coincidence, it was about the time the new Metroliner service between New York and Washington was inaugurated. As a Philadelphian, I was included on the VIP list in the lead car (which was also a club car) with the president. Notwithstanding the availability of cocktails, Nixon refused all drinks except soda water. He told me that he didn't want a drink to take the edge off his appreciation.

I remember sitting behind Nixon at the close of the concert, Tchaikovsky's *1812 Overture*, which includes cannon shots near the end. I suddenly recalled that Hitchcock movie, *The Man Who Knew Too Much,* when the would-be assassin's shot comes at the same time as the symphonic clashing of cymbals. I inwardly winced, and scrunched down in my seat.

Afterwards, in presenting Ormandy with the Presidential Medal of Freedom, Nixon told the Austrian conductor how he had admired him since boyhood. Ormandy told him that the regard was mutual, and added this affirmation: He was an anti-communist, and appreciated the way Republicans had restored Austria's freedom in 1954.

Edward Kennedy "Duke" Ellington: Jazz Composer, Pianist, and Band Leader

I only saw the Duke once—at a White House dinner given in his honor, on the occasion of his seventieth birthday in April 1969. Other famous musicians had been invited to perform at state banquets, but Ellington was the first to be the reason for the dinner. It all happened because of Charlie McWhorter, a jazz enthusiast. Besides jazz, McWhorter's other love was the Republican Party. It was said in the 1960s that if you wanted the list of key GOP workers, operatives, and activists in all fifty states, you could find them in GOP National Chairman Len Hall's business-card file and Charlie McWhorter's Christmas card list. (The cards were sent out on the day after

Thanksgiving, every year without fail.) McWhorter's close friend was fellow Republican and jazz virtuoso Lionel Hampton. He first wanted to honor Hampton at the White House, but Hampton demurred and suggested his friend, Duke Ellington, the giant of jazz.

As a White House writer, I was asked to compose the words that would be used in bestowing the Presidential Medal of Freedom, to be awarded to Ellington that night. I have written before that much of a presidential speechwriter's job is drafting remarks for ceremonial occasions, such as honoring retiring Cabinet officers or saluting historic anniversaries. If the event was a state dinner, oftentimes President Nixon would invite the writer to join the White House guests for after-dinner coffee in the East Room. I introduced the president by saying, "President Nixon, I want to honor one of the country's historic names—Edward Kennedy . . . Ellington." The audience broke out in laughter at the allusion to Nixon's putative Democratic rival, the senator from Massachusetts. Then Nixon delivered the remarks I had written for him: "In the royalty of music, no one swings more or stands higher than the Duke."

Ellington said he was moved by the words. His mood was one of high jubilation when I met him, certainly not "Mood Indigo." His white teeth and wide smile beamed a young man's radiance—hardly that of a seventy-year-old—especially when Nixon serenaded him by playing "Happy Birthday to You" on the piano!

Claus von Bülow: Society Playboy and Movie Villain

In 1991, Jeremy Irons won an Oscar for his portrayal of a Newport socialite who was charged with trying to murder his heiress wife. The film, *Reversal of Fortune*, was released in October 1990. Three decades later, the alleged events on which it was based still intrigue the public.

In 1982, I was in Newport, on the coast of Rhode Island, doing my communications seminar. I walked into the dining room of the hotel where I was staying, to have breakfast. A somewhat familiar transatlantic voice called out: James Humes! Then the owner of this voice asked me to join him. While I recognized the face, I couldn't recall the name. But with an old campaigner's practice, I masked my ignorance with a gush of amenities: "You're looking as great as ever." He was fairly tall, slightly balding, and wore a Norfolk tweed jacket with twilled tan trousers. His blue shirt was topped with a paisley ascot at his throat.

He reminded me of the drinks we had together at the Ritz in London some years before, and later at my club—The Brook—in New York. He asked how the Churchill book I was writing in London was coming along. I answered, "It's published and is coming out in trade paperback this year."

Finally, having exhausted every small-talk gambit, I resorted to the politician's favorite ploy: "Tell me, how's the family?"

When I saw the stunned look on his face, I realized my gaffe. It was Claus von Bülow, the aristocratic playboy, who was on trial in Newport with respect to the death of his wife, Sunny. His two stepchildren were heading the witnesses for the prosecution. The question in court was whether von Bülow had contrived to make his drug-dependent wife die, or whether he had let her go into a diabetic coma by intent or neglect.

Years later, when I was doing my one-man Churchill show in New York, von Bülow revealed the wit that made him such a charming dinner guest. In response to knocking on my dressing-room door, I opened it to hear him say that his family was fine, thank you!

Anne Brown, a doyenne of Rhode Island society and the wife of John Nicholas Brown (whose family had founded Brown University), shocked her peers by standing up for von Bülow as a character witness. Newport is one of the haunts of the upper class, and there, von Bülow found his fabulously rich, beautiful wife, utilities heiress Martha "Sunny" Crawford. His first case ended in a mistrial, and in the second, he was acquitted. But, like O. J. Simpson, Claus von Bülow trailed doubts and suspicions in the wake of his trial. Sunny lay in a coma for twenty-eight years, her hair coiffed every day by her attendants, until her death in 2008.

My son-in-law and daughter in London still sight the carefree Claus dining at one of London's posh bistros near Sloane Square.

Notes

1. William Shakespeare, *The Tragedy of King Richard the Third*, in *The Oxford Shakespeare, Second Edition*, edited by John Jowett, William Montgomery, Gary Taylor, and Stanley Wells (Oxford, UK: Oxford University Press, 2005), 194.

2. William Shakespeare, *The Tragedy of Antony and Cleopatra*, in *The Oxford Shakespeare, Second Edition*, edited by John Jowett, William Montgomery, Gary Taylor, and Stanley Wells (Oxford, UK: Oxford University Press, 2005), 1005.

3. Samuel Taylor Coleridge, "The Rime of the Ancient Mariner," in *The Rime of the Ancient Mariner and Other Poems* (Mineola, New York: Dover Publications, Inc., 1992), 9.

4. Johann Wolfgang von Goethe, *Faust*, in *Goethe's Werke, Band 41* (Stuttgart and Tübingen: J. G. Cotta'schen Buchhandlung, 1832), 544.

Chapter Ten

Stadium

Jackie Robinson: Baseball Hall of Famer

My wife and I first met the baseball legend Jackie Robinson in July 1960, at the Blackwood Hotel in Chicago. He was in town for the Republican National Convention, working on behalf of Vice President Nixon.

Rachel Robinson, Jackie's wife, and top Nixon Aide Loie Gaunt (a friend of the Robinsons) introduced us. The muscular black man was an arresting figure of dignity and grace. After Robinson starred in the winning World Series for the Brooklyn Dodgers against the hated Yankees in 1955, he was sold to their cross-city rival, the New York Giants. Robinson quit, and took a high-salary vice president's position with Chock full o'Nuts, the coffee-shop chain.

With the help of baseball executive Branch Rickey, who signed him up, Robinson had broken baseball's color barrier right after the war, via the Montreal Royals, a minor-league team that supplied players to the Dodgers. As the first black man to play in modern major-league baseball, as opposed to the segregated ball clubs of the past, Robinson had to learn how to discipline his inner rage so as to brook the insults and taunts that came his way. Thirteen years later, he vented some of the frustration he still harbored. He was bitter at the northern Democrats, who pontificated on civil rights while letting their southern allies in the Senate bottle up many bills that would have advanced the civil-rights agenda.

He also was embittered by baseball. The Dodgers boasted of their unique hometown greatness, then shipped off Robinson in a cynical move, choosing profits over civic pride.

Robinson disdained Senator John Kennedy, whose bid for vice president against Estes Kefauver four years earlier was backed by southern senators who opposed the only Democrat below the Mason-Dixon Line who was pro-civil rights. As for Johnson, he was the typical plantation owner who expected all blacks to vote Democratic. This was despite the fact that Johnson, as Democratic majority leader, arranged the Senate voting calendar so that Vice President Nixon would have to make the deciding vote in the case of ties, to insure southerners' hatred of Nixon and his party. The Republican administration under Eisenhower, which had sent in troops to open Arkansas schools to black children against the entrenched opposition of Governor Orval Faubus, had far more to offer blacks than the Democrats did.

In 1972, when I represented President Nixon at the Little League World Series in Williamsport (my home town) by throwing the first pitch, I said: "If Jackie Robinson made baseball the All-American game, it was Little League that made it an All-World game."

John "Jack" Kelly Jr.: Olympic Sculler and Brother of Grace Kelly

It was the first day of March 1985, and the last full day of Jack Kelly's life. The former Olympic sculling champion had been selected as president of the U.S. Olympic Committee, and he had recruited me to write some speeches for him. I had dinner with him that day at the Union League in Philadelphia. When he met me in the foyer, I asked him, "Jack, will you walk to the table alone? I want no comparisons of physiques from all the women." A little later, you could hear a collective sigh from all the ladies who were lunching there before the Wednesday afternoon symphony.

Jack was happy that night. He had left the running of the family brick works to others, so that his only 'work' was working out every morning and afternoon. The result was a perfect Adonis, a star athlete like his father and namesake. At the annual Christmas Day re-enactment of American troops crossing the Delaware in 1776 to surprise the Hessians, the tall, husky Jack would play George Washington. Talent, beauty, literary gifts, athletic prowess—the Kelly family seemed superhuman, but like many such families, they were touched by tragedy. Jack's sister Grace enjoyed a brief but spectacular career as a Hollywood actress, whose finale was her coronation as a real-life princess. Yet she would die at age fifty-two of a stroke suffered at the wheel of her car, leaving her tiny principality and its prince, Rainier of Monaco, overwhelmed with grief.

Jack relayed one recent regret: He would have to root for Harvard against his own alma mater, the University of Pennsylvania, in the coming crew race, because his son Jack was captain of the Crimson crew. He felt pride in his son's engagement to a Harvard co-ed; I knew from my daughter Mary that his fiancée was a stunning and very bright African-American woman, the former Karen Spencer of Chicago, now Mrs. Jack Kelly III.

Though he was a Philadelphia city councilman, Jack shocked me when it came out in our conversation that he didn't know the difference between a state senator and a U.S. senator! He was also inclined to drop names. On one occasion, he joined me when I was flying from Philadelphia to DC. When the stewardess came to get our cocktail requests, he said he would have that drink his sister the princess in Monaco liked to order. (This was a Cosmopolitan: a blend of vodka, lime juice, cranberry juice, and triple sec, served in a chilled glass with a garnish of citrus rind.)

"Jack," I said to him, "your physique and looks are enough to gain the stewardess's eye and fixed attention! If Grace was my sister, I might have to drop her name, but for you, it's an A-bomb, when you don't even need a cap pistol!" Jack grinned.

At the Union League, he invited me to join him for dinner at a future date, to meet his new girlfriend Rachel Harlow, who was a transgendered woman. She was the proprietor of Harlow's, a glamorous club in Philly, and also a model—blonde like an earlier Harlow, beautiful, smart, and funny. Jack proudly took her to Monaco to meet Princess Grace, but his mother, old Mrs. Kelly, threatened to disinherit him. So the engagement was ended. The day after our dinner, Jack was found dead outside his center city apartment, in jogging clothes. He had suffered a massive heart attack.

Ted Williams: The Greatest Hitter Who Ever Lived

He was known as the "Splendid Splinter," a sobriquet coined by sportswriters when the lanky young Red Sox player hit .401. This was the last time *anyone* ever hit more than .400—although he would again come close in 1957, when he hit .388 at age 39.

This star performer of the Boston Red Sox referred to himself in conversation as "Teddy Ballgame." I met him once, in 1958, after Dianne and I had come back from a wedding in Brattleboro, Vermont, where we had socialized with the Gannet family. Sarah Gannet was the granddaughter of Teddy Roosevelt, while her son, Billy, was a Red Sox fan. Ted Williams was Billy's hero. So, I went on the field at Griffith Stadium in Washington, DC some weeks later and asked Ted Williams to sign a ball, adding, "Ted, the boy's a great-grandson of Teddy Roosevelt." He seemed surprised. Signing the ball, he asked me why the boy had *him* for his hero when he had Teddy Roosevelt as a great-grandfather. Williams told me that his Mexican mother had named him after the rugged and outspoken American president.

Years later, in 1992, I was asked to deliver my Churchill show, "Never Give Up," in Fall River, Massachusetts, to honor a retiring doctor. Afterwards, a man in his sixties came up to me and asked me to autograph my Churchill biography for a friend. When I asked to whom I should inscribe it, he answered "Ted Williams. I was his roommate, a batting coach for the Red

Sox." I signed the book: "To my first hero—a biography of the hero who replaced him."

On receiving the book, Williams called me from Florida, and told me that he wholly approved of Churchill as his replacement.

Ted had retired from baseball in 1960. Twice, he left the ball field to fly for his country—during World War II and in Korea, where he garnered a dozen medals. They said that as a batter, he could read the name "Spalding" on the ball as it came to the plate. "Best eyes ever examined by the navy," or so they said. He was the hero that John Wayne played in films.

Chapter Eleven

Press Box

Michael Smerconish: Political Analyst, TV and Radio Host, Author, and Attorney

I first met Michael Smerconish in the gym of the Union League of Philadelphia during the 1990s. He was a more regular patron than I—and with better results—but we both loved talking about politics to pass the time on the treadmill. Back then, Michael was practicing law and had a talk radio program. Today, he is editor and publisher of *Smerconish.com,* a columnist for *The Philadelphia Inquirer,* and the host of CNN International's *Smerconish* TV show, along with SiriusXM Radio's POTUS Channel (124)—a broadcast venture dedicated to the politics of the United States.

Michael's Pennsylvania political heroes run the gamut from former Philadelphia Democratic Mayor Frank Rizzo on the political right, to Senator Arlen Specter in the liberal wing of the Republican Party. A caring father and loving husband, this freethinker and maverick embodies the family values for which he fights, and the importance of civil discussion and debate. As the foremost voice of reason on the right, Smerconish is the one to watch and listen to as America adjusts to the controversial presidency of Donald Trump.

A Republican supporter of Presidents Nixon, Ford, and Reagan, Smerconish opposed Donald Trump's run for president. In Smerconish's view, Trump was too volatile a risk in a time of turmoil when division and dissent were splitting the nation asunder. Any cooling of the rhetoric and rage would not be coming from a President Trump—who, in the pundit's view, would further ignite the flame of protest and conflagration of riots and rampage boiling over in this country.

Smerconish would have backed Governor Jeb Bush of Florida or Governor John Kasich of Ohio, but once Trump was elected president, this widely heard and respected political analyst muted his criticism, opting not to join the legions of politicians and pundits who would remove Trump by impeach-ment—or the rogue government officials who have whispered of stooping to other means. Removal of Trump (or any other president) by ballot is the preferred method. Ouster of Trump by impeachment and conviction without conspicuous grounds for doing so would be difficult, if not disastrous, for our republic. In Smerconish's view, one may oppose Trump, but be civil about it. Smerconish believes that discourse should not be vitriolic or venomous, but evince more reason than rage.

Smerconish is a Republican, not a radical who would blow up the govern-ment and eradicate our democratic institutions. If he has become more muted in his opposition to Trump, he is not silent, choosing to voice the concerns of the moderate and middle-of-the-road Republicans who decry the excesses of Trumpism. He does this not with rancor but with the reasoning of an attorney appearing before a jury of his peers: Smerconish is a lawyer and officer of the court, under oath to uphold and defend our laws.

Opposition to the Trump regime has need of at least one informed voice against monarchical antics. British MP Edmund Burke—the founder of mod-ern conservatism—attacked the tyranny of George III in support of the American colonies' struggle to achieve representative government. Burke was no radical. Neither is Smerconish. He harbors no ambition for elective office, and would rather emulate Thomas Paine, or Pennsylvania's greatest printer and Founding Father, Benjamin Franklin, in waging war through reasoned argument. Smericonish remains a law-and-order Republican, and is sure to chastise any who would take the law into their own hands against our system of justice.

John LeBoutillier: Congressman, Author, and TV Pundit

In 1981, at the age of twenty-seven, John LeBoutillier became the country's youngest legislator, representing New York's Sixth District in the House of Representatives. He had first won fame a few years earlier with his book *Harvard Hates America*—an indictment of the hypocrisy and elitism he found as a student at that venerable institution. His tales of the left-wing bias on campus earned him appearances in which he was asked to defend these allegations. In the course of one panel discussion, Gore Vidal declared that if LeBoutillier had been from one of the old families, he wouldn't have taken such an anti-establishment position. LeBoutillier could have replied that he was a scion of Commodore Cornelius Vanderbilt and a great-grandson of Gertrude Vanderbilt Whitney, but he is loath to trade on his lineage.

Known to his TV and Internet fans as "Boot," the political pundit and blogger (*Boot's Blasts*) now lives in Gertrude Vanderbilt Whitney's former art studio in Old Westbury, New York, which his mother inherited from her own mother, Flora Whitney Miller. I have vivid memories of Mrs. Miller, who had a commanding presence even as an octogenarian. During World War I, she became engaged to Quentin Roosevelt, a pilot in the U.S. Air Force who was a son of President Theodore Roosevelt. The young Roosevelt was shot down behind German lines in France and killed instantly. Following this tragedy, Flora remained close to the Roosevelt family, through her past engagement to Quentin as well as a slightly more tenuous link with other members of Roosevelt's circle. Thanks to connections in Aiken, South Carolina, Flora was a friend of Lucy Mercer Rutherfurd, Eleanor Roosevelt's former social secretary, who began an affair with Franklin Roosevelt during World War I. Lucy and FDR resumed their relationship in 1944, after the death of Rutherfurd's husband. Rutherfurd had arranged to drive from Aiken over to Hot Springs, Georgia, to see FDR in April of 1945, and she was with him when he died. Not wanting to be found at the scene, Rutherfurd drove all night to Old Westbury in order to escape to the home of her friend Flora Miller.

When first elected to Congress, the twenty-seven-year-old LeBoutillier was considered an *enfant terrible* by Speaker of the House Thomas ("Tip") O'Neill. One reason might have been the opening words of a speech in which Boot said that Tip O'Neill and the federal government were very much alike: big, fat, and out of control. The powers that be reapportioned Boot's congressional district in 1982, and he lost the subsequent election.

Boot's passions are pitching and politics. His proudest moment was hurling a masterful set of innings in the Congressional Baseball Game, a match that pits Republicans against Democrats in a charity fundraiser. He still does weekly turns on the mound for a crack amateur suburban team. Boot's biggest regret is that he could never learn the knuckleball. At one point he organized a group of investors including Ted Williams to buy the New York Mets from his cousin, Joan Whitney Payson, but publishing CEO Nelson Doubleday topped his bid and bought the franchise.

After his service in Congress, LeBoutillier struck up a friendship with Richard Nixon in New York. He has also been active in helping families of Vietnam POWs/MIAs, and has organized missions to Vietnam to find out what became of them.

In addition to his role as a TV and on-line commentator, Boot keeps a hand in Nassau County politics by hosting a weekly luncheon for local politicians. Nationally, he hosts a weekly television show for Fox News, *Political Insiders,* with Pat Caddell and Doug Schoen. He is devoted to family members, and cared for his half-brother, Timmy Secor, who was a paraplegic following an accident, for over twenty-five years until Timmy's death in 2016.

Lady Jeanne Campbell: Correspondent and Convert

I was on a charter plane to San Francisco, on my way to the 1964 Republican Convention, when I heard a very feminine British accent. It belonged to Lady Jeanne Campbell, granddaughter of Lord Beaverbrook, the British publishing mogul. I could not resist interrupting a conversation between Lady Jeanne and Senator Jacob Javits, who was entranced by the sexy Lady Jeanne.

She introduced herself to me as just "Jeanne," a correspondent for *The Daily Sketch*—a British tabloid newspaper. Suddenly the pilot announced that the plane would make an unscheduled landing in Los Angeles, before heading on to San Francisco. After we landed in Los Angeles, the rumor of a bomb on board seemed to be fact, as the plane stood on the tarmac.

"Jeanne, this is a perfect story for the *Sketch*," I told her. "Imagine the headline, 'MY KNICKERS RANSACKED FOR A BOMB!'" (Knickers are what they call panties in Britain.)

Jeanne seemed puzzled, and asked me what I meant.

"Jeanne," I replied, "they're going through the luggage—examining all apparel—and that has to include underwear!"

She hauled out a portable typewriter to punch out her story, while I added my advice. She told me that she loved the name Jamie, which she knew to be Scottish. Then she told me she had a confession to make: She had no hotel reservation. She hadn't thought to ask her grandfather for one, as her trip had been arranged at the last minute. (Her grandfather happened to be Lord Beaverbrook.) Then she looked at me with wide, innocent eyes, and asked whether my room had two beds. But I mustn't worry: She knew I was married, and promised not to be a distraction.

The bomb scare having been diffused as a false alarm, we flew on to San Francisco. When we got to my economy lodging, we both checked our bags at the lobby, keeping the taxi-meter running. Then we were off to the St. Francis Hotel, where there was to be a press conference, and Henry Cabot Lodge Jr.—LBJ's ambassador to Vietnam—would endorse Scranton. With her press credentials, and my Scranton connections, we were able to squeeze into the front row. When we got to the Q & A session, I wrote out a question for her. Lodge took a look at the beauty with the British accent, who asked him if he would campaign for Goldwater if he was nominated. Unmoved by her charms, Lodge thundered that he would neither campaign nor vote for him.

We were then off to Ernie's, a seafood restaurant on the waterfront, where we both ordered shrimp cocktails. Before our order came, Stewart Alsop, the reporter and brother of Joe, came over. He knew Lady Jeanne, and invited us to his suite in the Mark Hopkins Hotel for a party. (When we got there that evening, one glare from Alsop told me that "three's a crowd.") Finally, in this jam-packed restaurant, we ate our shrimp cocktails. While we were waiting for our paella, Jeanne suddenly stood up, and told me that we had to go: Her husband had just entered the room! At that point, I didn't know she was married, nor did I know the gentleman's name. She went on to say that her husband was Norman Mailer, the author, and that he had once taken a knife to a guy she was seeing.

We left Ernie's through the kitchen, and I never saw her again. Years later, my literary agent wanted me to contact her for a possible book. But after three husbands, this ball of sexual energy had become reclusive. She converted to Catholicism late in life, and became active in the practice of her new faith at St. Joseph's Church in Greenwich Village. Having lived in reduced circumstances herself for many years, she made it her special mission to care for the poor at St. Joseph's homeless shelter. Her funeral mass was held at St. Joseph's in June 2007.

George Plimpton: Writer and Society Gadfly

George Plimpton was America's best-known participatory journalist. Circus trapeze artist, cymbalist in the symphony, football player for the Detroit Lions, golfer, goalie, boxer—he did all this, and more, to explore different fields and then write about his experiences. His actual persona was New York socialite, and in that capacity, I had two occasions to talk with him extensively. Both were at The Brook, in 1987—the first at the bar at night, and then later at the common lunch table.

When I told him my name, he asked if I was any relation to Harold Humes—a co-founder of *The Paris Review,* which Plimpton edited for decades after its creation in 1953. No relation, as I told him; and it surprised me that Plimpton made no mention of my cousin John Humes, Nixon's ambassador to Austria, a squash-playing and yachting sportsman. The wife of Harold Humes had been my wife Dianne's classmate at Wellesley College.

In planning his pranks and performances, Plimpton's active imagination was most drawn to competitive sports, sometimes as an athlete, other times simply as a joker. On April 1, 1985, the cover of *Sports Illustrated* featured a hoax article on "Siddhartha Finch," a phenomenon at the Mets training camp in Florida, who was supposedly throwing baseballs at 168 miles an hour. "Sidd," as he was known, was a former cricket bowler at Stowe, and he had learned his fastball technique while living with his father in India.

At The Brook, I asked Plimpton why he had picked Stowe as Sidd's school for this celebrated spoof. He said he had chosen the British prep school because he had a friend who had gone there, and also because it was not as well known as Eton or Harrow (and therefore, less likely to attract attention). The baseball world believed Plimpton's hoax report on the lightning-fast pitcher, ignoring the fact that it came out on April Fool's Day.

The story reveals Plimpton's insouciant laughing at the world. His antics were frequently reported in *People* magazine, and broadcast on ABC Television. Yet he was chiefly known for his myriad adventures in professional sports. He played quarterback in a pre-season exhibition for the Detroit Lions, and later wrote a book about it (*Paper Lion,* 1963). He also did a stint for the Boston Bruins as a goalie, took to the golf course (written up as *The Bogey Man,* 1968), and boxed a round with former light heavyweight world champion Archie Moore, who bashed his nose.

Plimpton was a tall figure of striking appearance, which he used to his advantage in commanding an audience on the lecture circuit, at book readings, or in talk-show interviews. A Democrat and close friend of the Kennedys, he was expansive, full of himself, and opinionated. When I asked him to describe his hardest athletic ordeal, he told me about playing guard for the Boston Celtics. The boards for basketball, unlike grass, have no give, and running up and down the court for a fifty-year-old just about did his legs in.

A patrician descendant of English Puritans, and the son of a corporate lawyer and UN ambassador, he took pride in his early antecedents in Massachusetts. One was the Reverend Comfort Starr, a founder of Harvard University, whose family home was the setting for Harvard's first classes in 1636. When he said he had been invited to London for the anniversary of Starr's ordination as a minister in the Church of England, I volunteered that I had been another one of his many descendants. He asked whether I had gone to Harvard myself, and I said "No," but mentioned that my daughter had excelled there.

Plimpton then volunteered that the hardest challenge he ever underwent was not in sports but at the symphony. He was the cymbalist one Sunday afternoon for the New York Philharmonic, where his one contribution was the closing clang of a work by Beethoven. Although air-conditioned, Avery Hall seemed excessively hot to him. The usually cool Plimpton admitted that he was sweating bullets, because, as he told me, playing the cymbals is a matter of exquisite timing: One can't be too soon or late—just the right second—then BOOM!

During World War II, Plimpton was a demolitions expert, and later, Mayor John Lindsay's unofficial fireworks commissioner for the city of New York. In 1975, his attempt to launch the world's largest Roman candle resulted in an on-ground explosion that left a ten-foot-deep crater on Long Island. His second attempt broke seven hundred windows in the town of Titusville, Florida. Characteristically, Plimpton turned his experiences with pyrotechnics into book copy: *Fireworks: A History and Celebration,* which was published in 1984, and may be considered an authoritative work on the subject. Per his request, Plimpton's ashes were loaded into a "Japanese Willow" golden fireworks rocket and scattered over the Hamptons on July 4, 2006.

Kay Halle: Journalist, Washington Grande Dame, and Friend of the Churchills

If not for Kay Halle, there would have been no honorary American citizenship for Winston Churchill. Nor, for that matter, would a statue of Churchill stand where it does outside the British Embassy—one half on British soil, one half on American. This was in recognition of Churchill's strong friendship with America, but also as a tribute to his American mother, Lady Randolph Churchill—the former Jennie Jerome of New York.

A freelance writer, radio broadcaster, and World War II intelligence operative, Kay Halle became an expert on Churchill, and a close friend of the great man. Her Georgetown house on Dent Place was the stopping point for all Churchill kin staying in DC, such as the prime minister's grandson Winston II, and John Churchill, his nephew. That's how I first met her back in 1971, when the American Platform Society, founded by Daniel Webster, honored Kay for her writings, as well as her lifelong friendship with the Churchill family. She was the author of two books about the prime minister (*Irrepressible Churchill: Winston's World, Wars, and Wit*, 1966, and *Winston Churchill on America and Britain* , 1970), and a collector of Churchill memorabilia. With us was her guest Sir William McVey, the sculptor of the Churchill statue. (He later gave me the original cast of the cigar.) I fully believed her when she told me that Randolph Churchill was the love of her life, and she had never married because of that.

Half Irish and half Jewish, Kay was the heiress of a Cleveland department store magnate. (Churchill himself had told her that some Jewish blood would enrich their thinning bloodline.) She possessed beauty and wit (along with connections) that led to a series of remarkable friendships. Luminaries including George Gershwin, Averell Harriman, and Joseph P. Kennedy became her confidants, and possibly more.

Before she died, Kay asked me to write a book about Churchill's prophecies, and so I did.

Chapter Twelve

Pentagon

Colin Powell: Four-Star General and U.S. Secretary of State

If John Kennedy's eloquence made Americans believe in themselves and reach for the stars, it was Richard Nixon's accomplishments that made their aspirations a reality: sending astronauts to the moon, funding gender equality in education, and setting the Affirmative Action programs in motion. It was a Republican administration that first promoted the African American Colin Powell as "their" black general, following his promotion to four-star rank in 1989.

Powell had heard me do my "Evening with Churchill" presentation once, and when Walter Annenberg asked him what he wanted to hear on our visit to Sunnylands, he said he wanted to see my Churchill show. Annenberg knew me from Philadelphia. So, in March 1994 I flew from Philly to L.A., then to Palm Beach, and on to Sunnylands to join a party of guests including Powell. Annenberg's driver picked me up at the airport. Once we were through the gate at Sunnylands, it was another mile before we got to the house. The room where I spoke was walled with Impressionist paintings—the originals, not copies. Present in the living room were President Gerald Ford, President Ronald Reagan, his wife Nancy Reagan, Colin and Alma Powell, and Regan's secretary of state, George Shultz, and his wife Helena.

Powell could deliver an inspiring speech about his career and the American Dream, but I lost some respect for him when he pandered to Walter Annenberg on that weekend I shared with him at Sunnylands. Not surprisingly for a Harlem-born son of Jamaican immigrants, Powell seemed overawed by his billionaire host. He is rightly a hero to Americans, but as secretary of state, he was often ambivalent and two sided in his support for George H. W. Bush during Desert Storm, and, later, in his leaks against the

Iraq war after his initial support. Moreover, as secretary of state, he often showed one face to President Bush and another to the media.

My favorite Powell is his wife Alma, an audiologist, child advocate, and children's book author. If not glamorous like Michelle Obama, she is a friendly, lovable woman who radiates warmth and affection. She told me that as long as she was Mrs. Powell, her husband would not run for president or vice president. She was sure that some crazy assassin would shoot him if he ran for president, or after he became president.

David Petraeus: Afghan War General and CIA Director

I sat at a roundtable next to General Petraeus when he was the featured speaker for a meeting of The Ends of the Earth. I must say that he did not have a prepossessing appearance. This was in 2009. The surge in Iran planned and orchestrated by him had worked, and now the new president, Barack Obama, had urged the winning general on to victory in Afghanistan. Petraeus, sitting down, delivered a cogent advocacy as to why the Afghanistan war was necessary and why the United States would win. Following the attacks on September 11, 2001, and the subsequent invasion of Afghanistan as a haven for terrorists, American troops had already been fighting there for some time.

Petraeus was mobbed afterwards by the military-friendly crowd. I too had found him impressive, but not persuasive. For almost a thousand years, Afghanistan had been a quagmire for its invaders. The valleys and the cities may be subdued, but not the mountains. The surge had worked on the flat desert terrain of Iraq, but in Afghanistan?

I shall never forget how this slight general with seemingly little presence kept the audience rapt, commanding a standing ovation with his understated analysis of the battle situation in Afghanistan. Notwithstanding his cogency and persuasive manner, he did not overcome my skepticism of military involvement in this tribal, mountainous terrain. Two world powers, Britain and Russia, had already proved the long-range futility of winning over its proud and independent people.

Initially, General Petraeus was proved right. The surge did achieve results in Afghanistan, and by the end of 2010, he would say that American forces had their teeth in the enemy's jugular vein and were not about to let go. But following the death of terror leader Osama bin Laden in a strike by Navy SEALs in May 2010, President Obama had already begun to "let go," scheduling drastic troop reductions for the Afghan war in 2011 and 2012. By 2015, the Taliban forces that bin Laden had led were resurgent, and as of January 2018, they were active in 70 percent of the country.

General Petraeus retired from the U.S. Army in August 2011, and was appointed Obama's CIA director that September. In 2012, it was reported that Petraeus was resigning as head of the CIA after little more than a year, because the FBI had come across his telephone calls to his mistress. I was dumbfounded. I would have suspected Presidents Nixon, Ford, or even Carter of having an inamorata. Petraeus looked more like a supply clerk than a Casanova. But you never know.

George S. Patton IV: Major General and Namesake of "Old Blood and Guts"

The great General Patton of World War II was many things: brilliant strategist, grandstander, inspirational leader, flamboyant four-star general, poet, mystic—but he wasn't a stuffed shirt. Yet his son and namesake—who attended The Hill School a decade before I did—could be pompous and socially awkward. Decades after the elder Patton's World War II victories, I had come to hear his son deliver a talk on his famous father at a dinner meeting of the Ends of the Earth. Before he spoke, I passed him a note describing how my father had introduced his father at the Hill–Lawrenceville football game, when young Patton was playing for Hill in 1941. He never read the note, because he thought I wanted his autograph. So he wrote on a napkin, "Best wishes, George Patton."

The note I handed to him also related a story about my father and his father at this Hill homecoming match in October 1941. The way I heard it, young Patton played end. At the close of the game, Hill was losing to Lawrenceville by six points. Standing in the end zone, he caught and then dropped a Hail Mary pass thrown by Hill. Colonel Patton, standing between my father and Hill's headmaster Jim Wendell, let loose a screed of Anglo-Saxon expletives directed at his own son.

The younger Patton curtly corrected me: His father had been a general at the time, not a colonel, and when he reamed his son out it was Lawrenceville who threw the game-ending pass. Young George had been the safety who missed the tackle that won the game for Lawrenceville.

We talked about the Patton memorial windows in the Episcopal Church of Our Savior in San Marino, California, featuring Nazi swastikas on the dragon that St. George is slaying. A smaller image of Patton riding one of his Third Army tanks appears in the same window. Commissioned by Patton's family after his death, this window symbolizes Patton fighting the dragon of evil. (I think Eisenhower was wrong in holding Patton back on the drive to Berlin. He should have been allowed to go after the Russians, but I understand the diplomatic restraints of Eisenhower.)

Young Patton had the opinions of his father, if neither his personality nor flair. But he served bravely in Vietnam, earning two-dozen military awards, including the Purple Heart and Bronze Star. He spent his last years as a gentleman farmer at Green Meadows, the family estate in South Hamilton,

Massachusetts. Visitors could buy fresh produce, honey, and other groceries in the large farm store, and gaze at a unique war memorial: Each of the farm's fields was named for a fallen soldier.

Alfred Gruenther: Four-Star General and Eisenhower's Head of NATO

Superficially, Al Gruenther was a smaller version of his close friend and military colleague. Both were prairie-raised, West Point-educated soldiers (Gruenther from Nebraska, Ike from Kansas) who could disarm with an engaging grin. Gruenther succeeded Major General Matthew Ridgeway as head of NATO in 1953, a position Eisenhower had left the previous year to run for president.

When I lunched with Gruenther at the Metropolitan Club in 1969 and greeted him as "General," he beamed, and told me to call him Al. (As a mark of respect, I didn't.)

Like Eisenhower, he was no showoff, as were Patton and even Mark Clark (under whom he was deputy commander of Austria at the close of World War II). He had risen to the acme of the military profession—a four-star general at age fifty-three, the youngest in U.S. Army history.

When he retired from NATO and from the army in 1956, he was selected for the best civilian post in Washington, the head of the American Red Cross. There, he could spend time with his old friend Ike, now the president. In spite of being nine years younger, Gruenther was Ike's best companion for relaxing, which usually meant playing bridge while sipping scotch at the White House or at Ike's Gettysburg farm.

Although these two descendants of the old settlers had much in common, there were differences. Underneath his disciplined facade, Ike had a smoldering temper. Gruenther was always genial. It wasn't a pose like Ike's. Eisenhower hid his barbed tongue from politicians, but when relaxing with his friends, their stupidities in bidding or playing bridge invited his sarcasm. (Never with Gruenther, however, who was a champion bridge player.)

Despite the close superficialities, Gruenther was a Catholic, the son of a well-to-do Platte Center newspaper editor and publisher. He had attended an elite Catholic prep school, the St. Thomas Military Academy in St. Paul, Minnesota. Unlike Ike, who graduated near the bottom of his class, Gruenther was fourth in his class at West Point. His intellect and powers of analysis led to his being nicknamed "The Brain" by his army colleagues.

I was not in a position to ask Gruenther questions about General Eisenhower and the war. So, instead, I asked him about Churchill and his visits to NATO headquarters outside Paris. He laughed, and told me a story about both leaders.

Gruenther met Churchill after he was re-elected in 1951. This took place in France, at Churchill's first meeting with Eisenhower since 1946, when Ike had joined Churchill in Virginia after the British statesman's Iron Curtain Speech in Fulton, Missouri. When Eisenhower met with Churchill and Gruenther, they sat down for lunch. Ike wanted to know how much Churchill was going to increase the British military contribution to NATO.

Churchill instead took note of the credenza behind the seated Eisenhower, and asked him whether it was a Louis XV.

Ike replied that he didn't know: The fancy sideboard had been there when he moved in. He went on to frame, in somber words, the Soviet military threat to Europe and to the world at large.

Churchill looked thoughtfully at the decanter on the credenza, and asked Ike whether it was made of Waterford crystal.

Meanwhile, Gruenther was kicking Ike under the table, to no avail. Ike continued on about military needs. Then Churchill interrupted again, asking Ike what was inside the decanter.

Ike turned around, saw the brandy-filled carafe, and realized his lack of hospitality. The brandy was dispensed, and Churchill lifted his glass in a toast to the military, and more importantly, its morale—a toast to lift its spirits.

Gruenther and I shared a laugh over Churchill's mischievous ragging of his old friend and ally.

Jean MacArthur: The General's Widow

For many years, I served on the board of the Pilgrims Society with Jean MacArthur, widow of the World War II five-star general. The society gathered once a year for a dinner meeting at the Waldorf Astoria. Jean lived in the suite on the top floor, where she and the general had resided since Truman dismissed him from the United Nations Command in the Korean War (for his alleged insubordination) in 1951. On his return to America, she rode with him in the biggest ticker-tape parade held in New York City since Lindbergh's in 1927.

It was my honor to usher her down in the elevator, although she could walk by herself to the table. On this evening in 1985, I told her that she looked much like an older version of Nancy Reagan: petite, elegant, with silver hair, still a stunning beauty. She smiled and thanked me for the compliment. She always referred to her husband as "the General." She liked Nixon and appreciated the warm handwritten letter he had written her on the general's death.

At the Waldorf dinner, I gave a toast. Jean's husband had been awarded the Congressional Medal of Honor for his gallant defense of the Philippines, and for battling the Japanese in the Pacific. When the Philippines fell, he

famously declared that he would return, a promise he kept—and which cul-
minated in his overseeing both the surrender and postwar reconstruction of
Japan. In 1942, he and his family escaped to Brisbane from the Philippines in
a PT boat, which took them through Pacific waters infested by Japanese subs.
In toasting the general's widow, I said, "But just as valorous was his young
wife, holding their two-year-old in her arms the whole while." She was
embarrassed by these words, because she thought they diminished "the General."

When I asked about her son, Arthur, she sadly admitted to having lost
contact with him—not even a Christmas card. After the general's death,
Arthur changed his name and disappeared; rumors swirled as to why. Some
say he simply got tired of the spotlight that had been fixed on him since
childhood, others that he is a concert pianist hiding out in Greenwich Village.
But it is more likely that he is working anonymously for The General Douglas MacArthur Memorial, a history museum and research foundation created
in memory of his heroic father.

Chapter Thirteen

Foreign Capitals

John Diefenbaker: Prime Minister of Canada

I met John Diefenbaker in December of 1964. He had served as prime minister of Canada from 1957 to 1963—the first conservative Canadian Prime Minister in more than two decades. I had been invited to address the Young Progressive Conservatives at the annual conference of the Canadian Conservative Party. The rightist party in America had almost been wiped out of existence in Goldwater's landslide defeat. But in Canada the previous year, Diefenbaker had been defeated by the Liberals in almost as close a race as Alec Douglas-Home in his loss to the Labourites in Britain.

Still, adding "Progressive" to the party name may have been a mistake in the long run. The Canadian Conservative Party had a choice: Lean left and possibly win a single contest, or campaign like Goldwater and lose overwhelmingly, but build a party for the future. This tendency to pass over true conservatives in favor of more liberal party members was brilliantly depicted, and condemned, in a definitive work within the canon of American conservatism: Phyllis Schlafley's *A Choice, Not an Echo* (1964). I delivered that same message to the Young Progressive Conservatives, but then Progressive Conservative Party Chairman Dalton Camp called on me to talk to the senior party delegates. Some of them were moving for the resignation of Diefenbaker, who was now their party chief and leader of the opposition. A motion by Progressive Conservative MP Leon Balcer called for a vote. Dalton interrupted, and said that a speech by James Humes had been scheduled (at very short notice!).

Halfway through my speech, Camp handed me a note that said, "Stop." I stopped, and Camp adjourned. Thus, there was no vote on ousting Diefenbaker. I wasn't allowed to talk to the press. My room reservation at the Château Laurier was canceled. I was hustled out by the Royal Mounted

Police and sent to the opposition leader's official residence to spend the night. Next day, the Mounties showed up and escorted me to the plane—no press, no questions, and no comments by me. I had done my duty for the conservative cause, and it was time for me to go.

The previous evening, Diefenbaker and his wife Olive had entertained me at their home. Olive, who was the domestic type, served us his favorite treat: a chocolate cake. Diefenbaker was a shaggy man with a voice like Everett Dirksen's, his skill for oratory, and his values. A trial lawyer from the Saskatchewan prairie, his hero was Lincoln. He loathed Kennedy as a jet-set type with "Hollywood" values, but admired Eisenhower. And he gave me a timely warning: Don't let Hollywood destroy the Norman Rockwell virtues of America!

Anatoly Gromyko: Son of Andrei Gromyko, Russian Diplomat

The scientist Anatoly Gromyko was a leading intellectual of the Institute for U.S. and Canadian Studies, a think tank within the Russian Academy of Sciences in Moscow. He was the son of Andrei Gromyko, the long-lived Soviet diplomat who served under every Soviet leader from Stalin to Khrushchev to Gorbachev, and retired as communism fell. The senior Gromyko somewhat resembled Richard Nixon. But the son, unlike the dour father, was dapper and genial. As the expert on American society in Russia, he spent most of his formative years in New York, when his father was the Soviet envoy. Anatoly's accent was American and his attire cosmopolitan. Though Marxist trained, he had absorbed the manners, values, and style of an American capitalist.

In June 1972 I was Anatoly's guest at the Institute for U.S. and Canadian Studies in Moscow. Even though I had recently retired from my post in the U.S. State Department, I was treated as a VIP, probably because I had once been a speechwriter in the Nixon White House. He told me that their required daily reading at the institute was *The Wall Street Journal*, whose very name proclaimed it a capitalist organ. He told me that he had liked the first page, third column, in particular—a report on American life.

In the summer of 1972, President Nixon had just completed the SALT arms talk pact with the USSR, and Gromyko made no attempt to mask his bias in the coming election between Nixon and Senator George McGovern, the Democratic nominee. Gromyko manifested his contempt for the American far left. His disdain was matched by his distrust of leftish intellectuals.

After the luncheon, Edmund Stevens, senior correspondent for Long Island *Newsday*, hosted American visitors on the lawn outside his log cabin house (one of the few left from the original Swedish settlement in Moscow). His son was Edmund Stevens Jr., a classmate of mine at Williams. I particularly remember the bearskin hat he wore in winter. He was a shy student, and I can't say we were friends.

His father, however, pretended that we were, and made me a guest of honor at this afternoon party.

I later said to some *Washington Post* reporters who were in attendance, "Ed Stevens is a nice guy, but he's a communist!"

They replied in chorus: "Oh, you Republicans, you always see communists everywhere."

"But when one of you attacked Nixon in your comments," I protested, "Stevens replied, 'No, he's a statesman,' and you countered, 'I remember in the Wallace campaign of 1948, you called Nixon America's number-one fascist.'" (This was during Nixon's exposure of Alger Hiss as a Soviet spy, and Henry Wallace's unsuccessful bid for the presidency as a Progressive Party candidate.)

I continued: "And Stevens responded: 'But he's matured since then.' I ask you this: Why would Stevens single me out—a low-ranking member of the State Department? Because he assumed I was close to Nixon, and for the Soviets, 'Nixon's the One' this year."

Aleksander Kwasniewski: President of Poland

To me, Aleksander Kwasniewski looked nothing like a president. With his piercing gray eyes and sharp features, he reminded me more of a city alderman as painted by Dürer than a heroic knight who could topple the legendary Lech Walesa in a free election. But maybe that's why he succeeded. Walesa had come to believe in the Lech myth—that he was a world symbol who could not be defeated by a former communist.

Kwasniewski had been an apparatchik in the Soviet-controlled Polish puppet government: sports commissioner, to be exact. The people mostly remembered him as the smiley, good-natured guy who told jokes and got himself photographed with Poland's soccer, track, and hockey stars. Unlike Lech, he was down to earth and not a bit preachy.

In 1995's upset election, Kwasniewski won, and Lech Walesa sulked. His rival was president of Poland for the next ten years.

I found myself sitting next to Kwasniewski at a dinner in March 2010 in New Zealand. I had no idea who he was, until the dinner host introduced him. I was there speaking about Churchill to a group of Asian premiers. Kwasniewski asked me about Churchill and was fascinated that I had met him. I asked him his opinion of Lech Walesa, and he told me that Walesa was a great man who became intoxicated with his greatness. When Pope John Paul died, Kwasniewski wanted Walesa to go to the funeral, realizing that if he didn't, it would make Kwasniewski look bad. So Kwasniewski arranged for a special plane to take Walesa alone, and he assented, but only if Kwasniewski guaranteed their paths wouldn't cross in Rome. Kwasniewski assured him of that, and they carefully orchestrated their schedules to achieve this. But, unfortunately, the call of nature intervened. The johns in the Vatican are not so grand as the outside marble would lead one to believe. Kwasniewski was led down various subterranean tunnels until the ultimate destination was reached. Pipes hung here on the ceilings and the urinals were cracked and yellow. To his dismay, Walesa was addressing one of them. When he was finished with his business, Kwasniewski paused, summoned up his courage, and extended his hand. Walesa gasped, shook his head, and then hesitantly grasped it.

The ice was broken. Some awkward amenities were exchanged. Eventually, the two men found some common agreement: They both cordially disliked Kwasniewski's handpicked successor, who appeared in 2005, because his policies were not what he promised. That successor was President Lech Kaczynski, whose twin brother Jaroslaw later became prime minister. In 2010, President Kaczynski died in a plane crash along with scores of Polish government and military leaders who were traveling to Russia on a mission of reconciliation and healing. Amazingly, both Walesa and Kwasniewski traveled together for Kaczynski's state funeral in Poland.

His Imperial Majesty Haile Selassie I: Emperor of Ethiopia

Haile Selassie was the only modern monarch to have inspired a religious cult. Standing only five feet four inches tall, and weighing about one hundred pounds, this devout Orthodox Christian dominated the world stage during the 1930s. The invasion of his kingdom by a fascist dictator would cause the League of Nations to collapse. Yet his name is hardly known today except to historians, and those for whom his cult endures.

I had the opportunity to approach him in the White House at the state dinner given for him by President Nixon in July 1969. At seventy-eight years old, the diminutive ruler radiated majesty, like the Biblical Solomon from whom he claimed descent. As Nixon's speechwriter, I cited the story from Kings: The angel of the Lord visits the boy Solomon and asks the lad what he needs to govern his country. Is it riches, strength, or power? Solomon answers, "I want the gift of an understanding heart"—in other words, the gift of wisdom (1 Kings 3:9).

As I wrote for Nixon: "So it is with His Majesty. He has wisdom. He has had a long life, and, I know from personal experience, an understanding heart." Nixon was referring not only to the hospitality he and his wife Pat had received on their visit to Ethiopia, but also to the hospitals and universities its emperor had founded. When Selassie was told that I had helped craft the toast, his penetrating eyes surveyed me appreciatively.

Known to his people as the "King of Kings, Elect of God, and Conquering Lion of the Tribe of Judah," Selassie lent his name to a worldwide cult, the Rastafarians, which derives from Ras ("Duke") Tafari, one of his titles. When Selassie was crowned in 1930, the Rastafarians saw this as fulfillment of a Biblical prophecy. To them he is immortal, God incarnate, a pan-African messiah who will lead the African diaspora back to their homeland. Selassie made no such claims about himself. But when this African royal leader visited Jamaica in 1966, he was credited with ending a drought, and the island-dwellers felt affirmed in their iconic worship.

In 1935, Italian fascist dictator Benito Mussolini sought revenge for Italy's defeat by Ethiopia in the First Italo-Abyssinian War, and a later failed attempt to conquer the African nation. Using a trumped-up border dispute with the Italian colony of Eritrea as his excuse, Mussolini sent armies to invade Ethiopia. Britain's Foreign Secretary Anthony Eden asked the League of Nations (a forerunner of the UN) to take action. But France, nervous about its southern border with Mussolini, chose to appease the fascist bully. Mussolini accused Selassie of barbarous un-Christian cruelties—for example, beheading as the punishment for capital crime. In fact, Ethiopia was the oldest Christian country in the world. Yet the League ignored his pleas for help, and stood by as Mussolini conquered Ethiopia. After that, the League of Nations never regained respect as a protector of peace.

British forces liberated Ethiopia in 1941, and Emperor Haile Selassie returned to the throne, where he would reign until his death in 1975.

David Lange: Prime Minister of New Zealand

When I was on a speaking tour of New Zealand for the United States Information Agency in 1985, I was invited to have coffee with Prime Minister David Lange at his office in Wellington. He asked me about Nixon and Reagan. He admired Nixon for his China breakthrough, but withheld praise for Reagan, whom he found to be shallow and simplistic. Lange hoped that Reagan would come to terms with Gorbachev, who was a new kind of communist, as he said.

Lange was a portly man with an infectious smile and a hearty laugh. He had this to say about America's Republicans, who were pushing for a balanced budget amendment: All Congress had to do was stop spending.

I replied, "As a fellow man of broad proportions, I have talked to a doctor about having my jaw wired shut."

Taking my cue, he told me that all I had to do was stop eating! We shared a good laugh at this joke.

I asked Lange about his role in the decision to cease having the U.S. fleet call on New Zealand. Was this peace move designed to pacify the left, when

New Zealand's treasury had no more resources for increasing pensions and welfare?

No, he told me: It was a popular move that had been approved in the Labour Party Convention, as New Zealand's contribution to maneuvering the United States away from confrontational policies. He had liked Nixon's words: to move from the era of confrontation to the era of negotiation, which I helped frame for the president while working in the State Department.

Paul-Henri Spaak: Belgian Prime Minister and Socialist

This Belgian statesman was one of the great diplomats of the post-war period. During World War II, he was a leader in the Belgian underground resistance against the Nazis. He was also one of the first Europeans to push the idea of a European Economic Community. In 1944, he would help unite Benelux (Belgium, the Netherlands, and Luxembourg) as a single economic entity, a forerunner of the later EEC. For these reasons, he is considered one of the founding fathers of the European Union.

Spaak might have been saddened to know what would become of his brainchild sixty years on: that the EU would increasingly be defined by majority-Muslim mass migration, with the nations of Europe reacting characteristically to this aspect of central control out of Brussels. Repercussions would include Britain's choice to "go it alone," with their June 2016 "Brexit" vote to leave the European bloc; Poland's reaffirmation of its identity as a conservative Christian nation; and Germany's elections of September 2017, which sent nationalists to the Bundestag for the first time since World War II.

In April 1953, I was at Stowe, and about to start my spring vacation of five weeks. Meg Fugit, a friend of my mother's, invited me to stay with her. Her first husband had been Ernie Fisher-Wood, the son of General Eric Fisher-Wood. He and his Russian wife, Vera, were the bridge-playing partners of my mother and stepfather in Bedford. Young Wood had died in the Battle of the Bulge, and his widow had married Warren Fugit, who operated as a lobbyist for organizations like NATO and Benelux that served to unite Europe.

The Fugits were wonderful to me. They took me to lunch atop the Eiffel Tower, on a picnic at Fontainebleau, and to a dinner with some visiting British MPs on a boat going down the Seine. One night when Warren was out, Mrs. Fugit cooked me a spaghetti dinner and played records from the new Broadway hit musical *Wonderful Town*. Then one night came a problem. The famous Paul-Henri Spaak was coming to Paris and needed a bedroom. So he shared the guest bedroom with me.

Spaak had a round face, a balding head, and black-framed glasses. I told him, "You look like Winston Churchill."

He agreed with that assessment, but said that while he looked like Winston Churchill and spoke like Charles Boyer, he would much rather look like Charles Boyer and speak like Winston Churchill. I instantly took a liking to him, and he quizzed me on politics; for example, what party I belonged to ("Republican"), and how I felt about Joe McCarthy ("I despise him").

I said I thought he would like our new president, General Eisenhower. He did indeed, and from personal experience, having worked with him at NATO. But Spaak was a socialist, and told me that he would have voted for Adlai Stevenson. His grudge against Eisenhower was that he shorted Belgium on NATO defense money. Yet he did add that Eisenhower, next to Churchill, was the most popular person in Belgium.

Soong Mei-ling, Madame Chiang Kai-Shek: First Lady of the Republic of China

At a lunch at The Brook club in 2005, I asked my fellow diners, "Who is the only world leader of World War II still alive?" No one could give the right answer: Madame Chiang Kai-Shek, wife of the Chinese president and Generalissimo. Some of the younger men questioned her designation as a "world leader," asserting that she was only a wife, like Eleanor Roosevelt or Clementine Churchill. But unlike those two great ladies, Madame Chiang attended all the major wartime meetings with her husband: the Cairo Conference in 1943, for example. And unlike most dignitaries' wives, when she visited the White House, she participated in the substantive discussions. Richard Nixon once told me that Chiang was the dull-witted one and his wife had the brains. Interestingly, she had nothing kind to say about Nixon after his 1972 mission to China!

She was born Soong Mei-ling, the daughter of "Charlie Soong," a Methodist missionary turned millionaire. Having been educated at Wellesley College (Class of 1917), at her thirty-fifth class reunion she was introduced by my wife Dianne. Of the three Soong sisters, one wed a descendant of Confucius, while the third married a financial wizard. Soong Mei-ling brought wealth to the Generalissimo, while, at her insistence, he converted to Christianity.

In 1998, I attended a dinner at the National Arts Club in New York, with Madame Chiang Kai-Shek in attendance; she was giving some of her art treasures to the club. When the Nixon visit to Beijing was mentioned, the eyebrows of the centenarian rose, and then she smiled. The frail but elegant lady would no longer voice political opinions. When she died at the age of 105 in 2003, the People's Republic of China sent a huge floral wreath to the Chinese Consulate in New York.

Mahmoud Abbas: President of the State of Palestine and Palestinian National Authority

I never personally met Mahmoud Abbas, but I did interface with him on closed-circuit television, in August 2005. His speechwriters had called the U.S. State Department, and they recommended me as a speechwriter to counsel him on a talk he was giving. Yasser Arafat had died in November of the previous year, and in January, Abbas had been elected his successor. He was considered dull compared to the charismatic and demagogic Arafat. The talk had been arranged by Colorado State University, to be delivered on a closed television circuit. Present on the Jerusalem end were a PLO press officer, a speechwriter, a woman aide, and Abbas. Abbas never spoke. I stressed that he could be eloquent without being demagogic. "Don't spout an anti-Israel rant," I counseled him. "Speak hope, not hate, as Doctor King did."

Abbas registered no response. He seemed nervous, playing with his hands, staring away from the camera. I talked about using Mohammed's vision of a new day for Jerusalem, and gave them this quote from the Koran, "Ye who voluntarily performeth worthy works, Allah is aware and appreciative" (al-Baqarah, 2:158). It got no response. Abbas seemed edgy and hesitant. "Rhetoric should not be rant," I told them. "Ignite dreams, not fears."

Abbas seemed like a technocrat, not a leader; a gray bureaucrat trying to succeed a vibrant, popular hero to his country. Accordingly, he felt he had to spew the "hate Israel" line.

Kurt Waldheim: United Nations Secretary-General and President of Austria

Kurt Waldheim served as UN secretary-general between 1972 and 1982, and later, as president of Austria. He resigned from the UN as rumors of a Nazi past rose around him, eroding his support. Revelations about his activities during World War II nearly derailed his 1986 presidential campaign: He had lied about the duration of his service in the Wehrmacht, and may have known about German atrocities committed against Jews and other civilians.

We hosted him at a dinner in 1971, when I worked for the U.S. State Department. My cousin John Humes, the U.S. ambassador to Austria, had known Waldheim in Vienna, and asked us to entertain the former Austrian foreign minister. Our other guests included personnel from the White House and the State Department.

Slim, hawk-nosed, and immaculately dressed, Waldheim claimed that he had met us at the U.S. Embassy in Vienna, but we had no recollection of it. He was urbane, polished, and accommodating, and gallantly kissed my wife's hand. He probably thought we were as rich as John Humes—not that we were living on my government salary. I made no attempt to dissuade him from his misperception of our status. On the contrary, I asked if he enjoyed sailing the Danube on John Humes's yacht, *Scoop*. His eyes lit up.

At that time, Waldheim had just run for president of Austria and lost. The year after our dinner, this forgettable bureaucrat of a man was elected UN secretary-general. Goethe said that all our earthly debts must be paid. Waldheim would find this out. Yet the perceived persecution of this long-serving diplomat caused a backlash in Austria, and in 1986, his countrymen elected him president—a position he would hold for six years.

Giovanni Leone: President of Italy

In August 1973, I was invited to a dinner at the Palazzo del Quirinale in Rome, the Buckingham Palace of Italy. I had arranged a meeting with Pope Paul for the chancellor of the Philadelphia Bar, my friend Joe Bongiovanni. We were taking a Uniform Reciprocal Peace bill, introduced by Pennsylvania Senator Hugh Scott, to Italy in order to get the pope's blessing. Because the president of Italy knew about our engagement with the secretary of the Vatican, we were special guests at this dinner with Nixon's ambassador to Italy, John Volpe.

I sat across from President Leone. Although as president, he might qualify automatically as a statesman, he didn't look like one. He was five foot two, with a rotund figure. His name means "Lion" in Italian, but it should have been "Teddy Bear." And he was a jolly old soul. He asked me where I was from. When I said I was born in Williamsport and lived in Philadelphia, the Neapolitan Leone claimed relatives in both places. In my toast I gave a quotation in Latin, since it was better than my Italian. To salute him, I cited a poet of ancient Rome in a distinctly American context: "The United States has these words on the dollar bill, 'Annuit Coeptis'—'favor our undertakings'—a quote from Virgil."

Leone reminded me of an American backslapping state senator from Philadelphia I knew in Harrisburg. Little did I know that five years later, Leone would resign due to an accusation of taking bribes from Lockheed Martin. This unproven charge was leveled at a number of high-profile Italian politicians at a time when the aircraft manufacturer was said to be urging a deal with the Italian military: the purchase of Lockheed Martin's Hercules aircraft. He was the first and only president of Italy to resign under such circumstances, and died in 2001 at the age of ninety-three.

Miklos Horthy: Admiral and Regent of Hungary

In January 1957, I was en route from Naples to Madrid, where I was attending classes at the university. While on the train in Spain, I happened to share a compartment with a distinguished-looking gentleman. He had thinning white hair, sat militarily erect, and was clad in a navy-blue double-breasted suit. It was Admiral Miklos Horthy, the former regent of Hungary. He had made himself the autocratic head of his country following the defeat of the Central Powers, during the Versailles Peace Conference in 1919. At the time, he denounced U.S. President Woodrow Wilson and French Prime Minister Georges Clemenceau for the harsh conditions they imposed on Germany, and the breakup of the old Austro-Hungarian Empire. This Hungarian nobleman did not rant, but spoke in a commanding voice that suggested both his military service and aristocratic origins.

Horthy announced himself regent in 1920, in lieu of the exiled Hapsburg monarchs, and served in that capacity until 1944, when he handed control of Hungary over to the Allies. He had joined forces with Hitler only reluctantly, due to his hatred of communism, and was the only Axis leader to survive the war. Following years of exile in Portugal, this Hungarian patriot was returned to his native country for burial.

Horthy told me that Franco copied his *in loco parentis* position, having acted in place of the Spanish King Alfonso, who was in exile in Rome. He admired Franco for defeating the Soviet-backed Republicans. But Horthy had harsh words for Eisenhower for not backing the Hungarians in 1956 against the Soviets, after all the "liberation" talk by those in his administration, including Dulles.

He liked Vice President Nixon, and thought he had a prominent future. He regretted Joe McCarthy's downfall and demise. This statesman of the old school was gracious and grandfatherly to a young college student from Pennsylvania.

Delegate Con: Confucius Descendant and Heir

In February 2012, Dianne and I traveled to China to celebrate the fortieth anniversary of Nixon's historic visit to the formerly inaccessible communist nation. In Beijing, we were introduced to Delegate Con, a direct descendant of Confucius, the Chinese sage and founder of Confucianism. Confucius was born around 550 BC, and developed Confucianism as a humanistic and ethical philosophy rather than a religion, but its students around the world have made it into a cult. The philosopher's descendant was born almost two millennia later, and lived in the northern province of Shantung. A man of scholarly pursuits, he looked more like a Tibetan Buddhist priest than a politician who had been elected as a delegate to the Chinese Assembly that met in Beijing. His position owed more to his ancestry than to his work for the Communist Party.

Con entertained us at his modest home, where we enjoyed some simple refreshments. I asked him about WEI-JI—two picture symbols for "danger" and "opportunity" in Chinese that signify "crisis" when joined together. The implication is that once the danger has been surmounted, the crisis may reveal itself as an opportunity in disguise. I used this concept in speeches for Nixon, and since then, it has gained worldwide popularity in many different contexts. Con thought that it could be attributed to Lao Tse, author of the *Tao te Ching*—the fundamental text of Taoism. This sister philosophy of Confucianism stresses a "way," or Tao, based on religious piety, humility, and harmony with the universe.

I shared one of my favorite anecdotes about Con's ancestor, who was minister and counselor to a new young ruler of China. Upon his accession, the emperor asked him, "What is the best advice you can give me about governing the Middle Kingdom?" Confucius answered: "The approach to any problem must be that you first must define the problem." Indeed, no problem can be solved, or even truly identified, unless one has determined the cause. Con agreed with me that this was wise advice for any leader, in any place and time.

He apologized that he had few relics in his humble abode, because the Nationalists had taken everything of value to Taiwan. I didn't say that it was a good thing, although I had seen some of these Chinese imperial pieces that had been appropriated from private homes. The Red Army of Mao—who were anti-Confucius—would have destroyed everything.

Li Min: Daughter of Mao Zedong

It was February 21, 2012, the fortieth anniversary of Nixon's opening visit to China. Four decades ago, in this same vast room of Diaoyutai—the state guesthouse—Premier Zhou Enlai had dined with President Nixon, who later spoke with Chairman Mao Zedong. And on this day, Mao's daughter Li Min was our hostess.

One look at Li Min could suggest that she was the daughter of the Red chairman, but she acted more like a grandmother. She was eager to see the pictures of our four grandchildren when my wife, Dianne, who was seated to her left, showed them to her. In fact, she asked my wife for her autograph, and the next day she had her son-in-law deliver a red cashmere scarf as her personal gift. The saturnine face of Li Min radiated a benignity that had been absent in her father. Her eyes twinkled with an animation and enthusiasm that were in contrast to the black-and-gray-patterned smock she wore.

About twenty-five guests were seated at the huge round table. They included officials from the Chinese Foreign Ministry, and notables from the United States, such as Edward Nixon, the late president's brother, and Devon Nixon, the great-nephew of both Edward and Richard. (Devon was fluent in Mandarin, and at that time, a resident of Shanghai.) My wife and I were also present: I as a former Nixon White House speechwriter, and my wife Dianne as a Nixon staff member when he was president, and earlier, when he was vice president.

I noticed that President Barack Obama had not sent representatives to observe the ceremonies that honored Nixon. Instead, Obama would later host a reception in Washington honoring President Carter, who had formally recognized China in January 1979. This was Obama's way of dismissing Nixon's efforts. A staff member from the Consulate General in Shanghai told Ed Nixon and me that the Chinese people honor Carter as much as Nixon. But we did not hear Carter's name mentioned by any Chinese people. And Li Min was hosting this banquet to honor Nixon, not Carter. With the help of the interpreter, who sat right behind her, she indicated pride in observing that this was the first time the two families—Mao's and Nixon's—were together.

Li Min stressed that this state banquet in honor of Nixon and his delegation was of great import. Certainly the choice of dining hall implied it—it had high ceilings with gold walls that were hung with ancient Chinese pen sketches. The floor was covered with a yellow oriental rug bearing a few rectangular figures. Our place settings, with our names in Chinese and English, were set around an immense lazy susan that featured a score of fish, eel, and shrimp delicacies. Our dinner plates were gold china that had come from the last empress's palace.

Li Min herself was modest and unassuming. She dismissed her sentencing in the Cultural Revolution as proper and just, as her father wanted her to experience firsthand what peasant life was like. Later, our Chinese friend—a Shanghai native who was both interpreter and guide—informed us that Li Min had hauled two honey buckets hanging on two ends of a stick across her shoulders as her penance in the Cultural Revolution. When my wife asked for the date of her birthday, Li Min replied that she didn't know, but that she was born in the Long March. She did reveal to us the untold story about her father's meeting with President Nixon that February. After her father's stroke in 1971, Mao had been moved into his daughter's house in the imperial and restricted enclave. Mao was in a coma, and Li Min wanted to be at his side to administer to him.

Later, she found out that press reports from the United States had criticized Nixon's decision to go to China because the Chinese gave no assurance of his meeting Mao. In the eyes of the media, the president would suffer a huge loss of face when he met with Premier Zhou Enlai rather than Mao, the Chinese chief of state. For their part, as she explained, the Chinese government could not let the people know that their leader was in a coma.

Oddly enough, Mao awoke about the time Air Force One was circling Beijing. Speaking in a croak, he told his daughter that he wanted to see President Nixon. His aides quickly phoned Zhou Enlai to let him know. Li Min also explained the mystery of the figures seen hovering around her father in photos, who were not identified as Mao's government advisors.

They were, she explained, doctors whom she could see sticking her father with needles and stuffing him full of pills. The physicians warned her father that he could tolerate only five, maybe seven minutes of conversation. Instead, Mao spoke with President Nixon for seventy-one minutes.

At the state banquet that evening, I delivered the toast: "To courage. For the physical courage of Chairman Mao, who rose from his near deathbed to greet President Nixon. And, for the spiritual courage of President Nixon, who, despite the opposition of the State Department, persisted in going!"

When the translator finished, Li Ming nodded and put both thumbs up. Later, she told us the two American names most revered by the Chinese people: Lincoln and Nixon.

His Serene Highness Heinrich IV, Prince Reuss of Kostritz: Head of the German Princely House of Reuss

Prince Heinrich's forefathers ruled the Principality of Reuss, a tiny royal realm in Thuringia that was part of East Germany during the Cold War. One of the oldest royal families in Europe, the House of Reuss dates to the year 1010, and names each of its princes Heinrich after a twelfth-century Holy Roman Emperor. At the Congress of Vienna, as the proud sovereign of this small state, an early-nineteenth-century Prince Heinrich of Reuss had insisted that he be accorded no fewer cannon salutes than the ruler of any other European principality.

I came to meet Prince Heinrich IV of Reuss (the fourth Heinrich in his branch of the family) through Eliska Hasek Coolidge, my colleague in the Nixon White House, who had emigrated from Czechoslovakia. Her grandfather, the mayor of Prague, was executed by the Nazis when he refused to turn over a list of Jews in the city. When the communists took over Czechoslovakia, the mayor's son and family escaped to Austria. Prince Reuss offered them refuge in his schloss, the picturesque Castle Ernstbrunn in Lower Austria, where he had moved after fleeing the Red Army.

In 1971, Dianne and I were staying with my cousin John Humes, Nixon's Austrian ambassador, at the embassy in Vienna. John told us to host Prince and Princess Reuss at the embassy because he and his wife had an engagement outside of the city. As if I were preparing for a toast to a visiting sovereign, I did my homework on him. Prince Reuss was married to Princess Marie Luise of Salm-Horstmar, who was a second cousin of Prince Bernard, the consort of Queen Beatrice of the Netherlands. He also had a child with her, another Prince Heinrich. Heinrich senior kept his own private zoo at the castle, with elephants, lions, giraffes, and monkeys, and also some diminutive Chinese deer. On his estate, he let European red deer range with the other varieties. After a little more research, I learned they were subject to disease, although a new preventive serum was effective with the red deer.

The dinner went well, and afterwards, I asked Prince Reuss about the deer and the serum. (Unfortunately, the princess spoke little English.) Since I had brought up deer, the prince suggested we visit the castle and do some shooting. I begged off, but we promised to do it the following year, if we returned.

The next year, in June 1972, we came back from Moscow to pick up our daughters Mary and Rachel in Vienna. I was tired, and didn't want to drive south without a rest, but "Circus! Circus!" were the cries I heard from the girls. They would go with their mother to the circus in Vienna (where they both volunteered to ride the elephant), while I pretended to be a game hunter on Prince Reuss's estate. Unfortunately, I had no clothes with me except the three-piece pinstripe suit I had worn to lunch with Soviet diplomat Anatoly Gromyko. Neither did I have a rifle. The next morning, Dianne, Mary, Rachel, and Princess Reuss went to the circus, while I planned to practice shooting with a loaned game rifle. Standing next to the target was the young heir! I felt like the Swiss hero William Tell shooting an apple off his son's head—I had better shoot straight. Fortunately, I declined. I was grabbed by the arm and taken to the tower from which I would shoot my deer. With me was the head game warden of Austria, and a professional guide who had escorted the King of Spain and Marshall Tito on shooting occasions.

Climbing up the steel-runged ladder in my three-piece suit and black dress shoes was a scary ordeal. I felt like Jack on the beanstalk, going up, up, and up. Awaiting me were the game warden and the world-traveled guide. As the afternoon turned to twilight, I fired and missed. Their pride was hurt—forget about mine—so I had to get my deer! They turned the searchlight on. Talk about a deer trapped in the headlights! I still missed.

My descent was one of despair and disgrace. For dinner, we had a stag bagged by the princess. We washed it down with some Georgia champagne I had brought back from Russia.

In 1975, Prince Reuss established a wild-animal park as a tourist attraction at Castle Ernstbrunn, and today, no one is shooting at anything.

Alexander Kerensky: Minister–Chairman of the Russian Provisional Government, July–October 1917

In September 1952, I was preparing to sail to England on the Queen Mary, to take up my English-Speaking Union fellowship at Stowe. Before we left on this most significant journey, my mother, stepfather, brother Graham, and I spent a long weekend in New York City. We stayed at the Hotel Pennsylvania across from the old Pennsylvania Station railroad stop.

While I was in town, I had been invited to pay a visit to my old school friend Dean Holbrook. Alphabetical seating in the Hill School Chapel had initially brought us together, and we remained good friends. When I arrived at Dean's apartment, he asked me if I would mind if we stopped by the apartment next door to look in on an elderly neighbor, a Russian emigré who had taught Dean to play chess. The neighbor turned out to be Alexander Kerensky, the last democratically elected Russian premier. At age seventy-one, his once-dark hair had turned snow white. A moderate socialist revolutionary in 1905, he became a prominent lawyer and was elected to the Duma.

In 1915, the war aims of Russia, now allied with France and Britain, were questioned within that nation's governing body. Kerensky supported the war effort, and because his dramatic oratorical skills resulted in popular support, he was made prime minister. He advocated women's suffrage and freedom of the press. When the Bolsheviks seized power during the October Revolution of 1917, Kerensky escaped to the front, from which he fled Russia. Following World War I, he emigrated to New York. Told later of his eloquence in the Duma, I found him to be a soft-spoken, distinguished man. In the election year of 1952, he preferred Adlai Stevenson to Eisenhower. He was not fond of either Churchill or Eisenhower because they had cooperated with Stalin, whom Kerensky hated bitterly.

Jack Lynch: Prime Minister of Ireland

I met the *Taoiseach* ("the chief," in Gaelic) on St. Patrick's Day in 1970. He was the featured speaker at the annual dinner of the Society of the Friendly Sons of St. Patrick in Philadelphia. Curiously, the society had as its founders both Protestants and Catholics who had emigrated from the Old Sod to America in the eighteenth century. Its stated mission was the relief of emigrants from Ireland, regardless of faith or creed, and the society's by-laws required it to have both Catholic and Protestant members. Today, few Protestants seek to join, but I was recruited, and—as a White House speechwriter at the time—asked to say a few words.

Lynch had spent the day in Washington, during which he stopped by the White House to greet President Nixon. He was offered the use of Air Force One to get to the dinner that evening in Philadelphia, and I managed to hitch a ride. Upon boarding, I berated the plane staff for not having any Bushmills (Irish whiskey) on board, but Lynch shamed me by ordering a single-malt scotch. Short and balding, he was not an imposing figure. But when you talked with him, he won you over with his open face and wide smile. He found Nixon to be well briefed and knowledgeable. Of course, we talked about the Irishman James Hoban, the architect of the White House.

I was most curious about Lynch's relationship with Eamon de Valera, the grand old man of the Irish Republic. De Valera had refused to sign the Anglo–Irish Treaty in 1921, and the violent conflict that followed ultimately led to Irish independence. Michael Collins, one of the delegates who supported the treaty, was later assassinated while fighting de Valera's Irish Republican Army, in his role as army commander of the Irish Free State.

Lynch told me he was from County Cork, and read Law at the National University at Cork. Upon completing his law degree, he decided to enter politics, although up until that point he had shown little interest in it. There were two major political parties in Ireland at the time, Sinn Fein and Fianna Fáil, the latter of which had been founded by de Valera. To choose which one he would join, Lynch flipped a coin, and the more conservative Fianna Fáil won the toss.

De Valera, tottering and almost blind, was still a towering figure in Irish politics. Lynch made friends easily, and showed the eagerness of someone who was ambitious. Despite this, or perhaps because of it, Lynch caught the attention of de Valera, who advanced him to the front ranks of the party. De Valera had warned him that he was no ideologue. Indeed, as Michael Collins had found to his cost, de Valera's methods were both pragmatic and subtle. Lynch told me that he liked Nixon, but that JFK was seen as a saint in Ireland. At the dinner that evening, his self-deprecatory style and easy manner charmed his audience.

Chapter Fourteen

Courthouse

Earl Warren: Governor of California and U.S. Supreme Court Chief Justice

I saw Earl Warren three times in my life, and of those, I talked to him on two occasions. The time I was simply an observer, I was watching him deliver the inaugural oath to President Nixon in January 1969, a ceremonial duty he must have loathed. On the California delegation's train to the Chicago Republican Convention in 1952, Senator Nixon had lobbied for Eisenhower despite the fact that the whole group was pledged to a favorite son, Earl Warren, who was then governor of California. The decades-long feud between Nixon and Warren (whose court Nixon characterized as being soft on criminals) lasted through Warren's retirement—and even onto his deathbed, from which he begged the remaining justices to release Nixon's Watergate tapes.

On my wife's birthday in March 1956, I took her to the best restaurant in DC—The Diplomat. We wanted chocolate soufflés for dessert, and they had to be brought from the Mayflower Hotel, two blocks away. Warren was at the next table, and we watched him drink two huge glasses of milk (the rest had wine), his hands as big as bear paws wrapped around the glass. He was with his daughter Virginia, who married TV anchorman John Daly. I congratulated him on his 9–0 Supreme Court decision in 1954's landmark desegregation case, *Brown v. Board of Education.*

The next time I talked to him was in Vienna in 1971, on the terrace of John Humes's ambassadorial residence. Warren had retired in the summer of 1969. I told him that I had written Nixon's introduction of his successor, Warren Earl Burger. Warren laughed when I told him that my brother Sam's crush on his honey-blonde daughter led him to campaign on his behalf for president in 1952. Aware that John Humes and I both worked for Nixon,

Warren and I avoided that subject. I brought up Dewey and his surprise loss in the 1948 campaign. Warren told me that in Truman's opinion, if the ticket had been Warren–Dewey, the GOP would have won. He confessed that he liked Truman, and thought Dewey was arrogant.

Partly because Governor Warren avoided personal partisan attacks against Truman, Californian went Democrat in the 1948 election. In fact, Warren divulged that some of his own family voted for Truman in 1948. He also said he was surprised when Ike picked him and not Dewey to be chief justice. Towards the close of our conversation, Warren told me that the legacy of his career on the court was fairness—that was his touchstone.

Antonin Scalia: Supreme Court Justice

I was first introduced to Scalia in 1997 at the Bohemian Grove, a campground of the Bohemian Club—an exclusive men's club in California. Revelers at the Bohemians' yearly gatherings among the giant redwoods of the Golden State include diplomats, entertainers, entrepreneurs, and former presidents. Later, I sat next to Scalia at an Ends of the Earth dinner at the Union Club in New York. He told me he was an originalist, as far as the Constitution was concerned. He told me that he took the Founding Fathers at their word, and didn't try to invent what they would have said if they had lived today. He also had little regard for amendments to the Constitution—be it the ERA, the balanced budget, or the 'defense' of marriage.

Scalia believed that under the Constitution, the states have jurisdiction over areas such as alcohol, marriage, abortion, and guns. He opposed amendments to forbid gay marriage because they trivialized the Constitution, as he told me. He went on to say that if Utah wanted to legalize polygamy, it would be all right with him, and that New York and California could approve gay marriage if they were so inclined.

He also told me that Supreme Court Justices cannot be eunuchs, and that while their politics are part of them, they must be ruled by precedent. In other words, he said, they should judicate, not legislate.

Brilliant and scholarly, he was definitely opinionated as well. I agreed with most of his opinions, except one: He was anti-Stratfordian. That is, he thought that Edward de Vere, Seventeenth Earl of Oxford, was the real Shakespeare, and Will the glove-maker's son was a sham cooked up to disguise the poet and playwright's true identity.

Harrie Brigham Chase: Jurist from Vermont

On the U.S. Court of Appeals for the Second Circuit, he had been the stupid one. The person who voiced this opinion was Judge Harrie Chase. We were staying at his house in Brattleboro, Vermont in July 1958, when I was an usher at a grade-school friend's wedding. By his own admission, he was no intellectual, but was known as a man of values and integrity who preferred competence over cronyism.

Chase, who was seventyish, looked to be about fifty—lean, distinguished, and handsome. He was a former associate justice of the Vermont Supreme Court. In 1929, President Calvin Coolidge appointed him to the noteworthy U.S. Court of Appeals for the Second Circuit, whose jurisdiction included New York, Connecticut, and Vermont. He was appointed Chief Judge on the court in 1953, with President Eisenhower's chief of staff, Sherman Adams, and Vermont Senator George Aiken endorsing him.

Also serving on the Second Circuit was the greatest judge never appointed to the Supreme Court: Learned Hand, author of "The Spirit of Liberty," a stirring patriotic speech delivered to one hundred and fifty thousand newly naturalized citizens in New York's Central Park on "I Am An American Day" in 1944. Hand's cousin was Augustus Hand, also an appeals court and district court judge. Another jurist on the court during Chase's term was Martin Thomas Manton, who bears the ignominy of being the first federal judge ever convicted of bribery. Chase told me that if he was the dumbest, Manton was the brightest one on that court. Shrewdly, he only took bribes in cases where he had the deciding vote. Then he would write the most scholarly and brilliant opinion. That's why it was hard for the government to nail him on taking money.

Chase was engaging, humorous, and far too modest about his own legal success. Another thing he told me was that Alger Hiss was guilty as sin. His court approved of the lower court's conviction of Hiss for perjury. He was, Chase declared, a proven communist. Later history has confirmed it.

Chapter Fifteen

Church

Marion Gordon "Pat" Robertson: Media Mogul and Evangelist

In 2000, I asked my son-in-law, a Phi Beta Kappa history and literature major at Harvard, "Who was the only winner in a 1988 primary whose great-grandfather was president of the United States?" He reflected on who ran in 1988 besides George H. W. Bush. He knew it wasn't Michael Dukakis. He ventured, "Al Gore." "No," I told him. The answer was Pat Robertson, who won the Iowa caucus. His presidential forebear was Benjamin Harrison. I had written some speeches for Robertson in 1987. One was for a meeting at the Copacabana in New York, where Robertson said, "My great-grandfather was right when he stated, 'The U.S. can't be a world policeman.'"

When many think of Robertson, the televangelist comes to mind: the man who said (along with Jerry Falwell) that 9-11 might have come about because of America's descent into sin. They associate him with other preachers such as Falwell, Oral Roberts, and Jimmy Swaggart. Robertson may have come from the South, but he was no cracker. He was a Phi Beta Kappa who attended Washington and Lee University and then Yale Law School. His father was Absalom Willis Robertson—Democratic senator from Virginia and chairman of the U.S. Senate Committee on Banking, Housing, and Urban Affairs.

Robertson wrote me after the release of my 1980 biography, *Churchill: Speaker of the Century*. Believe it or not, through his mother, Gladys Churchill Willis, he was a second cousin of the Duke of Marlborough—the noble title bestowed upon Churchill's ancestor. When I visited him, he displayed the coats of arms for two Scottish clans, Robertson and Gordon, as well as portraits of two Virginia presidents who were his forebears. In my visit to his home office, he never talked about God or prayed with me. But his fawning staff kept saying "May God bless you," and "Let the Holy Spirit be with you," *ad infinitum* and *ad nauseam.*

Robertson proudly pointed out that he was a direct descendant of a Puritan preacher who had come to this eastern Chesapeake point of Virginia. He had planted his university and headquarters on the very same land his ancestor had first settled.

After his Marine Corps stint following World War II, he went to Yale Law School and then Union Seminary. In 1956 he headed the Adlai Stevenson campaign for Staten Island, in suburban New York. After a call from God, Robertson moved his home from Westchester County to Bedford–Stuyvesant—a largely black inner-city neighborhood—to establish a church. No one can ever impute prejudice to Robertson.

If I were a Freudian, I would say that this political televangelist was strongly influenced by the estranged marriage of his parents. His father, a career politician in the Byrd machine of Virginia, lived in Washington, and his mother—a religious, Bible-reading recluse—stayed at home in Lynchburg. For one who is widely read and multi-lingual (in Greek and Hebrew), he is narrow in his religious obsession.

Now, I grew up in a devout home, know my Bible, and respect and admire the church-going folks who are the strength of this nation. But sometimes, too much of the "born-again" puts me on edge.

I had had my fill of religiosity after some days with Robertson's group. When I boarded a Piedmont flight for Philadelphia, and heard I could upgrade to first class for ten dollars, I took it. The stewardess asked me what I wanted to drink. I said "A double martini, and fast. I've had so much of 'Yours in Jesus' that I need some little taste of sin or I'll start hitting on you!" She laughed and brought me the gratis drink. As for Pat Robertson, he may want to ponder what his distant cousin Winston Churchill once said: Never trust a man who has not a single redeeming vice.

Ruth Carter Stapleton: Evangelist and Sister of Jimmy Carter

I only met the "born-again" evangelist Ruth Carter Stapleton once, on a trip to Boston in September 1976. I was a speechwriter for President Ford at that time, as he faced a difficult election battle against Georgia Governor Jimmy Carter. I was to be interviewed by a Boston TV station about my new book, *Roles Speakers Play: How to Prepare a Speech for Any Occasion.* When I arrived at the studio, I was greeted with a "great idea" to promote my book— a debate with Ruth Carter Stapleton.

My reaction to this promotional media stunt was one of horror. I had only barely gained permission to take the trip for book promotion, and I could imagine the liberal media manipulating and twisting my remarks so as to say: "Ford Aide Attacks Governor's Sister!"

But I did meet her—a lovely, gracious woman whose smile was as disarming as her modest demeanor.

She asked me if I knew her brother Jimmy.

I shook my head, but told her that I was certainly aware of the governor and his meteoric rise to be his party's candidate.

Then she queried me as to whether I had ever met her *other* brother, Billy.

"I understand he is his own personality," I replied tactfully.

She smiled, and went on to tell me the difference between the two of them: Some years ago, Ruth had experienced a personal problem. She went to Jimmy, who told her to pray about it, and they both got down on their knees in the governor's office in Atlanta and prayed long and hard. Then she went to Billy, and he asked her to excuse him for a moment. He went out and brought back a can of beer, popped it open, and then pulled out his checkbook and ripped out a check. Then he gave it to her, and told her to just fill out the number she needed.

Charles Colson: Politician, Prisoner, and Preacher

When Julie Nixon Eisenhower visited us in Pueblo, Colorado in 2001, we told her that Jonathan Aitken, her father's biographer, had already started his biography of Nixon's Special Counsel Charles Colson, who was a fellow born-again Christian and convict. She asked me if I thought Colson was really sincere about finding Jesus.

I replied with what I had told Jonathan: "Chuck would kill for the Marines, kill for Nixon, and kill for Jesus." Julie shook her head. She remembered when Colson formed the Herter for Vice President Committee in 1956 in San Francisco, to stop her father.

Colson was a super salesman—two people whom I admire sang his praises. The first was his former wife Nancy Billings, who was my wife Dianne's best friend at Concord Academy and the president of her class. Nancy never spoke a word against him, even after their divorce. Second was my close friend Don Whitehead, who worked for Colson in political campaigns. When Colson first came to the White House in 1969, he had dinner with me there. A disciple of de Tocqueville, that firm believer in democracy, Colson had the idea of mobilizing volunteer associations on behalf of Nixon. So he organized an office that still exists in the White House today, the political communications liaison. The proof of its efficacy was that in 1972, Nixon would carry forty-nine states in a landslide.

After his release from prison, Colson found Jesus, and organized a Christian outreach organization, Prison Fellowship. By all accounts, he did a superb job, and by the time of his death in 2012, Colson had become a world figure in prison reform.

Father M. J. Divine: Spiritual Leader

Pedantic purists and sticklers for the facts may be too blinded by the truth to report my encounter with Father Divine in May 1968. These unbelievers might assert that the African-American preacher had departed from the terrestrial realm three years earlier. But that contravenes the more than five hundred witnesses to that night's events—not to mention the *Philadelphia Tribune*, which reported the next day that Father Divine had endorsed Nixon.

It was an election year, and the Nixon campaign had asked me to deliver a speech to Father Divine's church, the International Peace Mission, on behalf of the former vice president. The invitation had been set up by Gaye Pendleton, a Pitcairn by birth, a scion of the noted manufacturer of paints and other products. The Pitcairns were Swedenborgians, members of an obscure Protestant sect, and they had lent their cathedral-like church to the International Peace Mission.

Peace Mission members thought that Father Divine was God. His blonde wife, the former Edna Rose Ritchings, was addressed as Mother S. A. ("Sweet Angel") Divine. Father M. J. ("Major Jealous") Divine had married this young white woman from Vancouver in 1946 as his second wife, proclaiming her the reincarnation of his first wife, Penninah.

At the Swedenborgian church in Philadelphia, Nixon aide Dwight Chapin handed me a speech by Nixon on black capitalism. We were seated at the communion table, which was at least twenty yards long, and we were served heapings of food—chicken, duck, beef, lamb, and goat (but no pork products), and juices including apple, cranberry, orange, and grape (but no alcohol). Gaye Pendleton had warned me to eat everything I put on the plate. During our meal, Father Divine's purple-robed Celestial Choir serenaded us with hymns to Jesus, America, and even the Constitution.

I soon began to understand this audience, which was about 90 percent women and just about all black. Despite the fact that they were drawn mostly from the African-American working class, and included many maids and cleaning ladies, their political and religious beliefs were far closer to those of the DAR (Daughters of the American Revolution) than those of the NAACP. In other words, this was a conservative audience.

From the jewel-encrusted lectern, Mother Divine introduced Father Divine, to the sound of uproarious foot pounding and cheers. Then a high-pitched voice with an Alabama drawl came over the microphone: It was Father Divine. He declared that while the congregation couldn't see him, he could see them, and that even if they couldn't see him, they could put out their hands and feel the love of God filling the room. Then Father Divine delivered his sermon to the faithful.

After a pause, Mother Divine introduced me, saying that I had come straight from the side of Richard Nixon. I came to realize, by the hymns of the Celestial Choir and the words of Father Divine, that a boring speech on black entrepreneurship would not stir this crowd.

I began: "When the Pilgrims landed on Plymouth Rock, their words were, 'In the name of God, Amen.' When Thomas Jefferson sat at Sixth and Market and wrote the words of the Declaration, he wrote, 'endowed by our Creator.' When Benjamin Franklin attended the Constitutional Convention, he offered this prayer, 'If no sparrow can fall from His sky without His notice, surely no empire can rise from the ground without His help.' Before Abraham Lincoln left for Ford Theater that Friday, he signed the Executive Order putting 'In God We Trust' on the nickel."

Shouts from the crowd of "God be praised!" and "Hallelujah!" followed each sentence.

Then I closed with this: "When I served in the Pennsylvania General Assembly, I often would look at the mural behind the speaker's rostrum. It showed one garbed with eighteenth-century cloak and breeches on a high platform on a tower underneath a bell. He was the sheriff of Philadelphia, and was reading a document to the audience beneath him. The document was the Declaration of Independence. John Hancock told the signers they faced jail sentences or probably death, and to circulate its message secretly, stealthily. But the sheriff, whose name was John Nixon, said, 'The words on the bell above us have the inscription from Leviticus, 'Proclaim liberty throughout all the land unto all the inhabitants thereof.' And John Nixon said, 'I'm not afraid to proclaim these words of freedom.' And I ask all of you to let his collateral descendant, Richard, again proclaim freedom across this country and this world."

The audience was quiet, rapt with respect and reverence.

Then Mother Divine said that she would now pray to Father Divine for guidance.

After a few minutes that seemed like an eternity to me, she raised her head and told the congregation that Father had asked them to give and vote for Richard Nixon.

Then I was carried on a litter to Father Divine's white Rolls Royce limousine, and driven home.

The next morning, the front-page headline of the *Philadelphia Tribune* reported the story, and Father Divine's endorsement of Richard Nixon.

Later, I learned more about Father Divine. Born about twenty years after the Civil War, he considered Lincoln a saint. His flock, which had adherents in Australia, Canada, and elsewhere, refused government handouts. In the 1940 presidential election, he erected a flashing neon sign on his upstate New York summer home, next to the Hudson River. It read, "WIN WITH WILKIE!" and was visible to his neighbors across the river in Hyde Park, Franklin and Eleanor Roosevelt.

Some Father Divine naysayers told me later that he had recorded sermons before his passing in 1965, which could be used after his death. But I swear that he was present that day. And after Nixon's aides watched me carried off in a litter, they would keep a respectful distance from me.

Chapter Sixteen

Art Gallery

Andrew Wyeth: American Artist

In October 2011, Dianne and I watched an episode of the TV hit *Antiques Roadshow*, in which a charcoal drawing by Andrew Wyeth was estimated to sell at auction for four hundred and fifty thousand dollars. In a way, I played a small role in Wyeth's advancement to world fame. I had served with Wyeth on Pennsylvania's Shakespeare Quadricentennial Commission in 1964, and was the only politician in the small panel's select roster. I had been appointed because in the course of backing an unpopular penny tax hike, I had revealed my knowledge of the Bard by quoting *Macbeth* in asking for a quick passage: "If it were done when 'tis done, then 'twere well / It were done quickly."[1] Other notables were Pennsylvania novelists Pearl Buck and Conrad Richter.

We had dinner at the governor's residence. I found Wyeth to be a slender, introverted figure, looking like a country squire from the horsey area west of Philadelphia—not some artist of a bohemian nature. I quoted him a line from Shakespeare's *Tempest*: "His art is of such power."[2] But later I admitted that I knew his father's works better than his son's oil landscapes: "Mr. Wyeth, my youth was colored by your father—N. C. Wyeth's illustrations of *Treasure Island*—and later, at the Hill School, by his murals in the school's dining room." A casualty of the leftist tenet that art must be chaotic and ugly, Andrew Wyeth was hurt by the self-appointed art critics who scorned his "representational" works but gushed over the abstractionists, whose daubs had little relevance for the people. That was why, as he told me, he voted for Nixon in 1960 over Kennedy—although in 1963, Kennedy bestowed the Presidential Medal of Freedom upon Wyeth, a first for an American artist.

At the White House, I suggested in a memo to Nixon that he honor the Chadds Ford painter. Nixon had already staged a dinner for Duke Ellington in which the great jazz musician was the honoree, not the entertainer. Kissinger got hold of the memorandum I wrote, blocked out my name, and substituted his own. At first, I wasn't even invited to the dinner, which took place in February 1970, augmented by a White House exhibition of twenty Wyeth paintings. This event would garner a *TIME* magazine cover for Wyeth, and sow seeds of the Chadds Ford Brandywine Museum, featuring the entire Wyeth family of artists: N. C., Andrew, and Jamie.

Albert Barnes: Art Collector

Albert Barnes had the greatest collection of Impressionist art in America, most of which he assembled during the 1920s for a song. A physician who trained at the University of Pennsylvania, he turned to art collecting, having made his fortune in pharmaceuticals—in particular, the development of a treatment for infant blindness. He lived in Merion, only blocks from City Line Avenue, which divided Philadelphia from the western suburbs of the Main Line. There, in a lavish home, he displayed his art collection—to be viewed by invitation only.

This saturnine, gloomy man was befriended by Paul Chancellor, a teacher at Hill School who was also head of the Art Department. Chancellor taught a class in the humanities (art and music). One morning in 1951, he and his wife took ten of us Hill Schoolers in two station wagons from Pottstown to Merion. We carried our sandwich lunches with us. Barnes kept watch that we touched nothing. He was to die in a car accident later that year.

The painting I remembered most was "The Card Players" by the Post-Impressionist Paul Cezanne. The Barnes collection heralded my first discovery of the Impressionists and their use of light, and Impressionism has remained my favorite genre. When Barnes died, he left instructions that his house be open only one day a week, and only to those who sought written permission in advance. These rules were modified somewhat to allow it to continue its tax status as a museum.

In 2012, after a lengthy court battle in which interpretation of the *cy-près* doctrine[3] was stretched to new extremes, the bulk of the Barnes collection was removed to the Philadelphia Museum of Art. Previously, the collection had been run by Lincoln University, a majority-black college to the west of Philadelphia. Barnes might not have liked seeing his private collection submerged in the Philadelphia museum's more massive display.

J. Carter Brown: Director, U.S. National Gallery of Art

J. Carter Brown was predestined to be the director of a major art museum. By family and education, he was raised to be a leader in the art world. His family was one of Rhode Island's oldest, and founders of Brown University. His father, John Nicholas Brown—tall, hawk-nosed, with craggy, weather-beaten features—looked like he came from a long line of whaling captains or Puritan preachers. His mother, born Anne Seddon Kinsolving, whom Brown favored in looks and actions, was the beautiful daughter of a Baltimore Episcopalian bishop, and had many male admirers in her youth. One, to their family's consternation, was the dark, handsome son of an Italian fruit peddler. That romance was thwarted when her parents packed her off on a round-the-world cruise. The young man to whom they objected so strongly was Rodolfo Guglielmi, better known as Rudolph Valentino—"The Sheik" of silent-film stardom.

Carter Brown went to Groton, the famed Massachusetts prep school, and later to Yale. After Groton, he did a year at Stowe. For a boarding school, Stowe is an art connoisseur's paradise. Sir John Vanbrugh, who was also the architect of Blenheim Palace, designed the main house. The outside grounds were laid out by the great landscape architect Capability Brown, and featured sweeping vistas in between Greek temples and colonnades. Unfortunately, hardly any of the paintings by Allan Ramsey and Sir Joshua Reynolds were still on the walls when Carter Brown and I attended there in the early 1950s. After Yale, instead of staying on to get a Masters in Fine Arts, as many would do following the award of an undergraduate art history degree, Carter chose Harvard Business School. As Carter told me, those who donated to museums were businessmen, and would appreciate Carter's financial training.

But better than any degree in fine art, Carter would spend the year after he got his MBA studying with Bernard Berenson in Florence. Berenson, the nonagenarian art guru, was visited every year by scores of art connoisseurs.

I met Carter for the first time as he was leaving Stowe and I was arriving. He looked more English than his fellow students, with his gray suit cut by a tailor from the Eton High Street, and a blue-and-white-striped sixth-former tie. A Rolls Royce had come to return him to London. I, by contrast, didn't have to open my mouth to proclaim my background: My crew cut and burly lumbering figure said "All American."

Carter was unlike any other boy my age I had ever met. He could walk into a living room and identify a Chippendale chair or Sheraton table at a glance. He could distinguish a Tabriz oriental rug from an Afghan one, note the Tiffany candlesticks, or that the fruit bowl was a Waterford. When most boys my age had their head full of the statistics of baseball players, Carter knew the birth and death dates of artists ranging from Giotto to Gauguin.

Philippe de Montebello: Director, Metropolitan Museum of Art

Philippe de Montebello was elegantly slim and perfectly attired, from the kerchief square in his pocket to the faint scent of cologne emanating from his throat. His five senses were keen detectors of bad taste, which was signaled by a twitch of the nostrils and an almost imperceptible raising of the eyebrows. I met him in 1996, in the course of preparing the most bizarre speech I ever delivered.

Michael Egan, the president of a national car rental agency, Alamo, had invited me to speak at a dinner hosted at his house in support of the Museum of Art of Fort Lauderdale. The founder of Alamo told me he had chosen the name for his company because it came before Avis in the phone book, yet was a familiar American name. The motor-rental mogul and his young blonde wife were trying to make a splash in the social world. He had constructed a white mansion on Martha's Vineyard that appalled the neighbors, denizens of more modest shingled abodes.

But his major coup would be his philanthropy to the Museum of Art of Fort Lauderdale, where Egan resided. My job was to arrive at the cocktail party the night before the gala event and familiarize myself with all the guests. I was supposed to pass myself off as an old friend of the Alamo CEO. In addition, at this dinner I was to make a toast (without notes) using a quotation from Shakespeare to depict each of the attendees.

The mansion where he hosted the event consisted of two Norman chateaux imported from France and then joined together on delivery to Fort Lauderdale. At the table, the gold-trimmed china and Waterford goblets added to the grandiose opulence. Never had a more motley group of guests mixed. Florida associates and their fur-draped wives braved the city's fifty-degree winter to mingle with effete curators in the Impressionists, Renaissance, Modernists, and American portraitists. When Egan introduced me to de Montebello, I saw the connoisseur's nostrils contract with disdain. My burly frame caused Montebello to lump me with Egan's similar rotund features. If Egan missed Montebello's aghast look, I didn't. I tried to make him reassess me by dropping to him that I was Carter Brown's schoolmate at Stowe. That shattered his earlier stereotype. Montebello then asked where I got my quote for him: "His art is of such power."[4] "From *The Tempest*," I replied. "I wrote a biography of Shakespeare." This seemed to reassure him further.

Later, it occurred to me that the comparison of Carter Brown and Philippe de Montebello was striking. Carter Brown was an aristocrat, to the manor born, always secure in his purpose and goal. Still, the Harvard MBA was undaunted by the realities of doing business, including the need to mingle with a wide variety of types. He would have enjoyed the party.

Yousuf Karsh: The Photographer "Karsh of Ottawa"

In 2000, *Who's Who in the World* named the one hundred most eminent personages of the twentieth century. A single photographer had portrayed over half of those listed. He was Yousuf Karsh, an Armenian who emigrated to Canada in 1925 as a seventeen-year-old fleeing Turkish persecution.

His most famous subject was the statesman who was universally regarded as the greatest man of the century—Winston Churchill. The thirty-five-year-old photographer made Churchill's portrait on December 31, 1941. This was not long after the wartime prime minister had delivered his memorable address to the Canadian House of Commons, in which he told his audience how French generals had predicted that England would have its neck wrung like a chicken within two weeks. Then Churchill paused and said: "Some chicken. Some neck."[5] The members rose in uproarious applause.

After his speech, Churchill went into an anteroom, where the apprehensive Karsh was waiting. Mackenzie King, the Canadian premier, had arranged the shoot. He had warned the photographer that he had only two minutes to get his shot. Churchill, who was looking forward to his usual post-rhetorical smoke, strode into the room, scowling. He regarded the camera as his enemy, with his cigar in his teeth as a weapon. Karsh told me a half century later that without thinking, he snatched the cigar from Churchill's mouth. The scowl deepened, his head was thrust forward, and he put his hand on his hip in a defiant pose. The image caught Churchill at a significant moment in time, defiant and indomitable. It would become not only Karsh's greatest portrait, but possibly the most famous photo ever taken.

I met Karsh when he was already Canada's most acclaimed citizen. It was at an English-Speaking Union luncheon at the Château Laurier in Ottawa. At eighty-two, he was no pussy-cat in appearance. With a large balding forehead over an oval face that narrowed into a prominent chin, he had eyes that appraised you like an eagle sighting its prey. I was a speaker on Churchill at that event, and Karsh introduced me. When we were seated at the head table, he also related to me how Churchill had told Karsh that he could make a roaring lion stand still and be photographed. In the signed print of the original photo Karsh gave me, he titled it "The Roaring Lion."

Notes

1. William Shakespeare, *The Tragedy of Macbeth*, in *The Oxford Shakespeare, Second Edition*, edited by John Jowett, William Montgomery, Gary Taylor, and Stanley Wells (Oxford, UK: Oxford University Press, 2005), 975.

2. William Shakespeare, *The Tempest*, in *The Oxford Shakespeare, Second Edition*, edited by John Jowett, William Montgomery, Gary Taylor, and Stanley Wells (Oxford, UK: Oxford University Press, 2005), 1227.

3. The *cy-près* doctrine refers to following the original terms of a bequest or will to the greatest extent possible.

4. William Shakespeare, *The Tempest*, in *The Oxford Shakespeare, Second Edition*, edited by John Jowett, William Montgomery, Gary Taylor, and Stanley Wells (Oxford, UK: Oxford University Press, 2005), 1227.

5. Winston Churchill, "Speech to the Canadian Parliament," December 30, 1941, Teaching American History, A Project of the Ashbrook Center at Ashland University, http://teachingamericanhistory.org/library/document/some-chicken-some-neck/, accessed August 7, 2018.

Chapter Seventeen

Lyceum

George Steiner: Philosopher of Language

The most compelling lecturer at Williams College in the 1950s was George Steiner, whose classes on English literature were nothing short of enthralling. Today Steiner is not a familiar figure to most Americans, unless they are regular readers of the *New York Review of Books,* where he is regarded as the intellectual's intellectual, possessing an erudition that is almost esoteric.

Steiner was not an arresting figure. Of stumpy stature with a moonlike face and somewhat deformed hand, Steiner was possessed of a singular voice. His thunderous tones could be mistaken for those of God in the Book of Job, much to the consternation of hapless undergraduates.

A refugee from Nazi-occupied France, the young Steiner had arrived on these shores in 1940 with his family. Having received his undergraduate degree from the University of Chicago, he pursued further studies in literature as a Rhodes Scholar at Oxford before arriving at Williams in 1953. European, intellectual, and absorbed in ideas, Steiner was something of an alien in the white-bread preppie culture of 1950s Williams. He reminded me of the seventeenth-century English poet and essayist Alexander Pope, who had moved within upper-class circles. (They admitted him at their peril; the short and ungainly Pope penned a mock epic lampooning the manners and mores of the aristocracy.)

When he found out that I had attended Stowe the year before matriculating at Williams, Steiner saw me as a fellow Anglophile, and took a liking to me. My brother Graham, a senior at Williams at the time, had a girlfriend at Vassar College by the name of Betsy, whom he later married. Betsy very kindly arranged get-togethers for Steiner and me, and the trio of Steiner, Graham, and I would set out each weekend for the drive from Williams to Vassar. I treasured these weekly drives, where the conversation touched on all aspects of literature and philosophy, and arguably contributed more to my education than any course I took at Williams. When we first arrived at Vassar and met up with Betsy's friends, George was shy and awkward. But by the end of the weekend, the Vassar undergraduates were in rapturous awe of the young academic, enthralled by his disquisitions on T. S. Eliot's *The Love Song of J. Alfred Prufrock*.

The last time I saw Steiner was in 1972 at the Savoy Grille in London. He was surrounded by some university "groupies" who were hanging on his every word. I introduced myself, but he waved me off. I think I must have reminded him of a time in his life when he was less than happy.

James MacGregor Burns: Professor and Presidential Biographer

In 1958, a professor of political science from Williams College ran for the open congressional seat in western Massachusetts, but lost to Republican Sylvio Conte. The scholar and author James MacGregor Burns was a partisan Democrat, yet he respected active Republicans for at least being involved in the political process. At Williams, he taught all three Humes brothers—Samuel, Graham, and myself. In 1971, he won the Pulitzer Prize for the second volume of his FDR biography, *Roosevelt: The Soldier of Freedom*.

I used to argue with Professor Burns in favor of history being a better major than political science. "The political scientist favors structures of governance that can accomplish his current political agenda," I told him. "The historian looks at political trends with a larger perspective." I cited examples, including the "spotlight investigations" favored by Congress in the 1920s (e.g., for the "Teapot Dome" scandal), which had fallen out of favor by the 1950s after the Army–McCarthy hearings, branded an anti-communist "witch hunt."

While I was a student at Williams, we remained on cordial terms. In 1954, I babysat Burns's two children when he traveled to Boston for a meeting of the Massachusetts ADA—Americans for Democratic Action. As President of the Massachusetts ADA, he had been designated to introduce Senator John Kennedy. Kennedy, to his chagrin, asked this ADA chapter to disband because they had favored recognition of Red China.

In 1958, Burns agreed to be Kennedy's biographer. (At the same time, the Polish-born journalist Earl Mazo, whose writings would later expose vote fraud in the 1960 election, was doing one about Nixon.) I did not see him again until the winter of 1980, when I was a visiting lecturer at Williams. When I delivered a talk on my White House speechwriting, Burns was seated at the head table. I stated that Nixon was a greater progressive than Kennedy, and supported my theory with examples such as Nixon's giving the District of Columbia the vote, instating Affirmative Action programs, creating the Environmental Protection Agency, ending the Vietnam War draft, banning gender-based discrimination in how public education funds are awarded (Title IX), so that women's school athletic programs were greatly expanded, withdrawing troops from Southeast Asia, and integrating 92 percent of young black students in the South by the end of his first term, versus 30 percent in 1968—not to mention his mission to open up China. As I left the podium, Burns ignored me.

Hugh Bullock: Philanthropist and Mutual Fund Pioneer

Hugh Bullock was a role model, a mentor, a friend. He died in 1996 at the age of ninety-eight. A 1921 alumnus of Williams College, Bullock remembered my father, his fellow student. Bullock was a native of Denver, Colorado. He served as a lieutenant in the U.S. Army during World War I, and again as a lieutenant colonel in World War II. He began his career in his family's investment firm, Calvin Bullock, Ltd., opening an office on Wall Street in 1927. He would go on to pioneer the field of mutual funds as a way for "the little guy" to invest in the financial markets, and was one of the authors of the Securities Act of 1940, which was developed to protect these small investors. But it was through his service to Anglo-American relations as the president of the U.S. branch of the Pilgrims Society that I knew him. And his career in this area was no less distinguished than his achievements on Wall Street. In 1976, he was the first American to be made a Knight, Grand Cross—the highest rank in the Order of the British Empire—for helping to promote Anglo-American relations.

Bullock's funeral ceremony at St. Thomas Episcopal Church in New York was a fitting celebration of his life. Of a proud Scots heritage, he was piped into the church to the tune of "Scotland the Brave." We then stood to sing "America the Beautiful," the patriotic anthem Katherine Lee Bates wrote while visiting Pikes Peak in Bullock's native Colorado. The Williams College Choir came to New York to sing his alma mater's song, "The Mountains," by Washington Gladden. Then a U.S. Marine Corps band performed a rendition of "The Marines' Hymn."

Bullock and I first met at an annual dinner of the Ends of the Earth, whose president I was at the time. The society's secretary general, Charlie West, introduced us, and as a result of this meeting, Bullock put me on the board of the Pilgrims. He had been asked to lead the American branch of the Pilgrims in 1951 when John W. Davis, former U.S. ambassador to the United Kingdom, had to step down due to the demands of appearing before the Supreme Court with respect to *Brown v. Board of Education*, the landmark desegregation case. At one Pilgrims luncheon, the British UN Ambassador was due to speak, but at the last minute sent his regrets and an aide to take his place. Bullock asked me to deliver the speech instead, and later said that it was the best luncheon we ever had. He always called me to speak at their board meetings, which were held at the Waldorf Astoria. It was Bullock who proposed the society's first women members: Edwina Sandys, the granddaughter of Churchill, and my daughter Mary Humes Quillen.

Bullock and I often met for lunch at the Downtown Club in Lower Manhattan, and Dianne and I were once his guests for lunch at his house on Martha's Vineyard. We found that we were both descendants of one Caleb Bullock of Massachusetts. I was delighted to find that we were related, however distantly, and I was honored when he asked me to be his pallbearer. His top choices for that honor had, of course, died by the time Bullock had reached his nineties; they had included Truman's secretary of state, Dean Acheson, his secretary of defense, Bob Lovett, and New York Governor Averell Harriman. At the crowded church service, I had to ask David Rockefeller where I should stand. His response was: right behind him. Along with America's rich and famous, European royalty were in attendance to pay their respects.

A patron of the arts, Bullock founded the Academy of American Poets, which gave stipends to writers. These words from Shakespeare fit him perfectly: "He is as full of valour as of kindness; / Princely in both."[1]

Note

1. William Shakespeare, *The Life of Henry the Fifth*, in *The Oxford Shakespeare, Second Edition*, edited by John Jowett, William Montgomery, Gary Taylor, and Stanley Wells (Oxford, UK: Oxford University Press, 2005), 615.

Bibliography

Churchill, Winston. "Speech to the Canadian Parliament," December 30, 1941. Teaching American History, A Project of the Ashbrook Center at Ashland University. http://teachingamericanhistory.org/library/document/some-chicken-some-neck/. Accessed August 7, 2018.

Coleridge, Samuel Taylor. "The Rime of the Ancient Mariner," in *The Rime of the Ancient Mariner and Other Poems*. Mineola, New York: Dover Publications, Inc. 1992.

Goethe, Johann Wolfgang von. *Faust*, in *Goethe's Werke, Band 41*. Stuttgart and Tübingen: J. G. Cotta'schen Buchhandlung. 1832.

Housman, A.E. "XXIII," in *A Shropshire Lad*. Mineola, New York: Dover Publications, Inc. 1990.

Humes, James C. *Instant Eloquence: A Lazy Man's Guide to Public Speaking*. New York: Harper & Row. 1973.

———. *Nixon's Ten Commandments of Statecraft: His Guiding Principles of Leadership and Negotiation*. New York: Scribner. 1997.

Kennedy, John F. "Inaugural Address," January 20, 1961. Online by Gerhard Peters and John T. Woolley, *The American Presidency Project*. http://www.presidency.ucsb.edu/ws/?pid=8032. Accessed April 27, 2018.

———. "Speech of Senator John F. Kennedy, Houston Coliseum, Houston, TX," September 12, 1960. Online by Gerhard Peters and John T. Woolley, *The American Presidency Project*. http://www.presidency.ucsb.edu/ws/?pid=25772. Accessed May 3, 2018.

Robinson, Edward Arlington. "Richard Cory," in *Edwin Arlington Robinson: Selected Poems*. Edited by Robert Faggen. New York: Penguin Group. 1997.

Shakespeare, William. *The Oxford Shakespeare: The Complete Works. Second Edition*. Edited by John Jowett, William Montgomery, Gary Taylor, and Stanley Wells. Oxford, UK: Oxford University Press. 2005.

Index of Names

About the Author

James C. Humes, White House speechwriter for Presidents Eisenhower, Nixon, Ford, Reagan, and George H. W. Bush, has practiced the art of public speaking as an attorney, lecturer, diplomat, and Pennsylvania state representative. The author of numerous books, Humes wrote the Pulitzer-nominated biography *Churchill, Speaker of the Century,* which won an Athenaeum of Philadelphia Literary Award. Other Humes titles include *Presidents and Their Pens: The Story of White House Speechwriters*; *Speak Like Churchill, Stand Like Lincoln: 21 Powerful Secrets of History's Greatest Speakers*; *The Reagan Persuasion: Charm, Deliver and Inspire a Winning Message*; *My Fellow Americans: Presidential Addresses That Shaped History;* and *Confessions of a White House Ghostwriter: Five Presidents and Other Political Adventures.* Most recently a teaching fellow at the University of Colorado, Humes has shared his expertise on American government as guest lecturer at more than thirty universities in Asia and Latin America, on behalf of the U.S. State Department.

WORKS BY JAMES C. HUMES

Churchill: Speaker of the Century. New York: Stein and Day. 1980.

Churchill: The Prophetic Statesman. Washington, DC: Regnery History. 2012.

Citizen Shakespeare: A Social and Political Portrait. Lanham, MD: University Press of America. 2003.

Classic Podium Humor: Using Wit and Humor in Every Speech You Make. Edison, NJ: Castle Books. 2002.

Confessions of a White House Ghostwriter: Five Presidents and Other Political Adventures. Washington, DC: Regnery Publishing. 1997.

Eisenhower and Churchill: The Partnership That Saved the World. Roseville, CA: Prima Publishers. 2001.

How to Be a Very Important Person. New York: McGraw-Hill. 1979.

How to Get Invited to the White House . . . and Over One Hundred Impressive Gambits, Foxy Face-Savers, and Clever Maneuvers. New York: Thomas Y. Crowell & Company. 1977.

Instant Eloquence: A Lazy Man's Guide to Public Speaking. New York: Harper & Row. 1973.

My Fellow Americans: Presidential Addresses That Shaped History. New York: Praeger Publishers. 1992.

Nixon's Ten Commandments of Statecraft: His Guiding Principles of Leadership and Negotiation. New York: Scribner. 1997.

Only Nixon: His Trip to China Revisited and Restudied. With Jarvis D. Ryals. Lanham, MD: University Press of America. 2009.

Podium Humor: A Raconteur's Treasury of Witty and Humorous Stories. New York: Harper & Row. 1975.

Presidents and Their Pens: The Story of White House Speechwriters. Lanham, MD: Hamilton Books. 2016.

Roles Speakers Play: How to Prepare a Speech for Any Occasion. New York: Harper & Row. 1976.

Speak Like Churchill, Stand Like Lincoln: 21 Powerful Secrets of History's Greatest Speakers. New York: Three Rivers Press. 2002.

Speaker's Treasury of Anecdotes About the Famous. New York: Harper & Row. 1981.

Standing Ovation: How to Be an Effective Speaker and Communicator. New York: Harper & Row. 1988.

Sweet Dream: Tales of a River City. Williamsport, PA: Williamsport Centennial. 1966.

Target Churchill. With Warren Adler. New York: Stonehouse Productions. 2013.

The Ben Franklin Factor: Selling One-to-One. New York: William Morrow & Company. 1992.

The Reagan Persuasion: Charm, Deliver, and Inspire a Winning Message. Naperville, IL: Sourcebooks, Inc. 2010.

The Sir Winston Method: The Five Secrets of Speaking the Language of Leadership. New York: William Morrow & Company. 1991.

The Wit & Wisdom of Abraham Lincoln: A Treasury of More Than 650 Quotations and Anecdotes. New York: HarperCollins Publishers. 1996.

The Wit & Wisdom of Benjamin Franklin: A Treasury of More Than 900 Quotations and Anecdotes. New York: HarperCollins Publishers. 1995.

The Wit & Wisdom of FDR. New York: Harper Perennial. 2008.

The Wit & Wisdom of Ronald Reagan. Washington, DC: Regnery. 2007.

The Wit & Wisdom of Winston Churchill: A Treasury of More Than 1,000 Quotations and Anecdotes. New York: HarperCollins Publishers. 1994.

Which President Killed a Man? Tantalizing Trivia and Fun Facts About Our Chief Executives and First Ladies. New York: McGraw Hill Education. 2002.

Winston Churchill: A Biography. New York: DK. 2003.